COME AND SEE

Catholic Bible Study

The Gospel of John

by

Fr. Joseph Ponessa, S.S.D.

and

Laurie Watson Manhardt, Ph.D.

Emmaus Road Publishing
827 North Fourth Street
Steubenville, OH 43952

 First edition published 2002. Second edition 2004
Printed in the United States of America
09 08 07 06 05 04 1 2 3

Library of Congress Control Number:
ISBN: 1-931018-25-1

Cover design and layout by
Jacinta Calcut/Image Graphics and Design

Cover artwork:
Domenico Ghirlandaio, *Last Supper*

Nihil Obstat: Reverend Joseph N. Rosie, *Censor Librorum*
Imprimatur: Most Reverend John M. Smith, Bishop of Trenton
Date: October 8, 2004

For additional information on the "Come and See"
Catholic Bible Study series, visit www.CatholicBibleStudy.net

Come and See

Catholic Bible Study
The Gospel of John

PRAYER TO THE HOLY SPIRIT

O Holy Spirit,
Beloved of my soul,
I adore You,
Enlighten, Guide, Strengthen
and Console me;
Tell me what I ought to say
and do and command me to do it.
I promise to be submissive in
everything You will ask of me
and to accept all that You
permit to happen to me,
only show me what is Your will.

Amen

Introduction

"Thy word is a lamp to my feet,
and a light to my path."
Psalm 119:105

May God set His Word in your heart
and fill you with everlasting joy.

May you walk in His ways,
always knowing what is right and good,
until you enter your heavenly inheritance. Amen.

God bless you as you embark upon this ***Come and See: Catholic Bible Study ~ The Gospel of John***. Whether you have studied Sacred Scripture for many years or are opening the Word of God for the first time, trust that your efforts will be pleasing to God and prove to be rewarding for you as well.

God's Word enables you to study again and again and receive new insights and fresh understanding. If you are a beginner to Bible study, the Holy Spirit can give you insights that will astound you and also bless the veterans in your group. If you are a seasoned student of God's Word, you know that God always has more. Share what God gives you and expect to be surprised with even more blessings from Him through others in your group. Studying Scripture with others multiplies the possibilities of receiving fresh insights and blessings as well as storing God's Word deep in your heart.

What you need!

To do this Bible Study, you need a Catholic Bible, and a ***Catechism of the Catholic Church (CCC)***. When choosing a Bible, recall that the Catholic Bible contains 73 books, compared with others having only 66 books. The additional seven books from the Hebrew Scriptures, called Old Testament books, and extra chapters of Daniel provide inspiring passages that you will need to consult. If you find Sirach and Tobit in your Bible table of contents, you have a complete Catholic bible. ***The Council of Hippo approved these 73 books in 393 AD,*** and this has remained the official canon of Sacred Scripture since the 4th century. The Council of Trent authoritatively reaffirmed these books of the Bible in 1545 AD. The Douay-Rheims (DR) Bible was completed in 1609 AD.

For Bible study purposes, choose a word-for-word, literal translation rather than a paraphrase. Some excellent translations for Bible study are the Revised Standard Version (RSV) 1957, 1971, the Jerusalem Bible (JB) 1966, and the New American Bible (NAB) 1970. The Good News Bible, or Today's English Version (TEV), 1976 represents a paraphrase of the Bible, which will be difficult to use in this type of formal Bible study where specific verses will be referenced.

Browse in a Catholic book store to determine which translation reads best for you. Compare Psalm 1 in several translations before making your selection. Do you sense that Psalm 1 is preparing you to recognize Jesus, the righteous, blessed man who will save the world? Does the translation of Psalm 1 inspire you to want to emulate that Righteous One and walk in His ways? The entirety of the Old Testament points to Jesus, the Father's provision for the atonement of sin. The New Testament reveals God the Father through Jesus Christ in the power of the Holy Spirit. Choose a translation that makes the mystery of God come alive for you. Often an old Bible proves to be a precious treasure.

Seek a quiet place for prayer and study. Adoration of the Blessed Sacrament in a chapel near your home may enable you to do some Bible Study in the presence of Our Lord. Set aside time to pray and study God's Word. *1) Pray, 2) Read the Bible chapter and commentary and then 3) Write answers to the questions using the Bible and Catechism.* This year, you will read the entire Gospel of St. John as well as some references from the Hebrew Scriptures (Old Testament) and the New Testament. You will see for yourself how God's promises are fulfilled in the New Covenant. You may want to get some Bible tabs to help you move back and forth through these books quickly and easily.

Please, share aloud with your small group members "only" on those questions for which you have written answers!

Getting Started

- *Pray to the Holy Spirit.* Ask God for wisdom on when to have Bible study, whom to study with and when and where to meet.
- *Invite neighbors and friends to a "Get Acquainted Coffee"* and find out who will make a commitment to meet for 60 - 90 minutes once a week for group Bible study.
- *Determine a day of the week and time of day to meet.* For mothers and children, one morning from 9:30 to 11:00 might be best, or an afternoon from 1:00 to 2:30 pm. Working people may be well served in the evening from 7:30 - 9:00 pm. It may be impossible to find a perfect time for everyone, so go with what seems to work best.
- *Find an appropriate location.* Start in someone's home and then, as your group becomes larger, ask the pastor of your parish if you could meet in church or school facilities. Pray beforehand and offer this book to him for his review and approval.
- *Explore the possibility of hiring a baby-sitter* for young mothers and share the cost among everyone, or investigate whether some students might do childcare for the Bible study as a project for their Confirmation service requirement.
- *Consider a cooperative arrangement* in which women take turns caring for and teaching the young children. All women, even grandmothers and women without children should take turns to serve the little children as an offering to God.
- Gather a small prayer group to pray regularly for your Bible study and for your specific needs and challenges. Pray to discern God's will, brainstorm, and make plans.

Pray that God will anoint specific people to lead your study. Faithful, practicing Catholics are needed to fill the following positions:

- **Teachers** ~ take overall responsibility to read commentaries and prepare a 20-30 minute wrap-up lecture after the small group discussions each week.
- **Song Leaders** ~ plan and lead a short hymn that everyone can sing to start Bible Study each week.
- **Prayer Leaders** ~ begin with a prayer and ask someone to prepare a short five minute opening devotional each week. This could be an answer to prayer or personal testimony.
- **Children's Leaders** ~ hire babysitters, prepare lessons and teach pre-school children who attend Bible study with their mothers.
- **Coordinators** ~ communicate with parish personnel about needs for space and use of facilities. Put invitations in church bulletins. Make sure rooms are left in good condition.

Small group facilitators will be needed for each small group. Try to enlist two mature Catholics who are good listeners to serve together as small group leaders for each group. Small group facilitators must be practicing Catholics and share the following responsibilities for their small discussion group:

- Pray for each member of your small group each day.
- Make a name tag for each member of the group.
- Meet before the study to pray with other leaders.
- Discuss all the questions in the lesson each week.
- Begin and end on time
- Make sure that each person in the group shares each week. Ask each person to read a question and have the first chance to answer it.
- You might just go around in a circle, so that each person can look forward to his or her turn. After reading the question others should feel free to offer answers as well.
- Ensure that no one person dominates the discussion, including you!
- Keep the discussion positive and focused on this week's lesson.
- Speak kindly and charitably. Steer conversation away from any negative or uncharitable speech, gossip or griping. Don't badmouth anyone, any group or any church.
- Listen well! Keep your eyes and ears open. Give your full attention to the one speaking.
- Look at people while they are speaking. Get comfortable with silence and pauses in the discussion. Be patient. Encourage quieter people to share first. Ask questions.
- If questions, misunderstandings or disagreements arise, refer them to the question box for a teacher or the parish priest to research and discuss later.
- Arrange for a social activity each month.

Invite and Welcome Priests

Invite your pastor, associate, visiting priests and religious to participate in Bible study. Ask for their blessings. Invite them to come and pray with the Bible study members. See if they would like to come and answer some written questions from the question box periodically. Accept whatever they can offer to the Bible study. However, don't *expect* anything from them. Appreciate that the priests may be very busy and don't add additional burdens.

If a priest offers to give a devotional or closing lecture, accept with gratitude.

† Jesus chose a group of twelve apostles. So, perhaps small groups should be about twelve or thirteen people. When you get too big, break up into two groups.

† Women share best with women and men with men. If you plan a mixed Bible study, organize separate men's groups, led by men and women's groups, led by women. In a mixed group, some people may be uncomfortable sharing and sit silently.

† Offer a married couples group if two married couples are willing to act as small group facilitators and come together to every single class meeting. Each person should have his or her own book and share on his or her own home study answers.

† You may also want to consider a nursing mothers' group in which mothers can bring their infants with them and hold the babies while they share their home study work.

† A group of teenagers or young adult group could be facilitated by the parish priest or by a young adult leader.

† Family groups can work together on the home study questions on a given night of the week, with older children or parents helping younger children to find the passages in the Bible and the Catechism.

† Share the overall goal that *each person* in each group shares aloud each time the group meets. Everyone should contribute every time Bible study meets!

† Sit next to the most talkative person in the group and across from the quietest. Use eye contact to encourage quiet members to speak up. Serve everyone and hear from everyone. Listening in Bible study is just as important as talking! Evaluate each week, "Am I a good listener? Did I really hear what others shared? Was I attentive or distracted? Did I affirm others? Did I talk too much?"

Social Activities

God has created us as social creatures, needing to relate communally. Large churches present challenges for parishioners to get to know one another. Some people belong to a parish for years without getting to know others. Newcomers may never get noticed and welcomed. Bible study offers an opportunity for spiritual nourishment as well as inclusion and hospitality.

Occasional social activities are offered in this book. These socials are simple, fun and non-threatening. In planning your social activities, be a good sport, try to attend and share with your small group. Keep in mind the following when planning.

- Agree on a time when most of the group can meet. This could be right before or after Bible study or on a different day of the week, perhaps even Saturday morning.

- Invite people to come to your home for the social time. Jesus was comfortable visiting in the homes of the rich and the poor. So whether you live in a small apartment or a big mansion, as a Christian you can offer hospitality to those God sends along your way.

> *"Do not neglect to show hospitality to strangers,*
> *for thereby some have entertained angels unawares."*
> *(Hebrews 13:2)*

- Keep it simple! Just a beverage and cookies works well. Simplicity blesses others. People can squeeze together on a sofa or stand around the kitchen. The important thing is to offer hospitality and love one another as Jesus directed. Don't fuss.

- Help out the group leader. If Bible study meets in someone else's home, invite the group to come to your place for the social time. Don't make the group leader do it all. Jump right in and offer. Be a blessing to others.

- If your Bible study meets in church, do not fall into the convenience of staying at the church for socials. You might have to drive a distance to someone's home, but it may be the first time anyone from the parish has taken the trouble to come out to their home to visit. Trust God. It's worth it. God will bless your efforts at offering hospitality to your Bible study group and also your efforts in accepting the hospitality of others.

Consider the following times for your socials.

9:30 a.m. - 10:30 a.m.	Saturday coffee	11:30 a.m. - 12:30 p.m.	Luncheon
3:00 p.m. - 4:00 p.m.	Afternoon Tea	8:00 p.m. - 9:00 p.m.	Dessert

Challenges

As Christians, all of us are weak sinners in need of God's mercy. People come to Bible study with all sorts of problems and challenges. Often Christians can fall into the temptation of trying to be all things for all people. It is good to remember that Jesus Christ is the Savior and we are only His humble servants. When a person comes to us, whose problems are too large for us to handle, be they financial, emotional, spiritual or whatever, don't hesitate to direct them to seek out a priest for spiritual direction or a professional counselor for emotional, marital or financial problems. Bible study, the task at hand, requires us to be faithful in this one thing, while at the same time praying for the needs of others.

Saint Paul's Letter to the Ephesians admonishes us to *"speak the truth in love . . . and be kind to one another, tenderhearted, forgiving one another, as God in Christ forgave you." (Ephesians 4:15, 32).* Bible study affords us the opportunity to search God's Word for direction in our lives and the lives of loved ones, to pray for one another, encourage one another and sometimes gently admonish one another.

"All scripture is inspired by God and profitable for teaching, for reproof, for correction, and for training in righteousness, that the man of God may be complete, equipped for every good work." (2 Timothy 3:16–17)

As children of God, we long to be taught and disciplined by God's Word, and trained in righteousness, that we may be whole, complete, balanced human beings, equipped for every good work that our Heavenly Father might assign us. We desire wholeness, we long for holiness. Achieving holiness on our own strength, by our own power is impossible. But with God all things are possible. We learn from the angel Gabriel speaking to our Blessed Mother, Mary in the Gospel of Luke, Chapter 1

"For nothing is impossible to God." (Luke 1:37 JB*).*

Therefore, let us begin the Bible study of the Gospel according to Saint John, in expectant faith, constant hope and utter humility. Longing for sanctity and wholeness, pray to the Holy Spirit in the prayer of Cardinal Mercier of Belgium.

A Prayer to the Holy Spirit

O Holy Spirit,
Beloved of my soul, I adore You,
Enlighten, Guide, Strengthen and Console me;
Tell me what I ought to say and do and command me to do it.
I promise to be submissive in everything You will ask of me
and to accept all that You permit to happen to me,
only show me what is Your will.
Amen.

John 1

In the Beginning Was the Word

Memory Verses

**"In the beginning was the Word,
and the Word was with God, and the Word was God.
He was in the beginning with God; all things were made through Him
and without Him was not anything made that was made."**

John 1:1-3

**"But to all who received him, who believed in his name,
he gave power to become children of God;"**

John 1:12

In the Beginning was the Word. These insightful words begin one of the most profound books ever written, the Gospel According to John. At the opening of the book we have the words "in the beginning." This poetic device, known in poetry as the "objective correlative," describes something out there in the world that corresponds to the very term being used in the text. So there is an interplay between two beginnings here: the literary beginning of the book, and the beginning in which was located the eternal Word.

> This same poetic device is found at the opening of four books of the Bible.
>
> "In the beginning God created the heavens and the earth" (Genesis 1:1).
> "The beginning of the gospel of Jesus Christ, the Son of God" (Mark 1:1).
> "In the beginning was the Word, and the Word was with God, and the Word was God" (John 1:1).
> "This is what we proclaim to you: what was from the beginning" (1 John 1:1).

The first sentence of each of these books includes the term "the beginning." One of these examples is at the very opening of the Old Testament, and three of the examples are at the introduction of individual books within the New Testament. Certainly, both of the New Testament authors, Mark in one case and John in the others, were consciously imitating the commencement of the Book of Genesis. "In Genesis, God's work of creation reaches its peak when he creates man in his own image and likeness; in the Gospel, the work of the Incarnate Word culminates when man is raised to the dignity of being a son of God" (The Navarre Bible, *The Gospels and Acts of the Apostles*, [Princeton, NJ: Scepter, 2000], 523).

In the broader sense, Jesus makes this demand of every person on earth: "What are you looking for?" If we seek false gods of our own creation, we will find them and be disappointed by them. But, if we seek the one true God, we will find Him and be satisfied in Him. The first thing God desires of us, since it is the first question issuing from His mouth in the Gospel that calls him the Word, is to clarify our own purposes. This is our beginning, the beginning of our commitment to God. Just as marriage is the continual renewal of the married vows from the first moment they are uttered until the last breath taken by one of the beloved, so our faith requires the perpetual renewal of our commitment to God. As God creates the world anew in each moment, we need to renew our faith from moment to moment in response to God's action.

✤ The beginning of a personal relationship with Jesus the Messiah and the beginning of evangelism is introduced by the apostle, Andrew. "We have found the Messiah" (John 1:41). Andrew wants to follow Jesus and he brings his brother, Simon Peter, to meet Jesus. Jesus finds Philip and begins to gather His disciples around Him to teach them, redeem them, change them, and empower them.

The Beginning of the Public Life of Jesus. The poetry of John reads beautifully and yet challenges the reader to return again and again to prior passages to glean truths about God that remain mystery for the human mind, but give hope to the human spirit. Returning to previous verses, the plan of God in sending Jesus and His role and mission on earth are revealed. John Paul II says "Remembering that 'the Word became flesh,' that is, that the Son of God became man, we must become conscious of how great each man has become through this mystery, through the Incarnation of the Son of God! Christ, in fact, was conceived in the womb of Mary and became man to reveal the eternal love of the Father and to make known the dignity of each one of us" (Pope John Paul II, *Angelus Address,* June 5, 1979).

St. John Chrysostom proclaims "He that was Son of God became Son of Man so that He might make sons of men become children of God ... In no way did He diminish His own essence by this condescension, but He raised us, who had been in darkness and disgrace, to indescribable glory" (St. John Chrysostom [344-407 AD], *Homilies on the Gospel of John,* 11.1).

The Greek for "to dwell," *esk Enosen,* can be translated as 'to pitch one's tent' among us. Recall that in Old Testament times, God's people lived in tents throughout their exodus to the Promised Land, and God dwelt among them. God's presence was revealed in a cloud by day and a pillar of fire by night (Exodus 13:21-22) and ultimately in the tabernacle (Exodus 40:34). Now, God's presence manifests itself in Jesus Christ, perfect God from all eternity and perfect Man, dwelling in the midst of sinful men.

The purpose of Jesus' public ministry is foreshadowed in verse 12. "But to all who received him, who believed in his name, he gave power to become children of God" (John 1:12). Pope John Paul II explains that "Christ's union with man is power. . . . The Word gives power to become children of God. Man is transformed inwardly by this power as

the source of a new life that does not disappear and pass away but lasts to eternal life (John 4:14)" (Pope John Paul II, *Redemptor Hominis,* March 4, 1979, no. 18.2).

John the Baptist serves as a bridge, the last of the Old Covenant prophets to point to Jesus, the Messiah. John also testifies to the presence of the Holy Spirit in the life of Jesus (Matthew 3:11-17 and John 1:33). The Blessed Trinity emerges in beauty and mystery. John the Baptist testifies that Jesus is the Son of God (John 1:34). Andrew told his brother, Simon Peter "We have found the Messiah" (John 1:41). The next day, Philip tells Nathanael "We have found him of whom Moses in the law and also the prophets wrote, Jesus of Nazareth" (John 1:46). And finally, Nathanael proclaims "Rabbi, you are the Son of God! You are the King of Israel!" (John 1:49).

This is the beginning of Jesus' ministry to bring the world to Himself and to reconcile the world to the Father through His suffering and death.

These are the distinct beginnings in John 1, but they are representative of many, many beginnings that constitute our whole life, both here and hereafter.

- Every child that is born in the world is a new expression of God's hopes for humanity.
- Each New Year's Day we feel the beginning of new opportunities for repentance and self-improvement.
- Each morning is a new beginning, a new opportunity to do good and reject evil.
- Each time we sin, God holds out His hand so that we can make a new beginning of goodness.
- His grace renews us always, and the mission of the church in the world is to teach the world that, no matter how much violence takes place, there is always the possibility of a new beginning of peace.
- St. Paul says we are to "Make all things new in Christ" (Ephesians 1:10). Even when this world passes away, there will be a New Heaven and a New Earth perpetually renewed by God's grace.

Let us thank God for all the beginnings He has already given us, many of which we have failed to recognize, and thank Him for the beginning He provides us right now in starting this study of the wonderful and profound Gospel of John. Pray for new eyes with which to see the beginnings He lays out before us in the future. John 2 begins with the first of seven great miracles reported in the Gospel of John. We do see, don't we, that the miracle of John 1, the entry of the Divine Word into the world, is the supreme miracle from which all other miracles flow?

So, at the end of the first chapter of John, the Word of God speaks. Jesus is about 30 years old before John quotes anything. Jesus' first words in John are simple yet profound. First the simple question, "What are you looking for?" And then the invitation, "Come and see." So they went to stay with Him. For three years they were privileged to be His earthly companions, and now they enjoy eternity with Him. Come and see!

10. "And the Word became flesh and dwelt among us,

    full of ___________ and ___________;

    we have beheld his ______________,

    ______ as of the only Son from the Father." John 1:14 RSV

11. Which John is spoken of in John 1:6, John 1:15 and John 1:19-36?

12. What is this John's blood relationship to Jesus? Luke 1:13, 36, 41.

13. What sacrifice did God demand of the people of Israel? Exodus 12:3-5

14. What did the blood of the Passover Lamb do for the people of Israel? Exodus 12:23

15. To whom do the following references in Revelation refer?

Revelation 5:12	
Revelation 7:17	
Revelation 17:14	

16. How did the following people describe Jesus?

John the Baptist		John 1:29, 34
Andrew		John 1:41
Philip		John 1:45
Nathanael		John 1:49

17. What two things does Jesus ask in John 1:39 and John 1:43?

18. Recall some significant beginnings in your life.

19. How long has God known you? Psalm 139:1-17

20. Find a Douay-Rheims or Revised Standard Version Bible and write down the first four words of the Bible. Ponder them for awhile. Genesis 1:1

21. At the beginning of this study, can you pray the following prayer?

Lord God, You have known me from my beginning.
Forgive me for those times when I have ignored You or disobeyed You.
Open my heart and my spirit during this study.
Give me a new beginning.
Reveal more of Yourself to me.
Mold me, form me, change me.
Let Your light shine in me.
Let Your love transform me for Your glory.
Amen

JOHN 2

Jesus' Miracle at the Wedding

Memory Verse

**"His mother said to the servants,
'Do whatever he tells you.'"**

JOHN 2:5

The Wedding at Cana. Why would Jesus choose a wedding celebration for the scene of His first public miracle? Wine, the symbol of joy, anticipates the joy of the Eucharist, the new and everlasting covenant. Moses changed the waters of the Nile into blood (Exodus 7:14-22) in the Old Covenant. Jesus now changes water into wine, ushering in His New Covenant. At the Last Supper, Jesus gives Himself to His disciples and introduces the miraculous sacrament of the New Covenant, the Eucharist, in which wine mixed with water is transformed into the blood of Christ. "This is my blood of the covenant, which is poured out for many" (Mark 14:24). Jesus' sacrifice and death brings about the redemption of the world. "Truly, I say to you, I shall not drink again of the fruit of the vine until that day when I drink it new in the kingdom of God" (Mark 14:25).

Moreover, the wedding at Cana prefigures the marriage feast of the Lamb (Revelation 19:7). The first miracle gives a foretaste of the sublime miracle. Christ will offer spiritual drink from the chalice of His body. He offers the New Wine, the joy of salvation purchased by the shedding of His blood on the cross for our redemption.

Weddings play an important role in our lives as they do in Sacred Scripture. Have you ever slowed down on a Saturday afternoon to catch a glimpse of a bride leaving the church? And have you spent extra time in finding just the right gift and a special outfit for the wedding of a relative or friend? Whose idea was marriage anyway? Does the sacrament of matrimony make any difference from just living together? Or is it just a matter of a piece of paper as some suggest? Since Jesus and His Mother, Mary, chose to attend this wedding and then played instrumental roles in sparing the bridal couple and their families embarrassment in running out of wine for their guests, it might help to look at the sacrament of marriage while studying this first miracle of Jesus' public life.

Marriage in God's Plan. Sacred Scripture begins with creation of man and woman in the image and likeness of God and concludes with a vision of the "wedding-feast of the Lamb." The intimate community of life and love which constitutes the married state has been established by the Creator . . . God Himself is the author of marriage.

Vatican II, *Gaudium et Spes,* 48.1

John Cardinal O'Connor, the late archbishop of New York said "In a world in which marriage is frequently imperiled and denigrated in so many ways, it is imperative that the Church continually and faithfully announce the good news of marriage ... Herein lies the essence of the sacramentality of marriage: through the loving marital relationship, God continues to make known His presence in the world. Jesus announced the advent of His Kingdom as one of tenderness and intimacy. He speaks of a God whose love, mercy, and forgiveness is extravagant, limitless, and without reservation. Since marriage is the living, tangible, sacramental sign of this love, these characteristics are to be expressed and experienced in the marital relationship" (Cardinal John O'Connor, from Dietrich von Hildebrand's *Marriage, The Mystery of Faithful Love,* [Manchester, NH: Sophia Press, 1991], xix).

Philosopher Dietrich von Hildebrand said, "Love is the inmost core of the relation of the soul to God. Marriage has been chosen as the image of the perfect union between the soul and Christ because in marriage, the center and core is love. No other earthly community is constituted so exclusively in its very substance by mutual love." (Dietrich von Hildebrand, ibid., 4-5).

Marriage was at the heart of God's plan from the beginning. God said "It is not good that the man should be alone; I will make him a helper fit for him" (Genesis 2:18). So in the very act of creation, God creates woman and brings her to the man, that they may become one flesh. God has been in the matchmaking business from the very beginning, and God still brings people together to marry and cooperate in His plans for continuing the human race. Just as the couple at Cana invited Jesus to their wedding, it behooves married couples in this day to invite Jesus into the marriage relationship, for the scripture promises "Two are better than one. . . . For if they fall, one will lift up his fellow, but woe to him who is alone when he falls and has not another to lift him up. . . . A threefold cord is not quickly broken." (Ecclesiastes 4:9-10, 12). Invite God to be the third cord holding the marriage together.

St. Augustine said, "I suppose it was not without cause He came to the marriage. The miracle apart, there lies something mysterious and sacramental in the very fact. Let us knock, that He may open to us, and fill us with the invisible wine, for we were water, and He made us wine, made us wise; for He gave us the wisdom of His faith, while before we were foolish . . . The Lord, on being invited came to the marriage" (St. Augustine [354-430 AD], *Tractates on the Gospel of John,* 8.3-4).

Marriage has come under attack in contemporary society. The permanence and indissolubility of one man and one woman faithful until death is often discarded for a variety of arrangements in which partners stay together as long as they wish. So, how can marriage withstand the storms and tribulations that occur in life if the Lord is not invited? Without the presence of God and the grace of the sacrament, lives may be left to toss and turn amid the turbulent waves of societal whims. The couple at Cana invited Jesus to their wedding. The sensible Catholic married couple today invites Jesus into their marriage and family life to bless and sustain it and pour forth grace and

strength for whatever may come. In hard times, one spouse may lift up the other and when both are down, Jesus can hold them together in the midst of the storm. Whether in a happy marriage, or a difficult one, the grace of the sacrament enables God to be glorified in every situation. Human beings may fail and disappoint one another, but God never fails, never falls short. God's grace is always available in the sacrament, for those who call upon Him and seek His help.

St. Ignatius of Antioch (35-107 AD) said, "Tell my sisters to love the Lord and to be satisfied with their husbands in flesh and spirit." A Christian married woman may love God, but express dissatisfaction with her husband: "If only he was more spiritual, more industrious, more romantic." Similarly, a husband may wish his wife was younger, prettier, or more amusing. Dissatisfaction can rob one of the virtue of contentment. Gratitude, a thankful heart, nurtures the virtue of contentment.

In the Old Testament, Moses' first miracle before Pharaoh (Exodus 7:20) was to turn the waters of the Nile into blood. Moses turned something life-giving into something deadly. Jesus, by contrast, turns life-giving water into something better, wine which sustains life and brings joy. Isaiah 55:1 invites "Everyone who thirsts, come to the waters; come buy and eat! Come buy wine and milk without money and without price." And Joel 3:18 says, "And in that day, the mountains shall drip sweet wine and the hills shall flow with milk." An abundance of wine provides a foretaste of the messianic age and a restoration of the relationship with God lost in the Garden of Eden. The super-abundance of wine, some 120-150 gallons gives us a glimpse that God is doing something new and spectacular, which man has not yet imagined. Jesus ushers in the New Covenant with a lavish miracle of God's providential love and care.

In John 2:1-11 the wedding at Cana is described, and in John 19:25-27 we are told of Mary's presence on Calvary. In both passages, Mary is described as the Mother of Jesus and in both our Lord refers to her as "woman" with affection and respect. At both Cana and Calvary Jesus' "hour" is referred to—in the first case as something which has not yet arrived, and in the second as a present fact. This "hour" of Jesus marks His whole life until it culminates in His passion and death on the cross.

"Woman, what have you to do with Me? My hour has not yet come" (John 2:4). Jesus addresses Mary, His Mother, as "woman," the same title that was given to "Eve." The word "woman" may reference the proto-evangelium of Genesis 3:15 which promises the triumph of the "woman and her seed" over the serpent. Eve, the human mother of humanity, brought death into the world by her disobedience to God. Mary, the spiritual mother, the "new Eve," will bring life for lost souls, by her obedience to God. In accepting God's invitation and God's plan, Mary gave life to the Son of God, who brings about redemption for sinners and the opportunity for eternal life. Jesus identifies His Mother in her relationship to the whole of humanity and professes that His life also submits in total obedience to the Father. Jesus will not act, will not bring about the salvation of the world, at anyone's bequest until the Father's perfect time comes.

Prayer in an Unhappy Marriage

O God, Lord and Director of my life, You have placed me in the state of marriage. In it I had hoped for joy and happiness, but alas! I experience tribulation upon tribulation.

Place before my eyes Your only well-beloved Son, whose whole life here below was the hard way of the cross. You call me to follow Him. I will do, O Lord, what You ask of me. I thank You from my heart for Your love in treating me as You treated Your well-beloved Son, eternal with Yourself, and equal to You in essence.

Behold my weakness! Have pity on my cowardice! I know that without Your special grace, I am unable to bear my cross as I should.

Give me what You demand of me, and then ask what You will. Give me Your most amiable Son, as You gave Him to the most Blessed Virgin Mary, that He may be always with me, to counsel and assist me, to preserve and daily confirm me in Your love. Place me in the open wound of His Heart. Fill me with His meekness and humility. Grant me a share in His fortitude and I shall be able to endure all things.

Teach me after the example of my sweet Savior, to repay evil with good, angry words with silence or gentle replies; to merit Your favor by fulfillment of duty, and, by ready obedience and constant, faithful love, gain my spouse's heart for You.

Preserve us, Almighty God, from the deceits of the evil spirits and from the malicious, or perhaps well-meant, though foolish language and counsels of silly people.

Grant us peace and harmony, true affection and forbearance, devout sentiments and holy fear, that we may cheerfully labor, pray and suffer with and for each other.

May we tread together the way of Your holy Commandments and together reap the reward of our good works for all eternity! Grant us this, Heavenly Father, for the love of Jesus, Mary and Joseph, as also of all the saints who, in the married state, sanctified themselves and attained eternal life.

Amen.

1. What does the Catholic Church say about the goodness of marriage? ***CCC 1604***

2. Who confers the Sacrament of Matrimony? ***CCC 1623***

3. Did Mary make a request of Jesus or state a need? John 2:3
   What does she tell the servants to do?

4. In Tobias' prayer on the night of his marriage to Sarah, what was his motive for marrying? Tobit 8:5-8

   What two things did Tobias ask God for? Tobit 8:7

5. What attitude did Michal have toward her husband, David, when she saw him dancing before the Lord? 2 Samuel 6:16 or 1 Chronicles 15:29

6. What happened to Michal after criticizing her husband, David? 2 Samuel 6:20-23

17. Jesus expressed righteous indignation at religious leaders who made religion into a business. Can you identify similar dangers for religious people today, using things of God for one's own personal profit and gain?

18. What could you do to show more reverence in the church, the house of God?

19. What did Jesus foretell in John 2:19-22?

20. What does Jesus know about all individual human beings? John 2:24-25

21. How does St. Paul describe Christians in 1 Corinthians 3:16 and 6:19?

22. What could you do to make that temple more pleasing to God?

JOHN 3

Jesus, Source of Eternal Life

Memory Verse

**"For God so loved the world that he gave his only Son,
that whoever believes in him
should not perish but have eternal life.
For God sent the Son into the world, not to condemn the world,
but that the world might be saved through him."**
JOHN 3:16-17

Jesus Offers Nicodemus Eternal Life. Nicodemus, a Pharisee, among the most devout of the Jews, and member of the Sanhedrin, comes to see Jesus at night. Perhaps he was embarrassed to question this young, unschooled, itinerant preacher in broad daylight. Or perhaps, as a scholar, he was studying well into the night and came to Jesus with his queries while he was reading and praying. In any event, the contrast of night and day, darkness and light, sets the stage for repenting of sin and coming to believe in Jesus, the light of the world, the source of enlightenment and the revelation of God the Father. Nicodemus acknowledges that God is with Jesus, for no one can perform the signs that Jesus does, unless God is with him.

In school, a teacher may say "Listen up! Pay attention. This is important. This will be on the test!" to get the students attention. Jesus piques our interest and alerts us to the fact that something essential will be required, when He says "Truly, truly I say to you . . ." or "Amen, amen I say to you . . ." The repetition of words alerts the reader to pay attention. Listen up! This is important!

Jesus presents the concept of being born from above, being reborn or born anew. We must be born of water and the Spirit in order to enter the kingdom of God. The Spirit brings us to faith in Christ. This mystery of the Holy Spirit working to give the gift of faith and bring us to repentance is the free, divine gift of God. However, a response is required. The Christian must believe in the Son of Man, the Lord, Jesus Christ lifted up on the cross for the salvation of souls, repent of personal sin and be baptized.

In the Acts of the Apostles, the Jews asked Peter what they should do to be saved. And Peter said to them "Repent and be baptized every one of you in the name of Jesus Christ for the forgiveness of your sins; and you shall receive the gift of the Holy Spirit." (Acts 2:38).

John the Baptist deflects praise from himself and points to Jesus. He states clearly that he is not the Christ, but the precursor, the one who is sent before Him to prepare the way. "He must increase, but I must decrease" (John 3:30). John knows that all glory belongs to God and God alone. He resists the temptation to exalt himself and bask in the adulation of others. John models the virtue of humility for believers of all time. John knows who he is and he knows who the Messiah is and he doesn't confuse the two. He has a very healthy appreciation of discipleship and his role in God's plan.

In the movie, "Rudy," about a young man who wants to play football for Notre Dame, Rudy approaches a priest for counsel. The priest models John the Baptist when he says, "I know there is a God. And I know I'm not Him."

This example is helpful for all Christians. God assigns each a task for the building of His kingdom. The temptation is to compare and covet the task of another. Some forget that Jesus is the Messiah, the Savior of the world. Some might take on their shoulders the responsibility to try to save one's child from disappointment or one's spouse from failure. Like John the Baptist, God might call us to pave the way and then get out of the way and let God work. We can pray and serve and obey. But, only God can save.

Are you born again? Have you renounced Satan and all of his works and empty promises? Have you acknowledged your personal wrongdoing and repented of your sins, asking God for His forgiveness and mercy? If you have been baptized in the name of the Father and of the Son and of the Holy Spirit, then you are born again. You are a new creation.

If you don't feel like you've had a born again experience, examine your conscience. Is some unconfessed sin or lack of forgiveness on your part blocking you from experiencing all the love and grace that God has for you? If you are in a state of grace, know that God always has more for you. Ask God to reveal Himself to you in a more personal way. Ask the Holy Spirit to refresh you and give you a greater outpouring of His gifts and grace. Pray the following prayer aloud.

Come Holy Spirit,
Fill the hearts of your faithful;
Enkindle in us the fire of Your Love.
Send forth Your Spirit and we shall be created
and You shall renew the face of the earth.
O God, who by the light of the Holy Spirit
did instruct the hearts of the faithful,
Grant us by that same Holy Spirit
to be truly wise and ever to rejoice in His consolation
through Christ Our Lord. Amen.

A Good Samaritan

Janet entered the hospital the day before her minor surgery was scheduled. After settling into her hospital bed, she asked her nurse if she could see the hospital chaplain and go to Confession. Janet asked her roommate, Lynn, who was also scheduled for surgery the following day if she would like to speak with the priest as well.

"Oh no, I'm not into that stuff anymore," retorted Lynn.

The priest arrived and heard Janet's confession. He asked if there was anything else he could do for her.

"Yes, please talk to my roommate. She'd like to go to Confession, too," quipped Janet.

The priest moved to the next bed and drew the curtain. Janet turned up the radio and couldn't hear what transpired. When the priest left, Lynn admitted that she had gone to Confession too, for the first time in many years.

After surgery the following day, Janet was returned to her room, somewhat groggy from the anesthesia. When the nurse came to check on her, Janet was surprised that it was already evening and that Lynn, whose surgery was earlier had not yet returned to the room. Janet asked the nurse whether Lynn was still in the recovery room.

The nurse hesitated and then said, "I'm sorry no one has told you. But, your roommate Lynn did not survive her surgery today."

1. Why do you need a Savior? Romans 3:23

2 What did Elisha, the man of God, tell Naaman, commander of the Syrian army, to do when Naaman was stricken with leprosy? 2 Kings 5:10

   What was the result of Naaman's obedience? 2 Kings 5:14

3. When we are baptized, what are we baptized into? Romans 6:3-6

4. What is necessary for the grace of Baptism to unfold? *CCC 1255*

5. Does the Church offer any hope of salvation for those who have not been baptized? *CCC 1258, 1260, 1261*

6. What are some things that a godparent could do for a godchild? *CCC 1255*

7. Why must the Son of Man be lifted up on the cross? John 3:15

8. Why would someone refuse to come into the light and believe in Jesus? John 3:19-20

9 What are some examples of darkness in our society? Galatians 5:19-21

10. List some examples of light that Christians bring to the world today? Acts 4:32-35

11. When asked if you are saved or "born again," how would you respond?

12 Has there been a time in your life when you felt God was asking you to recommit your life to Him or make an adult commitment to Christ? Matthew 11:28-30

13. John the Baptist refers to himself as the friend of the bridegroom in John 3:29. How does John respond to the voice of Christ, the bridegroom? John 3:29

14. The word "Trinity" does not appear in the Bible. Can you identify the three Persons of the Blessed Trinity in John 3:34-35?

15. If you have not had a "born again" experience or don't feel alive in the Holy Spirit, how could you experience greater intimacy with God? Acts 3:19

16. Have you had any positive experiences with renewal movements such as Cursillo, Marriage Encounter or the Catholic Charismatic Renewal?

17. If you were to describe an excellent example of a Catholic "born-again" Christian, who would it be?

18. St Francis of Assisi said "Preach the Gospel always. When necessary use words." What do you think he meant by that statement?

19. Explain John 3:21 in your own words.

20. Describe one way that you try to share the Gospel or let your light shine.

John 3:16-17

(personalized)

For God so loved ____________ ,
(insert your name here)

that he gave his only Son,

that if ____________ believes in Him,
(insert your name here)

s/he should not perish

but have eternal life.

For God sent the Son into the world,

not to condemn ____________ but that
(insert your name here)

____________ might be saved through Him.
(insert your name here)

she stops running around and carrying on so shamefully. Perhaps the Samaritan woman was longing for a child or feverishly hoping for intimacy or perhaps she was simply looking for sexual pleasure or adventure. Perhaps she longed for affirmation or a purpose for living or a sense of meaning for her life. Whatever her motives, her sin had further isolated her as sin always does. The forbidden fruit that seems to be so desirable becomes deadly once eaten. Someone once said "Nobody ever really breaks the Ten Commandments. We simply break ourselves against them."

Jesus approaches the well in the heat of the day. The Samaritan woman comes to the well alone. It's hard for Westerners, who simply turn on the tap for a drink of cool, clear water to grasp the importance of water in this dry and arid land. The luxury of turning on the tub to sponge-bathe a feverish child in the middle of the night is unimaginable to women in many parts of the world even today. Women come to the well in the cool of the early morning to draw their water for drinking, cooking, washing and cleaning. The fellowship of the women, sharing news with one another, announcing engagements, discussing weddings, pregnancies, children's achievements, illnesses of the elderly and so on, would be missed by this poor outcast woman, coming to the well later in her shame and isolation.

In this chapter, St. John reveals to us both the humanity and divinity of Jesus Christ. Jesus displays the human condition that we all experience, identifying with fatigue, thirst and hunger. Despite His weariness, Jesus reaches out to a poor, sinful woman and asks her for a drink. Since rabbis avoided speaking to women in public and Jews disdained Samaritans, Jesus demonstrates astonishing charity. Jesus also shows that He is not bound by the cultural expectations or restraints of the place and time in which He lived. Jesus had no problem speaking with women, children, the rich, the poor, the prominent or the outcast.

Frequently, St. John uses dual imagery in writing his gospel. While telling an important story on the surface, he also provides a parallel, deep theological truth. So, Jesus speaks of water, which is essential for physical life and also living water, Jesus' gift of Himself and the gift of grace, which provides supernatural, everlasting life.

Jesus displays His supernatural powers and His divinity in speaking with the woman. *Jesus sees* the woman's heart. He knows her sins, her history and her need for redemption. The woman said to Him, "Sir, I perceive you are a prophet" (John 4:19). Jesus is a prophet of God, but so much more than a prophet, and He does not leave her with incomplete information or partial understanding about His identity. When speaking about the Messiah, who is called the Christ, who is to come, Jesus says to her "I who speak to you am He" (John 4:26). I AM recalls the way in which God revealed himself to Moses. "I AM WHO I AM" (Exodus 3:14). Jesus clearly identifies His oneness with God the Father and manifests His divinity. When Jesus explains "God is spirit, and those who worship him must worship in spirit and truth" (John 4:24), He prepares the woman for belief in Himself as the standard for true worship, which is acceptable to the Father. Jesus says "I am the way, and the truth, and the life; no one comes to the Father, but by me" (John 14:6).

When the disciples arrive, they marvel that Jesus is speaking with a woman, but they do not question Him. The woman leaves her water jug and goes into the town to tell the people all about Jesus and bring them to Him. After having met Jesus, she becomes an evangelist and strives to bring others to Jesus as well. The joy of a personal encounter with the Lord, Jesus Christ, and a taste of His mercy and love spills out to others.

St. John provides another dual message when the disciples ask Jesus to eat something. The disciples think of physical food, which is necessary for life and strength. Jesus, however, shows that His food is to do the will of His Father. Bringing souls into the kingdom invigorates and strengthens. Some harvest crops to feed people. Yet the harvest is ripe for laborers to proclaim the gospel and gather souls for eternal life. Because of the woman's testimony, many Samaritans come to believe in Jesus. So, Jesus is the first apostle to the Gentiles. The Samaritan woman at the well becomes a believer and an evangelist to her fellow Samaritans.

Jesus Heals the Official's Son. After two days Jesus leaves to return to Galilee. The Galileans welcome Jesus since they remember the fine wine that He provided for them at the Wedding Feast at Cana and the signs and wonders He performed. At Capernaum, there was a Gentile military official whose son was dying. When the official learned that Jesus had come to Galilee from Judea, he went and begged Jesus to come down with him to his home to heal his son. Jesus points out that people don't believe in Him unless they see signs and wonders (John 4:48). But, the official persists in begging Jesus to come with him before his child dies.

Jesus does not accede to the man's wishes. He does not come to the official's house to heal the man's child, as the official had hoped. Jesus does not meet this Gentile's demand. Nonetheless, Jesus sees the man's heart. He knows the man's level of faith. Jesus speaks to the man, "Go; your son will live." The man believed the word that Jesus spoke to him and went on his way toward home (John 4:50).

The official obeyed Jesus and returned to his home without having Jesus accompany him as he had requested. While on his way, his servants met him and reported that his son had been healed. On questioning the servants, the father learned that his son had been healed at the very hour that Jesus spoke to him. In response to God's word in healing his son, the official believed in Jesus and his whole household also became believers. So, more Gentiles came to know the saving power of Jesus.

John 4 describes two very dramatic accounts. The woman at the well epitomizes someone unlucky in love and steeped in sin. St. Augustine said "You made us for Yourself, Lord, and our hearts find no peace until they rest in You" (St. Augustine, *The Confessions of Saint Augustine*, 1.1).

Many dramatic conversion stories abound in the Bible and in contemporary society. Perhaps colorful sinners have an advantage in that their sin is so obvious and apparent to everyone. Their misery causes so much pain that they may be eager to respond to

8. Living water can be a reference to life in Christ Jesus, a life filled with grace. Use the *Catechism of the Catholic Church* to define "grace." ***CCC 1997, 1999***

9. The Jews worship the God of Abraham, Isaac and Jacob. In awaiting Messiah, explain the significance to the Jews of verses 6 and 12 in Chapter 4. John 4:6, 12

10. What evidence can you cite for the divinity of Jesus? John 4:21-26

11. How does Jesus reveal Himself in John 4:25?

12. What did Jesus' disciples find surprising about Jesus' behavior? John 4:27

13. What did the Samaritan woman report to the townspeople? John 4:28-29

14. Describe her question and the response of the townspeople. John 4:29-30

Judaism, a monotheistic religion, professes one true God rather than the many gods of mythology and false religions. In the Jewish tradition, every good Jew prays the Shema each day, which begins "Hear, O Israel: The LORD our God is one LORD; and you shall love the LORD your God with all your heart, and with all your soul, and with all your might" (Deuteronomy 6:4). Likewise, Christianity, also a monotheistic religion, confesses one God in three persons, each whole, entire and divine.

St. Fulgence of Ruspe (467-527 AD) explains. "See, in short you have it that the Father is one, the Son another, and the Holy Spirit another; in Person, each is other, but in nature they are not other. In this regard He says: 'The Father and I, we are one' (John 10:30). He teaches us that one refers to their nature, and we are to their persons. In like manner it is said: 'There are three who bear witness in heaven, the Father, the Word, and the Spirit; and these three are one'(1 John 5:7)" (St. Fulgence of Ruspe, *The Trinity,* 4.1).

> Christians are baptized in the *name* of the Father and of the Son and of the Holy Spirit: not in their *names,* for there is only one God, the almighty Father, his only Son, and the Holy Spirit: the Most Holy Trinity.
>
> *CCC 233*

The mystery of the Trinity, incomprehensible to the human mind, nonetheless can be pondered and cherished. Catholics accept on faith the testimony of Jesus and the Sacred Scriptures this teaching of the Church from the time of Jesus and the Apostles. The fact that the truth of the Trinity is a mystery should not cause undue concern to Christians. God chooses to reveal truths to His children that could not be discovered apart from His divine revelation.

> A story is told of St. Augustine, walking along the seashore, pondering the Trinitarian mystery. A little boy had dug a hole in the sand and was running back and forth to the sea, trying to fill his hole with water. St. Augustine became exasperated with the child and asked what he was trying to accomplish. The child explained that he was going to put the entire sea into the hole he had dug. When Augustine explained that it would be impossible to fit a huge body of water into such a little hole, the child responded that it is equally hopeless to try to fit the mystery of the Trinity into one human mind!

Because Jesus is the Son of God, we believe in the truth of His word and His witness. However, in perfect humility, Jesus accommodates the needs of the doubters with many other proofs of His divinity.

6. Before Jesus raised Lazarus from the dead, who did Martha believe Jesus to be? John 11:27

7. What verb tense is used to indicate a belief in Jesus and possession of eternal life as promised in John 5:24?

8. What criteria does Jesus give in John 13:35?

9. Write key phrases from the following Old Testament scriptures.

   Isaiah 7:14

   Micah 5:1-2

   Isaiah 16:5

   Psalm 22:17-18

   To whom do they point?

10. How does God the Father characterize Jesus in the following scriptures?

    Matthew 3:17

    Matthew 17:5

    Mark 1:9-11

    John 12:27-30

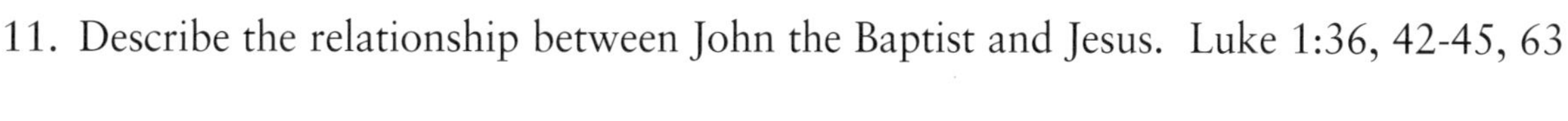

11. Describe the relationship between John the Baptist and Jesus. Luke 1:36, 42-45, 63

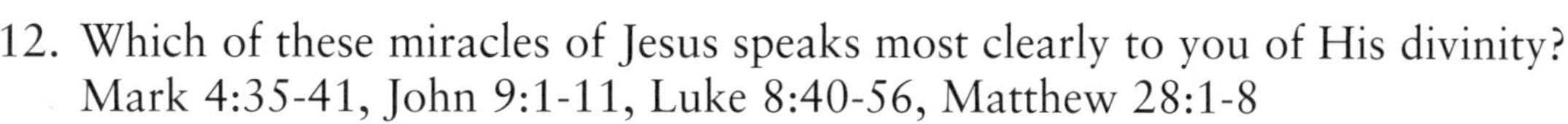

12. Which of these miracles of Jesus speaks most clearly to you of His divinity? Mark 4:35-41, John 9:1-11, Luke 8:40-56, Matthew 28:1-8

13. Explain the dogma of the Holy Trinity as clearly as you can. ***CCC 253-258***

14. Which persons of the Blessed Trinity can be identified in the following verses?

    John 14:26

    John 15:26

15. What is the physical manifestation of the Blessed Trinity that each Catholic makes at the beginning of each Mass? ***CCC 1145***

16. How do parents teach even young children to worship the Holy Trinity?

17. Which person of the Blessed Trinity is easiest for you to pray to? Why?

18. Which person of the Blessed Trinity is most difficult for you to comprehend?

19. This week, pray each day that God will give you greater affection and devotion for another person of the Blessed Trinity. ***CCC 260***

the very Life of God Himself. For all eternity, God will be our feast, and that banquet is spread out for us already here on earth. Just as we need Heaven hereafter, so do we need Eucharist now. Peter said he believed. Shall we stand with him and say the same? "The Body of Christ." "Amen. I do believe."

The Spirit Gives Life. When Jesus says, "it is the Spirit that gives life" (John 6:63), remember that God uniquely creates a human soul at the moment of the conception of each human being. We receive our bodies from our parents, but we receive our souls in a direct act of creation from Almighty God. Flesh begets flesh, but Spirit begets spirit. It is our souls that make us human, not just our DNA. Jesus goes on to say, "The flesh is useless." Here He is referring not to His own Flesh, but to sinful flesh. Now if my flesh died on the cross, you would not be saved, and if yours had done so, I would not be saved, because our flesh is subject to original sin. The flesh of Jesus on the Cross was anything but useless, however, because the spirit of God was in it. Now when we receive Communion we truly receive this useful Flesh of Christ, but we receive also the Spirit that made His Flesh useful. The real scandal of the Eucharist is not that Jesus gives us His Body and Blood as food (if He can do anything, He can do that too), but that His Soul and His infinite Divinity enter our small souls. How can something so large as God enter someone so small as I am? We humbly receive a Gift so far beyond our merits.

How did Christians in the first century of the Early Church understand these words?

No one may share the Eucharist with us unless he believes that what we teach is true, unless he is washed in the regenerating waters of baptism for the remission of his sins, and unless he lives in accordance with the principles given us by Christ. We do not consume the Eucharistic bread and wine as if it were ordinary food and drink, for we have been taught that as Jesus Christ our Savior became a man of flesh and blood by the power of the Word of God, so also the food that our flesh and blood assimilates for its nourishment becomes the flesh and blood of the incarnate Jesus by the power of His own words contained in the prayer of thanksgiving.

St. Justin the Martyr (100-165 AD),
First Apology in Defense of Christians, 66-67

Because of this Body I hope for heaven, and I hope to receive the good things that are in heaven, immortal life, the lot of the angels, familiar conversation with Christ. This Body, scourged and crucified, has not been fetched by death . . . This is the Body which He gave us, both to hold in reserve and to eat, which was appropriate to intense love . . . Reverence, therefore, reverence this table of which we are all communicants! Christ, slain for us, the Sacrificial Victim who is placed thereon!

St. John Chrysostom (347-407AD)
Homilies on Corinthians, 24.4-7,
and *Romans,* 8.8

One reason that Catholics do not routinely invite people of other faiths to share communion stems from this early church practice. Receiving Holy Communion in the Catholic Church presupposes belief in the Real Presence of Christ in the Eucharist, baptism and obedience to Catholic Church teaching. If a person does not believe in the Real Presence, does not adhere to the teachings of the magisterium or is not living in accordance with the principles handed down by Christ to His Church, it is appropriate to refrain from receiving the Eucharist and first speak with a priest about the issues.

Catholics are mystified why some who maintain the literal interpretation of the Bible can have such trouble in embracing the literal meaning of the words of Jesus repeated again and again in John 6. Ancient patristic authors from both the Greek and Latin traditions, from the East and the West, affirm the literal sense of the Eucharistic passages from the days of the early Church down through the centuries.

He [Jesus] Himself, therefore, having declared and said of the Bread, 'This is My Body,' who will dare any longer to doubt? And when He Himself has affirmed and said, 'This is My Blood,' who can ever hesitate and say it is not His Blood? St. Cyril of Jerusalem (315-386 AD), *Mystagogic,* 4.1	You may say: I see something else; how can you assure me that I am receiving the Body of Christ? . . . Could not Christ's word, which can make from nothing what did not exist, change existing things into what they were not before? It is no less a feat to give things their original nature than to change their nature. St. Ambrose of Milan (340-397 AD), *The Mysteries,* 9.50

Since Jesus Himself states plainly and repeatedly "This is my Body" (Matthew 26:26) and "the bread which I shall give for the life of the world is my flesh" (John 6:51), who would dare contradict Jesus and say that it is not so? Therefore, with complete assurance in the words of Jesus, Catholics receive the Body and Blood of Christ and having His Body and Blood, become Christ-bearers and sharers in the divine nature.

If God could create the universe out of nothing, if Christ could change water into wine at Cana, Christ can also change bread and wine into His very flesh and blood! If God can do all things, if God can save sinful human beings, God can also provide the spiritual nourishment necessary for the pilgrim's journey to heaven. To ponder this sacred mystery requires faith built upon reason. If you struggle to have faith in the Real Presence in the Eucharist, pray the prayer: "I do believe; help my unbelief" (Mark 9:24).

During the lifetime of St. Thomas Aquinas (1224-1274 AD), the Catholic Church introduced the Feast of Corpus Christi on the second Thursday after Pentecost. For this feast, St. Thomas wrote Eucharistic hymns which remain dear to Catholic devotional life—Tantum Ergo, O Salutaris Hostia, and Panis Angelicus. In these hymns, and in his Summa Theologica, the Angelic Doctor affirmed the credibility of the Real Presence. "Faith will tell us Christ is present, when our human senses fail" (*Tantum Ergo).*

The Fourth Lateran Council (1215) created a term to describe this marvelous Eucharistic change: "transubstantiation." The Council of Trent (1551) reaffirmed that "in the most Blessed Sacrament of the Eucharist the body and blood, together with the soul and divinity of our Lord Jesus Christ, and therefore the whole Christ, is truly, really and substantially contained."

Dissent and Defections Follow. After Jesus presents this amazing discourse, the crowd begins to murmur and grumble (John 6:41, 52), and the doubting continues to this very day. The dissenters query "How can this man give us his flesh to eat?" (John 6:52). Rather than softening His words or explaining them away, Jesus becomes more insistent, using verbs that in the Greek become more graphic, meaning to "chew" or "gnaw." Jesus reiterates "For my flesh is food indeed and my blood is drink indeed. He who eats my flesh and drinks my blood abides in me, and I in him" (John 6:55-56).

Aware that the disciples are murmuring about His words, Jesus confronts them. Look also at what is not said in this chapter. Jesus does not say that He is speaking symbolically. He does not say that this is a metaphor. Jesus does not run after the dissenters and invite them to come back. Jesus doesn't try to reassure them that they have misunderstood a concept that could easily be cleared up. Jesus says nothing about "symbolism." Jesus simply acknowledges that some will not be able to accept what He is saying. Some will take offense at His words and leave. Jesus confronts The Twelve; "Will you also go away?" (John 6:67). Peter, demonstrating his leadership and primacy among the twelve apostles, answers for the group, in a compelling profession of faith and allegiance, "Lord, to whom shall we go? You have the words of eternal life; and we have believed and have come to know that you are the Holy One of God" (John 6:67-69).

People who have the faith to believe in the Real Presence of Jesus Christ in the Blessed Sacrament praise and thank God for such a great gift and so precious a treasure. For, those who doubt the truth of Jesus' words "For my flesh is food indeed" (John 6:55), God provides continuing miracles to reinforce the truth of His word in Sacred Scripture and Tradition. Since the gift of the Eucharist is preceded by miracles, and the gift is itself a miracle, isn't it only right to expect that miracles should also follow?

In Lanciano, Italy, around 700 AD, a Basilian priest suffered recurring doubts about the mystery of transubstantiation. One day, during Mass, the host suddenly appeared as a circle of flesh and the chalice filled with blood. Many verifications of this miracle occurred over the centuries. In November 1970, scientists again examined the Eucharistic species and declared the host to be human myocardial (heart) tissue and the blood in the chalice, type AB matching the blood type of the heart tissue. You can see the relics of this miracle for yourself in the Church of St. Francis in Lanciano, Italy,

Similarly, in O Cebreiro, Spain in the 14th century a crofter braved a snowstorm to enter St. Mary Royal Church at the moment of Consecration. The officiating priest disdained the man for making such a heroic effort for just a piece of bread and a drop of wine. At that instant, the bread became flesh and the chalice overflowed with blood before their very eyes. The Eucharistic species were saved and remain on display in two ampules donated by the Catholic monarchs on pilgrimage to Santiago de Compostela.

The Catholic Church continues to reaffirm the truth of Jesus' words in John 6. Since the time of Christ, it has remained a central dogma of the faith. This teaching of the Church has been reiterated for almost 2,000 years without change.

> The Second Vatican Council declared that the Eucharistic sacrifice is "the source and summit of the Christian life. For the most holy Eucharist contains the Church's entire spiritual wealth: Christ Himself, our Passover and living bread. Through His own flesh, now made living and life-giving by the Holy Spirit, He offers life to men."
>
> Vatican II, *Lumen Gentium,* 11, and *Presbyterorum Ordinis,* 5

Pope John Paul II has, throughout his long papacy, encouraged frequent, worthy reception of the Eucharist by the faithful as well as adoration of the Blessed Sacrament. He has issued two major encyclicals on the Eucharist, one at the beginning of his papacy and another twenty-three years later.

> The Church and the world have a great need for Eucharistic worship. Jesus awaits us in this sacrament of love. Let us not refuse the time to go to meet Him in adoration, in contemplation full of faith, and open to making amends for the serious offenses and crimes of the world. Let our adoration never cease.
>
> Pope John Paul II, *Dominicae Cenae,* February 15, 1980, no.3

> The Church draws her life from the Eucharist. This truth does not simply express a daily experience of faith, but recapitulates the heart of the mystery of the Church. In a variety of ways she joyfully experiences the constant fulfillment of the promise: 'Lo, I am with you always, to the close of the age' (Matthew 28:20), but in the Holy Eucharist, through the changing of bread and wine into the body and blood of the Lord, she rejoices in this presence with unique intensity. Ever since Pentecost, when the Church, the People of the New Covenant, began her pilgrim journey toward her heavenly homeland, the Divine Sacrament has continued to mark the passing of her days, filling them with confident hope.
>
> Pope John Paul II, *Ecclesia de Eucharistia,* April 17, 2003, no. 1.1

The Eucharist provides an immense treasure for Catholics that staggers the imagination. Jesus humbles Himself each day to come in an intimate way to His beloved in churches all around the world. Christ meekly reposes in the tabernacles of the world. The Lord rests on the tongue of the believer. Jesus comes again and again. The Eucharist may be the greatest treasure of the Catholic faith. Catholics believe that what Jesus said in the Bible in John 6 is literally true. Jesus is the Bread of Life. The Eucharist is real food for the journey to nourish pilgrims on their way toward eternal life.

Catholics not only consume the Blessed Sacrament in Holy Communion, but also worship and adore Christ in adoration of the Blessed Sacrament. Miracles, answers to prayer and personal transformations accompany adoration. Stubborn sin patterns are broken and troubled marriages healed. Vocations flourish. Jesus is still a miracle worker!

Grace, Prayer, and Charles Kuralt

LaCrosse, Wisconsin is a busy little city on the Mississippi River. Not many people there have any idea that just at this moment, they are being prayed for.

And you, by the way, just at this moment, are being prayed for, too.

In the little chapel of Maria Angelorum, every minute, every hour, every day, two nuns kneel before the altar, praying. A clock chimes the hour. The Sisters conclude: Bring peace to the world. They stand and leave, but not before their places have been taken by others.

The chain is never broken.

These are the Franciscan Sisters of Perpetual Adoration. They have been praying—without interruption—for more than 100 years.

This began in 1878. I first visited the chapel in 1978. By then, every hour of every day and night for a century, two sisters had been on their knees side by side, always praying for the same things--for an end to sickness and hunger, for an end to social injustice, for wisdom in high places, for their city and their country, for their friends, for their enemies, for all people, including you and me.

We are talking about passion. What passion exists in the hearts of these women! I was back there not long ago to visit Sister Mileta, a scholar and writer, who first took her place in this chain of prayer in 1915. I asked her, "Aren't you discouraged to think that you've been praying for world peace for 100 years, and there's been so little peace?"

"Yes," she replied, "and we think God must be discouraged, too, after all these years of waiting. But discouragement is no reason to give up."

"So," I said, "you're going to go on praying for another hundred years?"

"Yes," she said, "for another hundred years, and another hundred years, till the end of time."

"Till the end of time" is not an idea most of us think about very much, but I have visited the Chapel of Maria Angelorum a few times now, and the intention of these women has begun to sink in.

The years go by. Bright sunshine gives way to soft snowfall, and day to night, and night to morning, and always the ticking clock in the chapel, and always the angels looking down from the stained-glass windows, and always the two Sisters on their knees. They mean to pray forever.

I am not Roman Catholic myself, but I know passion when I see it. And grace. And solemn, lifetime determination. And if I ever forget that such things exist in the world, I know now where I can go to be reminded.

Charles Kuralt in *FSPA Perspectives*, Spring/Summer 1997

1. Define "transubstantiation." *CCC 1413*

2. Consult a dictionary, and explain in your own words "communion."

3. What can you learn from the following passages?

Exodus 16:4 The Lord said to Moses, "Behold I will ____________________."

Nehemiah 9:15 You gave them ____________________________ for their hunger.

Psalm 78:23-24 He opened the doors of heaven and ____________________

____________________________________.

Psalm 105:40b He satisfied them with ________________________.

4. How does Jesus describe Himself in John 6:35 and John 6:51?

5. What does Jesus promise?

in John 6:35 ____

in John 6:40 ____

and in John 6:51b ____

6. What does Peter tell us to do to come into the presence of the Lord? Acts 3:19

7. When was the last time you celebrated the Sacrament of Reconciliation? Ideally, how often should you plan to go to Confession in order to receive Communion worthily?

8. Do the following Bible passages support the belief that Jesus Christ is really present in Holy Communion? ______ Write down key phrases from each verse below.

Matthew 26:26-28	
Mark 14:22-24	
Luke 22:19-20	
John 6:35	
John 6:48	
John 6:51	
John 6:53-55	
John 6:58	
1 Corinthians 11:23-29	

**Place a star in front of your favorite verse above.

9. Use the ***Catechism of the Catholic Church*** to explain the Blessed Sacrament.

CCC 1374	
CCC 1376	
CCC 1377	
CCC 1378	
CCC 1379	
CCC 1380	

10. What does St. Cyril of Alexandria say about doubts in the Real Presence? ***CCC 1381***

11. Can you find any Scripture passages to suggest that Jesus intended Holy Communion to be only a symbol? (This is a trick question. There aren't any!)

12. What could a Catholic do to receive the Blessed Sacrament more worthily?

13. Have you ever worshipped in front of the Blessed Sacrament?

14. Share with your group opportunities for Adoration near your home?

15. What one thing could you do this week to prepare for an encounter with the Living God, Jesus Christ, in the Blessed Sacrament on Sunday?

___ Go to Confession
___ Arrive at Church a few minutes early to pray
___ Remain a few moments to offer thanks to God
___ Pray a new prayer before or after Holy Communion
___ Dress more carefully to celebrate the Eucharist
___ Other ideas? *CCC 1386*

16. Why is it essential that a person who is not in the state of grace or who is guilty of mortal sin refrain from receiving the Eucharist? 1 Corinthians 11:27-29

17. What does *CCC 1385* advise?

18. What must a person in mortal sin do before receiving Communion? *CCC 1415*

19. Share your favorite Communion prayer. Then write your favorite verse from Adoro Te Devote by St. Thomas Aquinas, which is partially recorded in *CCC 1381.*

20. Share your favorite Communion hymn.

Prayer before Holy Communion

Lord Jesus Christ,
take all my freedom,
my memory, my understanding, and my will.
All that I have and cherish You have given me.
I surrender it all to be guided by Your will.
Your grace and Your love are wealth enough for me.
Give me these, Lord Jesus, and I ask for nothing more.

St. Ignatius Loyola

Adoro Te Devote ~ After Holy Communion

I devoutly adore You, O hidden God,
truly hidden beneath these appearances.
My whole heart submits to You
and in contemplating You it surrenders completely.
Sight, touch, taste are all deceived in their judgment of You,
but hearing suffices firmly to believe.
I believe all that the Son of God has spoken:
there is nothing truer than this word of Truth.
On the Cross only the Divinity was hidden,
but here the Humanity is also hidden.
I believe and confess both and ask for what the repentant thief asked.
I do not see the wounds as Thomas did,
but I confess that You are my God.
Make me believe more and more in You, hope in You, and love You.
O Memorial of our Lord's death!
Living Bread that gives life to man,
Grant my soul to live on You and always to savor Your sweetness.
Lord Jesus, wash me clean with Your Blood,
one drop of which can free the entire world of all its sins.
Jesus, whom now I see hidden,
I ask You to fulfill what I so desire:
that on seeing You face to face I may be happy in seeing Your glory.

Monthly Social Activity

This month, your small group will meet for coffee, tea, or a simple breakfast or lunch in someone's home. Pray for this social event and for the host or hostess. Make every effort to offer hospitality and accept the hospitality of others. If this is hard for you to do, ask God for the grace to step out of your comfort zone for His greater honor and glory.

Prepare to share about the following:

- What do you remember about your First Holy Communion?
- Did you have expectant faith?
- Were you given new clothes or a prayer book or rosary?
- Was there a party or celebration?
- Were special loved ones present who are no longer with us?
- Do you have a picture of yourself on that day? Share it with the group!

Please remember to take a concern that *everyone share* some reflections!

JOHN 7

Jesus, Our Thirst for Living Water

Memory Verses

"Do not judge by appearances, but judge with right judgment."
JOHN 7:24

**"If any one thirst, let him come to me and drink.
He who believes in me, as the scripture has said,
'Out of his heart shall flow rivers of living water.'"**
JOHN 7:37-38

Jesus Goes to the Feast of Booths. The action of John 6 took place on the Feast of Passover; the action of John 7 takes place on the Feast of Booths, or Tabernacles. Exactly six months transpire between these two feasts. The Book of Leviticus specifies that "The Passover of the Lord falls on the fourteenth day of the first month" (Leviticus 23:5) and the "fifteenth day of the seventh month is the feast of Booths to the Lord" (Leviticus 23:34). Hence, these two feasts divide a year's time into two equal halves. John the Evangelist was perfectly aware of this phenomenon, and he made use of the lunar-solar Jewish calendar to establish a structure for his narrative. He shows that exactly six months have transpired in the life of Jesus between Chapters 6 and 7.

We know how important Passover was, but Booths was also a very great festival. It is frequently called simply "The Feast" (Leviticus 23:39, Ezekiel 45:25, John 7:37). Another ancient source, not found in our canon of scripture, Josephus Antiquities 8.4.1 also refers to this feast. During more than 3,000 years of history, this feast acquired different customs, according to the differing circumstances in which the Jewish people found themselves.

When the Jews were an agricultural people, this festival celebrated the autumn harvest of grapes and olives. The oldest name for it is "The Feast of Ingathering" (Exodus 23:16 and 34:22). The rest of the year, the people lived in fortified villages and towns, for protection from marauding Bedouin, but during harvest they would build temporary huts ("booths" or "tabernacles") for themselves out in the fields. The vineyards and olive gardens were sometimes miles away from their homes. They were too tired at the end of a long workday to walk back to their own beds, just to get up a few hours later and return to the fields, so the "booths" were simple shelters for temporary use.

As the Jewish people became increasingly urbanized, even though they no longer gathered the harvest, they continued to celebrate the festival at harvest time, and even kept building huts, but now on their rooftops or in their backyards. Then, the name of the

feast became "Booths" or "Tabernacles." The customs of this phase became codified in the Talmud, in a treatise, which was written a century or more after New Testament times.

There are many interesting aspects of the Festival of Booths.
- In connection with the moon ~ it takes place at a time of full moon.
- In connection with the sun ~ it takes place soon after the autumn equinox.
- Octave ~ the festival is spread out over eight days.

The most important aspect of Booths was that the ceremonials were spread out over a period of eight days. "For seven days you shall offer an oblation to the Lord, and on the eighth day you shall again hold a sacred assembly and offer an oblation to the Lord" (Leviticus 23:26). In the Christian tradition, such an eight-day festival is called an "octave." The current Catholic liturgical calendar has two official octaves, the Octave of Christmas (which begins on Christmas Day and ends eight days later on New Year's Day) and the Octave of Easter (which begins on Easter Sunday and ends eight days later on Mercy Sunday). Every day of those octaves is a feast day, with the singing of the Gloria. There are other minor octaves in the calendar, when the first and eighth days are related to one another. The current calendar contains such an octave beginning with the Feast of the Assumption (August 15) and ending in the Feast of the Queenship of Mary (August 22).

The only mention of the Festival of Booths in the entire New Testament is in the Gospel of John, Chapter 7. This is not surprising, in view of the fact that it is mentioned in only eight books of the Hebrew Bible. The name which John, and John alone, uses for the feast is "Booth-Building" (John 7:2).

The whole of John 7 is spread out over the days before and during the eight-day celebration of the Feast of Booths. Let us proceed and examine what Jesus does at each stage of the celebration.

(A) Before the Festival (John 7:1-10). There is a disagreement between Jesus and His kinsmen about whether to go to Jerusalem. Despite the fact that some of the Jews were plotting His death, the relatives pressure Jesus to go to Jerusalem anyway. This is interesting in light of what St. Luke tells us (Luke 2:41) of the Holy Family's custom of going to Jerusalem every year for Passover. In John 7 we have the festival of Booths rather than of Passover, but again the relatives of Jesus are anxious to go to Jerusalem. Family custom was at work here, but something more than custom, too.

Three festival days in the Jewish calendar required sacred assembly. "Three times a year, then, every male among you shall appear before the Lord, your God, in the place which He chooses: at the feast of Unleavened Bread, at the feast of Weeks (Pentecost) and at the feast of Booths" (Deuteronomy 16:16). Deuteronomy does not specify the

place of assembly, because at the time of Moses, the Israelites were nomadic, so the place of assembly could vary from year to year. When Solomon built the temple, he specified the temple in Jerusalem as the place of assembly (2 Chronicles 8:13). When the northern tribes broke away, they built a rival temple, which the Samaritans continued to use. During the exile, the Jewish people became scattered into different countries, and it was no longer possible for all the males to gather in one spot three times a year. After the temple was rebuilt, as many as possible would gather there, all the males of Judea along with as many from other countries who would be able to come.

Certainly Jews from Spain or Babylon could hardly travel to Jerusalem three times a year. They would consider themselves privileged to be able to make the journey once in a lifetime, or every several years if they were very wealthy. On any given festival day, representatives from each of the far-flung Jewish communities would be present at the temple to offer sacrifice on behalf of their home communities.

Apparently the Jews of Galilee were just close enough yet just far enough away that it was an open question whether they would go to a particular celebration at the Temple in Jerusalem. It would depend upon family circumstances, business activities, and so forth. For young, healthy people the 160-mile round trip was not impossible. The infirm or elderly, on the other hand, would have to celebrate at home. Since Jesus was a healthy young man in His early thirties, relatives would have expected Him to go to Jerusalem in accordance with family custom. Elderly or ill family members, who could not travel themselves, would have pressured Jesus to go, to offer sacrifice on their behalf. His reluctance to go does not reflect rebellion against Mosaic law, or against His family, or fear of His enemies, but a simple sense of timing: "because the time is not yet ripe for Me" (John 7:6).

(B) The first four days of the Festival (John 7:11-13). In fact, Jesus does go to the feast, secretly. John briefly describes the muffled conversations about Jesus. Everyone seems to have been expecting to see Jesus, and His apparent absence throws them off balance. No doubt, that was precisely what Jesus had in mind.

(C) The last four days of the Festival (John 7:14-36). On the fourth day of the festival, Jesus enters the temple area and begins to teach. He demonstrates that His enemies have not intimidated Him, but He also knows that the time remaining in the celebration would not be long enough for them to execute a plan of action against Him. Jesus displays strategic genius befitting a very great general.

Jesus brings into His teaching the topic of circumcision, which has relevance to the time and place. If Jesus is teaching in the Court of the Gentiles, the outer courtyard of the temple, there are both circumcised and uncircumcised people in His audience. Jesus is still being criticized for having healed on the Sabbath in John 5. He points out the rite of circumcision is performed on the Sabbath, in accordance with Mosaic Law. If a boy is born on a Sabbath day, then according to Mosaic law, he is to be circumcised exactly eight days later, again on a Sabbath day. His mother labored on the Sabbath to give

9. What tribe of Israel, what city will the Savior come from? Luke 1:69-70, 2:11

10. What town did the Virgin Mary come from? Luke 1:26-27

11. What town did Joseph come from? Luke 2:4

12. What tribe of Israel did Joseph belong to? Luke 2:4

13. Where was Jesus born? Matthew 2:1

14. Where did Jesus grow up? Matthew 2:21-23

15. Whom is the Messiah descended from and from where was He to come? John 7:42

16. What does the Lord command in Leviticus 23:42-44?

17. Compare John 4:14 with John 7:37. What does Jesus offer us?

18. What Jewish leader came to see Jesus at night in secret? John 3:1-2

19. Who comes to offer a word in defense of Jesus now? John 7:50-51

20. The Pharisees judged Jesus wrongly. Have you ever made a first impression of someone and later found out that you lacked some significant information?

21. Have you ever been misjudged by others?

22. Can you pray that God would forgive those who misjudged you and pray that God will forgive you for your judgments of others?

23. Who is referred to in John 7:38-39?

24. List practical manifestations that this living water is flowing. Galatians 5:22-23

spiritual process, in which man matures 'in true righteousness and holiness' (Ephesians 4:24). Truth is important not only for the growth of human knowledge, deepening man's interior life in this way; truth has also a prophetic significance and power. It constitutes the content of testimony and it calls for testimony. We find this prophetic power of truth in the teaching of Christ"(Pope John Paul II, *General Audience,* February 21, 1979).

St. Thomas Aquinas, the Angelic Doctor, comments on this passage by identifying three types of freedom. "In this passage, being made free does not refer to being freed of every type of wrong, it means being freed in the proper sense of the word, in three ways:

- first, the truth of His teaching will free us from the error of untruth;
- second, the truth of grace will liberate us from the slavery of sin;
- third, the truth of eternity in Christ Jesus will free us from decay."

St. Thomas Aquinas, *Commentary on St. John*

The plain, sober truth which every human must face is who he is and who God is. Many of the Jews could not face the truth that, despite their chosen race, they were sinners in need of a Savior. Many Jews longed for a political ruler who would triumph over their enemies. They could not recognize this suffering servant, sent by God the Father to save them from their sins and crush their enemy, Satan. Without a humble acknowledgement of one's own sinfulness, the need for a Redeemer is obscured. Perhaps some felt they were good enough by their own strength. They didn't really need Jesus. And they didn't like His familiarity with God the Father.

Chapter 8 begins with some self-righteous people wanting to stone an adulteress. She was a guilty sinner, deserving of this punishment. Yet, Jesus has the power and mercifully frees her from her bondage of sin and the punishment that awaits her. The chapter ends with the Jews wanting to stone Jesus, the Innocent One (John 8:59), for they perceive Him to be a blasphemer and possessed by a demon (John 8:52).

At the end of this chapter, try to identify with the woman caught in adultery. How would it feel to have one's secret sin exposed in front of everyone? What would it be like to face death for one's crime? What would it be like to look into the face of Pure Love and see an ocean of mercy? Have you ever been like the Pharisee, a sinner picking up a stone to throw at another? Have you ever been like Jesus, showing love and mercy to someone who didn't deserve it?

1. How did Jesus respond when the Pharisees asked what He had to say about the woman caught in adultery? John 8:6-7

2. What did the Mosaic law prescribe for those who committed adultery and why? Deuteronomy 22:22

3. Adultery is displeasing to God. What three things are beautiful in the sight of the Lord? Sirach 25:1-2

4. Sirach gives some practical advice and warnings on how to avoid falling into sexual temptation. List four admonitions from Sirach 9:1-9.

5. Read the story of Susanna in Daniel 13.
   What choice did Susanna face in Daniel 13:22-23?

6. How did Daniel prove Susanna's innocence in the face of two witnesses? Daniel 13:51-59

21. What can you learn about Jesus from the following "I AM" passages?

John 4:25-26	
John 6:35	
John 8:12	
John 8:58	
John 10:7	
John 10:11	
John 11:25	
John 13:19	
John 14:6	
John 15:1	
Revelation 1:8	
Revelation 1:17	
Revelation 2:23	
Revelation 22:16	

John 9

The Man Born Blind

Memory Verse

**"It was not that this man sinned, or his parents,
but that the works of God might be made manifest in him.
As long as I am in the world, I am the light of the world."**

John 9:3,5

Chapter Nine of the Gospel of John, one of the finest pieces of writing in the New Testament, has been called "dramatic," in the sense that it could almost be used as a stage play. The comings and goings of the characters, their verbal interplay, and the climactic discourse of Jesus resemble the kind of drama that might be found in ancient Greco-Roman plays, or in the works of Shakespeare.

The LOCATION of the drama occurs along the street in Jerusalem, outside the temple area. Jesus had just slipped out of the temple precincts at the very end of John 8. This seems to be a very public setting, with many characters coming and going, rather than a rural setting like the Garden of Gethsemane.

The TIME of the drama is a Sabbath after the Feast of Booths, which takes place usually in September (John7) and before the Feast of the Dedication three months later, usually in December (John 10:22).

The CHARACTERS of the drama are:

- Jesus (John 9:1-17, 35-41), who despite His initial reluctance to come to Jerusalem for the Feast of Booths remains for a seemingly lengthy period of time.

- A blind man, whom the Evangelist is careful to point out has been blind from birth (John 9:1-17, 24-39), setting up the theological problem which is at the heart of the chapter.

- The disciples of Jesus (John 9:2), who have not previously been mentioned in connection with this festival. At the beginning of John 7, it had been the relatives of Jesus, not the disciples, who were mentioned. Perhaps John means the same people here, since some of Jesus' disciples were related to Him.

- The neighbors and acquaintances of the blind man (John 9:8-12).

The Pharisees (John 9:13-41), who are also called the Jews (John 9:18).

The parents of the blind man (John 9:18-23), who are brought in to testify to the fact that he was really blind from birth.

The ACTION of the drama revolves around the healing of the blind man, which is the sixth "sign" or miracle in the Gospel of John. The action takes place partially on stage and partially off stage. Jesus applies spittle to the man's eyes on stage (John 9:6), but the man leaves the stage to go wash in the Pool of Siloam, where the restoration of his sight actually takes place (John 9:7). Chapter Nine is a miracle story, but the core action takes place off stage. The man leaves the stage still blind, but returns moments later able to see.

The THEOLOGICAL PROBLEMS discussed by the characters on stage are of more interest to the Evangelist than the physical action of the miracle itself. After hearing this familiar story in Mass over the years, it would be helpful for us to delve into the deeper theological issues as well.

1) Is there always a causal relationship between sin and adversity? The disciples begin by assuming that that there is a connection between the physical affliction of blindness and the moral affliction of sinfulness (John 9:2). They don't ask Jesus whether sin is involved, but rather whose sin. Did God will for this man to be born blind as a punishment for his parents' sins, or as a punishment for the sins which God knew the man himself would later commit? Jesus does not address this question directly, and answers that the purpose of the man's blindness was to glorify God by being healed.

The disciples participate in the "blame game." If something is wrong, it must be someone's fault. There are "fear cultures," "shame cultures" and "blame cultures." Eastern Europe under Communism was a "fear culture." Medieval Japan was a "shame culture," controlling behavior by the weapon of shame. Ancient Judaism was a "blame culture," where behavior was controlled using the weapon of blame. Jesus does not participate in this cultural game of establishing dominance and control by imposing guilt. His purpose on earth is to take guilt away, not to lay it on.

2) Is Jesus a sign of the Divine Presence? Another theological problem for the Pharisees relates to who Jesus is and who He claims to be. Jesus heals a number of different blind people in the course of the gospels. Matthew recounts that there were blind people among the large crowds who came to Jesus and received healings, both along the Sea of Galilee (Matthew 15:30-31) and inside the Temple of Jerusalem (Matthew 21:14). Matthew also cites two pairs of blind people who were healed, one pair at Capharnaum (Matthew 9:27) and another pair at Jericho (Matthew 20:30). One of those healed at Jericho was the blind beggar by the name of Bartimaeus, who was also mentioned by Luke (Luke 18:35) and by Mark (Mark 10:46). Mark also mentions the healing of a blind man at Bethsaida (Mark 8:22). John mentions none of these healings, but only the healing of the man born blind in Jerusalem. John demon-

strates an economy of style in which the miracles are carefully selected for their theological implications.

The healing of the man born blind creates wonder in the crowd and also marvel for the man himself, who seems to grow in understanding of Jesus' identity under the interrogation he endures. The blind man affirms that Jesus is a prophet of God (John 9:17) and eventually bows down to worship Him as the Son of Man (John 9:38).

Isaiah prophesied the healing of the blind would be a sign of the Divine Presence:

- "In that day the deaf shall hear the words of a book; and out of their gloom and darkness the eyes of the blind shall see" (Isaiah 29:18).
- "Behold your God will come with vengeance; with the recompense of God. He will come and save you. Then the eyes of the blind shall be opened, and the ears of the deaf unstopped" (Isaiah 35:4-5).
- "I will lead the blind in a way that they know not, in paths that they have not known I will guide them. I will turn the darkness before them into light, the rough places into level ground" (Isaiah 42:16).
- "The Spirit of the Lord is upon me, because he has anointed me to preach good news to the poor. He has sent me to proclaim release to the captives and recovering of sight to the blind, to set at liberty those who are oppressed" (Isaiah 61:1 as quoted by Jesus in Luke 4:18).

For the synoptic writers, Matthew, Mark and Luke, the restoring of sight to the blind and other healings are clear signs of the coming of the Messiah, because it was prophesied that these things would happen. In Matthew 11:4-5 and Luke 7:22, Jesus says "Go and tell John what you hear and see: the blind receive their sight and the lame walk, lepers are cleansed and the deaf hear, and the dead are raised up, and the poor have good news preached to them" (Matthew 11:4-5).

For John, in both his Gospel and Epistles, the theme of light and darkness demonstrate the theological revelation of Christ, the light of the world. When Jesus gives sight for the first time to the man born blind, it calls to mind the first day of creation when God said, "Let there be light and there was light" (Genesis 1:3). The forces of darkness were defeated by Jesus in this miracle, just as the powers of nature were made subject to Him when He walked on the water. John's sign is one of cosmological significance. For John, Jesus has let His light shine into the darkness. The blind man can now see, and anyone illumined by Christ can see the significance of this healing, but those afflicted with spiritual blindness cannot see it.

3) Is it lawful to heal on the Sabbath? The Pharisees continue to fixate on the fact that Jesus heals the blind man on the Sabbath (John 9:14). Concerns over the letter of the Mosaic law and the day of the week overshadow the magnificent mercy of God displayed for them. Previously the Pharisees chastised Jesus for healing on the Sabbath, and now He does it again! His enemies are motivated by jealousy, not by love for the Law, because the Law allows emergency work on the Sabbath. Jesus' enemies try feebly to discredit Him and to keep Him away from the people. The Sabbath was "people day" for the ancient Jews. Since they could not work, they had plenty of time to visit the temple, gather at synagogues, mingle with the crowds and hear different teachers. If Jesus is not permitted to heal on the Sabbath, then His miracles will lose their sign value, because the people will be absent, away at their work in the fields or shops. Jesus works miracles on the Sabbath, when all of the onlookers can be blessed by the evidence of God's mercy and power. Jesus could easily have healed in private on a weekday, but then only the sick man would be blessed, not those others whose faith would be built up by seeing and rejoicing in his good fortune. The Evangelist does not emphasize this problem here, because it has already been thoroughly handled elsewhere. His economical treatment of the topic keeps it before our eyes, and helps us sense the growing crisis which will lead to the Passion.

The enemies of Jesus are guilty of self-contradiction, because while they associate the blind man's impairment with sinfulness, they do not associate Jesus' healing power with grace. Now, they cannot have it both ways. If the blind man must be a sinner because of his physical affliction, then Jesus must be holy because He works miracles. They attest the first half of the proposition, but deny the second, and they do not even see that they are contradicting themselves. By the end of the chapter, they themselves have become the problem. We continue to be propelled forward toward the Passion.

Jesus brief statement about the Pharisees at the end of John 9 becomes developed into the great discourse on the Good Shepherd in the next chapter. We should be aware that the Evangelist himself is not responsible for the division of the Gospel into chapters. The first subdivision of the biblical books was undertaken by Stephen Langton, Archbishop of Canterbury, in the early 1200's. The further division of the Bible into verses was done by the French printer Etienne in the 1500's. These divisions were done intelligently, but we must remember that there is nothing infallible about them. They are a form of interpretation which is imposed upon the Word of God, and which divides the material into handy little boxes. However, like cutting a piece of fine cloth, we must be careful not to ruin the fabric. The Sermon on the Mount in Matthew, for example, is divided up into three equal chapters, but this division has no relationship to the content. To use another comparison, it is just like cookie-cutters on dough.

The break at the end of Chapter Nine is unfortunate, because it interrupts Jesus' own discourse. A more sensible break would have been in the middle of Chapter Ten, but that would have made John 9 much longer than John 10. The point is, don't stop reading now! The next chapter continues to reflect upon the meaning of the "sixth sign" found in Chapter Nine.

1. What title do the disciples use to address Jesus in John 9:2?

2. How does Jesus refer to Himself in John 9:5?

3. How do the Pharisees respond to this miracle? John 9:16

4. Were the Pharisees unanimous in their judgment of Jesus? John 9:16

5. Does Jesus deliberately ignore the Mosaic Law? ***CCC 2173,*** Matthew 5:17-20

6. The Pharisees wrongly judged Jesus because He healed on the Sabbath. What did they say about Jesus in John 9:16?

7. As Jesus proclaimed to the Pharisees, who is really blind? ***CCC 588***

8. Has there ever been a time in your life when you were "spiritually blind" to what God was doing?

    _____ Failing to see God's mercy and love

    _____ Blind to your own sin or weakness

    _____ Unaware of the inherent goodness or good intent in others

    _____ Misreading another's attempt, albeit clumsy at being kind

    _____ Missing the big picture, while focusing on the little things

    _____ Judging another wrongly and finding out the full story later

    _____ Other, please explain

9. How does God speak to man? *CCC 1147*

10. What defense does the blind man, whose sight has been given to him, offer for Jesus? John 9:30-34

11. What two conditions exist for God to listen to man's prayers? *CCC 2827,* John 9:31

12. What title does Jesus use to identify Himself in John 9:35?

13. What two things does the healed man demonstrate in John 9:38?

14. Use the *Catechism of the Catholic Church* or a dictionary to define "worship."

15. The Old Testament prophet Micah explained three things that the Lord requires. What three things does the Lord require of you? Micah 6:8

16. How did Jesus evaluate the Pharisees? John 9:41

17. What person comes to your mind when you read Micah 6:8?

18. Can you think of anything that you could do to see yourself, your strengths and your weaknesses more clearly?

19. What did Jesus use to heal the blind man (John 9:6) and what does He use to heal us today? ***CCC 1504***

20. Christ the Physician, showed great compassion to the sick and suffering. But, Jesus didn't heal all of the sick. His healings were signs of the coming of something greater. Describe what Jesus had in store. ***CCC 1505***

21. John's Gospel presents seven signs, or miraculous deeds that Jesus performs which demonstrate His divine power. Please identify them below.

JESUS' SEVEN MIRACULOUS SIGNS

John 2:1-11	
John 4:46-54	
John 5:1-9	
John 6:5-13	
John 6:16-21	
John 9:1-11	
John 11:17-44	

JOHN 10

Jesus, Our Good Shepherd

Memory Verse

"I came that they may have life, and have it abundantly."

JOHN 10:10

Jesus, Our Good Shepherd. A slang expression floating around several years ago in response to the despondency and negativity in American culture admonished "Get a life!" Nihilist philosophers question whether there can be any meaning or purpose in life. Even the preacher in Ecclesiastes says "Vanity of vanities! All is vanity." (Ecclesiastes 1:2). Another translation of this Bible verse says "Meaningless! Utterly meaningless! Everything is meaningless!" Yet, Jesus says "I came that they may have life, and have it abundantly." (John 10:10) The Jerusalem Bible translation says "life to the full." The human heart longs for a rich, full, meaningful life. Jesus, alone satisfies that longing.

The French scientist Blaise Pascale once remarked: "There is a God-shaped hole in every human heart that can be filled by God and God alone." Sometimes people try to fill that void with money, sex, power, material goods, relationships, adventure, alcohol or drugs with unsatisfactory results. Even filling that void with good things—a good marriage and family life or the best Christian service—can't take the place of an intimate, personal relationship with Jesus, our Good Shepherd.

Even today in the Holy Land, shepherds bring their sheep through the sheep gate into the old city of Jerusalem on market day. These dumb animals need good shepherding to keep them from danger and harm. Wolves devour them. Sheep, lacking good vision, preoccupied with grazing on good grass can wander off over a cliff to their death if the shepherd doesn't protect them. Sheep need a shepherd. Sometimes, shepherds would gather their flocks together for the night and pen them in for protection. In the morning, each shepherd would call his own sheep and take his flock through the sheep gate out to pasture. Each sheep would recognize the voice of its own shepherd and follow that voice to the grazing land.

The Greek *kalos* means "good" in the sense of "noble" or "ideal," not simply "good at" something. Unlike some shepherds, who let the sheep be eaten by wolves, Jesus dies for the sheep. Unfortunately, even today people follow bad shepherds, whose words sound good, but fail to lead followers to abundant life. Just as sheep encounter danger, humans can also be led astray to their ruin by following false prophets and wrong voices. How many times have people been led astray by sweet sounding words

and novel ideas, which later turned out to be damaging and hurtful? Empty philosophies and foolish promises in any age can lead people to grave disappointments and ruined lives that can only be redeemed by Jesus, the Redeemer.

Jesus leads into good pasture those whom He knows by name and who recognize His voice, those whom He intends to defend against thieves and robbers. Jesus longs to join His sheep together into one fold because He is the Good Shepherd loved by the Father. Jesus will lay down His life for the sheep. Jesus' act of total, loving self-sacrifice to the point of offering His life on the cross to atone for the sins of all men and women is prefigured here.

Jesus identifies Himself both as the door or gate to the sheepfold and as the good shepherd for the flock. Jesus is the real, true, and genuine shepherd, in contrast to what is symbolic or fake. Jesus is our gateway to possession of the full revelation of God and the blessings promised in the messianic age. The door-keeper is God, who alone draws all believers to Jesus as a gift for Him to look after (John 6:39; 17:6). In the Old Testament God was the true shepherd of Israel, and here Jesus claims to be the true shepherd Himself, because He and the Father are one.

The Jews of Jesus' time would have remembered God's anger at the weak and irresponsible shepherds of Israel, who took care of their own needs rather than caring for the flock. In Ezekiel 34, God admonishes the shepherds of Israel for their lax pastoral care and promises that He, Himself, will come and search for His sheep and look after them. Who is the hireling that John speaks about? St. Augustine of Hippo (354-430 AD) reveals that the hireling is "the man who seeks his own glory, not the glory of Christ; the man who does not dare to reprove sinners. You are the hireling; you have seen the wolf coming and fled ... because you held your peace, because you were afraid" (St. Augustine, *In Ioann Evang.,* 46, 8).

St. Augustine gives a criterion for identifying the hireling. Does the messenger give God the glory or does he seek praise for himself? Does he point to God or draw attention to himself? Is he clear about the full gospel, the reality of sin and the need for repentance to find God's mercy, or does he offer a prosperity gospel or a sugar-coated gospel? Jesus, the Good Shepherd, seeks always to do the Father's will and bring glory to the Father while bringing His flock into the fullness of truth.

St. Thomas Aquinas reasons: "Surely it is fitting that Christ should be a shepherd, for just as a flock is guided and fed by a shepherd so the faithful are fed by Christ with spiritual food and with His own body and blood . . . Christ said that the shepherd enters through the gate and that He is Himself the gate as well as the shepherd. Then it is necessary that He enter through Himself. By so doing, He reveals Himself, and through Himself He knows the Father. But we enter through Him because through Him we find happiness"(St. Thomas Aquinas, *Exposition on John,* Cap. 10, lect. 3). And in Him, we come into life and experience life joyfully and abundantly. We can even experience joy in the midst of trials and tribulations.

Jesus and the Father are One God. Once again Jesus alienates some of the Jews by identifying with the Father. Some claim that He is demon-possessed or mad (John 10:20). But, could a demon do the miracles that Jesus does? Can a demon open the eyes of the blind? (John 10:21)

Jesus continues to live as a faithful, observant Jew. He goes to the temple for the feast of the Dedication. This is the feast that we commonly refer to as Chanukah or Hanukkah, the Feast of Lights, celebrated in December. This nine day feast commemorates the purification and reconsecration of the temple in Jerusalem by Judas Maccabeus in 164 BC after it had been desecrated and profaned by Antiochus Epiphanes some three years earlier (1 Maccabees 4:36-59, 2 Maccabees 10:1-8).

Jesus references His Father ten or eleven times in this chapter. His identification with God the Father could hardly be clearer or more bold. Some object to Jesus' intimacy with the Father, calling Himself the Son of God. Note that Jesus used the scriptures to prove His point. He also shows great humility and deference when He phrases His text proofs in the form of a question. "Jesus answered them, 'Is it not written in your law, 'I said, you are gods'?" (John 10:34) Jesus advances a biblical argument from a lesser to a greater case. If scripture speaks of humans as 'gods' how much more should the One sent by the Father, doing the work of the Father, redeeming the world for Him justly deserve to be called "Son of God" for in truth that is who He is.

Those who fail to accept the true identity of Jesus attempt to stone Him or arrest Him, but Jesus escapes from their hands. It is not yet the time for His suffering. And many continue to come to believe in Him and put their faith in Him.

The Second Vatican Council teaches that "The Church is a sheepfold, the sole and necessary gateway to which is Christ. It is also a flock, of which God foretold that he himself would be the shepherd, and whose sheep, although watched over by human shepherds, are nevertheless at all times led and brought to pasture by Christ himself, the Good Shepherd and prince of shepherds, who gave his life for his sheep"(Vatican II, *Lumen Gentium,* 6).

Reflect on the memory verse in question form. Do you experience the life of Christ abundantly? Do you hear His voice and rely on His protection and care? Are you one of the sheep of His flock, experiencing the protection of the Church and the shepherds that God has placed over you? Do you study the teachings of the Holy Father and the bishops in union with him? Or, have you wandered off into dangerous places? Have you listened to the voices of false shepherds? If so, what must you do to get back into the sheepfold? Listen to the invitation that Jesus gives:

Come to me, all who labor and are heavy laden, and I will give you rest.
Take my yoke upon you, and learn from me; for I am gentle and lowly in heart, and you will find rest for your souls. For my yoke is easy, and my burden is light.
Matthew 11:28-30

1. What does Jesus promise to those who come to Him in John 10:9-10?

2. Did the people listening to Jesus always understand Him clearly? John 10:6

3. List some of things that the shepherds of Israel failed to do.

Ezekiel 34:3	
Ezekiel 34:4	
Ezekiel 34:6, 8	

4. How will God remedy the situation of the sheep without good shepherds? Ezekiel 34:11-16

5. What titles identify God in Genesis 49:24-25?

6. Fill in the blanks from David's Psalm.

Psalm 23

The Lord is ___ __________, I shall not want; v 1

he makes me lie down in green pastures. v 2

He leads me beside still waters; he ________ ____ ________. v 3

He leads me in paths of ____________________ for his name's sake.

Even though I walk through the valley of the _________ ___ ________, v 4

I fear no evil; for _____ are ______ me;

thy rod and thy staff, they ___________ ____.

Thou prepare a table before me in the presence of my enemies; v 5

thou anoint my head with oil, ____ _____ __________.

Surely ___________ and ___________ shall follow me v 6

all the days of my life;

And I shall dwell ___ _____ ________ ___ ____ _________ for ever.

7. Christ has not abandoned His flock, but He keeps it under his constant protection and guidance today through whom? *CCC 1575*

8. The Christian faithful enjoy their own shepherd under whose authority? *CCC 2179*

9. Are Catholics free to pick and choose those truths of the faith which they prefer? Support your answer with the Catechism. ***CCC 88***

10. List all the verses in John 10 in which you find the word "Father."

11. What are some characteristics of the relationship between Jesus and the Father?

John 10:15	
John 10:17	
John 10:30	

12. Give an example of a hireling or a false shepherd in our day. John 10:8

13. Have you ever felt that you "heard God's voice" (John 10:27) leading you to do something or take a specific course of action in your life?

14. Was there ever a time in your life when you got sidetracked by following a false shepherd?

15. One way of determining whether a group or an individual is consistent with Christianity can be found in Philippians 2:10-11. Write down these verses and ask the question "Who do they say Jesus is?"

16. What did Eli tell Samuel to say to the Lord, to hear Him better? 1 Samuel 3:9

17. What does Jesus say in John 10:14? Do you feel like you know Jesus in an intimate way? What could you do to hear His voice more clearly?

18. What did Jesus establish to safeguard the truth and protect believers? Matthew 18:18-19

19. How can you be sure that Jesus will remain with the Church and not abandon her? Matthew 28:16-20

20. Who takes the place of the apostles in shepherding the Church today? *CCC 862*

21. Who is the shepherd that God has placed over you and your family? *CCC 2179*

**Pray for him daily. Ask God to bless him and keep him strong and faithful.

Monthly Social Activity

Some time between Advent and Epiphany, your small group will meet for coffee, tea, or a simple breakfast or lunch in someone's home. Perhaps some Christmas decorations will be up at that time. **Pray** for this Christmas social event and for the host or hostess. Make every effort to attend. Even though this is a very busy time of the year, God will be glorified by efforts to set aside time to meet with others in the Bible Study group to share about a Christmas memory or a family Christmas tradition.

Prepare to share about the following:

- One Christmas memory that I hold dear is ______
- One Christmas tradition that our family enjoys is

  ____

Please remember to take a concern that *everyone shares* some reflections!

JOHN 11

Jesus, the Resurrection and Life

Memory Verses

**"Jesus said to her,
'I am the resurrection and the life;
he who believes in me, though he die, yet shall he live,
and whoever lives and believes in me shall never die.
Do you believe this?'"**
JOHN 11:25-26

**"She said to him,
'Yes, Lord; I believe that you are the Christ,
the Son of God, he who is coming into the world.'"**
JOHN 11:27

Jesus Raises Lazarus from the Dead. Jesus manifests His Divinity decisively by raising Lazarus from death back to life after he had been buried for four days! Jesus had already raised Jairus' daughter from the dead (Matthew 9:23-25), but she had been dead for only a short time. So skeptics may contend that perhaps she was not really dead, but only in a comatose state. This skepticism falters when one considers that in Jesus' time people were more closely acquainted with death than we are today. Even young children watched lambs slaughtered to be cooked for dinner. The elderly died in their beds at home, not off in hospitals or nursing homes, far removed from the family. Jesus also commanded the dead son of the widow of Nain to rise from his burial bier (Luke 7:11-17). Now, the raising of Lazarus, who had been in the tomb for four days, proves, beyond a shadow of a doubt, that Jesus has power over life and death. God the Father, the Creator of the world, has power over life and death. Jesus reveals His oneness with the Father in this dramatic miracle of delivering Lazarus from death back to life.

Moreover, Jesus demonstrates His humanity in the emotion He displays in this chapter. "Now Jesus loved Martha and her sister and Lazarus" (John 11:5). Jesus speaks of friendship and identifies Lazarus as a friend in "Our friend Lazarus has fallen asleep," (John 11:11). And then in the shortest verse in the Bible, Jesus openly expresses human emotion: "Jesus wept" (John 11:35). In most cultures, men are not expected to cry, yet with deep emotion and troubled in spirit, "Jesus wept" publicly, thereby showing His compassion for those who grieve. Thus, in this chapter, Jesus reveals that He is true God, with power over life and death. Jesus, also is true Man, manifesting human emotions of love, friendship, sorrow and compassion.

Earlier in the Bible, St. Luke presents the familiar story of Martha and Mary (Luke 10:38-42). Mary sits at the feet of Jesus, listening to His teaching, while Martha does the work. Jesus admonishes Martha for worrying about so many things, while praising Mary for choosing the better portion, sitting at His feet, listening to Him. Many an overworked, distraught mother and homemaker has bristled at this passage. However, Martha is redeemed in this chapter. Jesus redeems Martha in John 11:5 when St. John tells us that "Jesus loved Martha." Those three words suffice for any Christian. To be loved by the Lord fills the deepest longings of the soul. Proactive Martha, busy in Luke 10, once again takes the bull by the horns. "When Martha heard that Jesus was coming, she went and met him, while Mary sat in the house," (John 11:20).

Martha goes out to meet Jesus and expresses total faith in Him. She announces that if Jesus had been present, her brother would not have died, but would have been healed by Jesus, as so many others had been before. Moreover, she professes that even now, she knows that God the Father will do whatever Jesus asks. Martha comprehends the way in which Jesus and the Father are one, acting in one purpose and one will. Martha demonstrates total trust and abandonment to the will of God. She does not ask Jesus to bring her brother back to life. She merely states her confidence that Jesus has the power to do so, if it is God's will.

In the Old Testament, Job said, "For I know that my Redeemer lives, and at last he will stand upon the earth; and after my skin has been thus destroyed, then from my flesh I shall see God," (Job 19:25-26). Jesus says, "I am the resurrection and the life; he who believes in Me, though he die, yet shall he live, and whoever lives and believes in Me shall never die" (John 11:25-26).

> Jesus links faith in the resurrection to His own person: "I am the Resurrection and the life." On the last day, Jesus Himself will raise up those who have believed in Him, who have eaten His body and drunk His blood Already in this present life He gives a sign of His power by restoring some of the dead to life, announcing thereby His own Resurrection, though it was to be of another order.

Jesus Is the Resurrection and the Life. Jesus' victory over death provides hope for the resurrection of all men. The miracle in raising Lazarus shows Christ's power to give life to all people. Hence, by faith in Jesus Christ, who arose first from among the dead, the Christian believes that he too will rise one day, like Christ. Therefore, for the believer death is not the end; it is simply the step to eternal life, a change of dwelling place, as the Roman Missal puts it: "Lord, for your faithful people life is changed, not ended. When the body of our earthly dwelling lies in death, we gain an everlasting dwelling place in heaven."

Catholics profess a belief and longing for the resurrection, when the just hope to see the face of God and live. Each Sunday in the liturgy, Catholics proclaim in the Nicene

Creed "We look for the resurrection of the dead and the life of the world to come." But, what does this resurrection entail? Perhaps contemporary movies, which show angels as re-cycled human beings and promote reincarnated people, sow confusion and falsehood in the place of pure truth. What is the truth?

St. Justin the Martyr (100-165 AD) says, "God calls even the body to resurrection, and promises it everlasting life. When He promises to save the man, He thereby makes His promise to the flesh: for what is man but a rational living being composed of soul and body? Is the soul by itself a man? No, it is but the soul of a man. Can the body be called a man? No, it can but be called the body of a man. If, then, neither of these is by itself a man, but that which is composed of the two together is called a man, and God has called man to life and resurrection, He has called not a part, but the whole, which is the soul and the body. The resurrection is of the flesh which died; for the spirit does not die. The soul is in the body, which cannot live without a soul. The body is the house of the soul; and the soul, the house of the spirit. These three, in those who have a genuine hope and unquestioning faith in God, will be saved" (St. Justin the Martyr, *The Resurrection,* 8, 10).

Jesus Is Lord of Supernatural Life as Well as Natural Life. Jesus offers grace and salvation from sin, and an opportunity to live forever in heaven. Lazarus receives his natural life restored, but he will have to die again at a later time. Jesus weeps over the natural death of His friend, Lazarus, how much more must Jesus weep over sin which can lead to spiritual death? People beg God for physical healing for loved ones. How much more should Christians pray for spiritual life and health for those they love?

St. Augustine (354-430 AD) sees the raising of Lazarus as a symbol of the sacrament of Penance. Sin binds man as death and the burial clothes bound Lazarus. When the sinner repents and confesses his sin, the Lord has given the priest power to forgive and unbind the sinner from the chains of sin. "Everyone who sins, dies. Every man fears the death of the flesh, few the death of the soul. In regard to the death of the flesh, which without a doubt must someday come, all guard against its coming: that is the reason for their labors. Man, destined to die, labors to avert his dying; and yet man, destined to live in eternity, does not labor to avoid sinning" (St. Augustine of Hippo, *Homilies on John,* 49.2).

While Jesus brings Lazarus back to natural life, this miracle prefigures the Resurrection of Jesus in John 20:1-18 and also the mystery that St. Paul speaks of: "Lo! I tell you a mystery. We shall not all sleep, but we shall all be changed, in a moment, in the twinkling of an eye, at the last trumpet. For the trumpet will sound and the dead will be raised imperishable, and we shall be changed" (1 Corinthians 15:51-52).

The Plot to Kill Jesus. Ironically, Jesus' action in restoring life to Lazarus precipitates the Sanhedrin's plan to take Jesus' life. Most scholars think it unlikely that the raising of Lazarus would have been the stimulus for plotting the death of Jesus. Jesus' cleansing of the Temple and turning over the tables of the money changers provides a much

more probable cause. However, the spectacular feat of calling forth a dead man from his tomb caused many of the Jews to believe in Jesus. This type of popularity did not bode well for the status quo. Hence, the chief priests and the Pharisees met to decide what could be done with Jesus before everyone started to believe in Him.

Caiaphas was the high priest from 18 AD until 36 AD. In deliberating with the Sanhedrin, Caiaphas makes a statement which holds a hidden, underlying, prophetic meaning. "It is expedient for you that one man should die for the people, and that the whole nation should not perish" (John 11:50). On the surface, this promotes the political peace of the people and survival of Israel. However, Jesus' death on the cross for all people brought about the establishment of the new Israel, the new Covenant, the Church. It is through the passion and death of Jesus that repentant sinners can hope to avoid eternal punishment and attain everlasting life in heaven.

Jesus moves in and out of this drama, fearlessly. He acts confidently, decisively in the Father's timing. Jesus does not rush to rescue Lazarus from his illness. Jesus does not fear or avoid death, but rather commands death to loose its hold on his friend, Lazarus. "O death, where is thy victory? O death, where is thy sting?" (1 Corinthians 15:55). However, as humans, it is natural to fear death, to fear the unknown. Prayer may be the best means of contemplating and preparing for death in light of the hope of resurrection to new life, everlasting life in Christ.

The Landowner and the Hired Man

Once there was a wealthy landowner with a hired man. The land owner had no faith, no family and few friends. The hired man lived in a small cottage with his faithful wife and several children. Sometimes the land owner would peer through the cottage window and see the man and his family in prayer.

One morning the hired man approached the landowner and relayed his dream of the previous night. In his dream, God had told him that the richest man in the valley would die before midnight. The man felt that he should warn his employer. Visibly upset, the landowner called his physician, was examined and assured of his excellent health. Nonetheless, the landowner stayed awake until midnight in utter fear.

Shortly after midnight, a storm broke out and there was a knock at the door. The man opened the door to the teen-age daughter of the hired man, who had been sent by her mother to report that just before midnight, her father, the hired man had died!

"Obviously, you will not escape death, whether you live well or whether you live badly. But if you choose to live well in this life, you will not be cast into eternal punishments. So while you are still alive choose wisely not to die forever!"

St. Augustine of Hippo

~ PRAYER ~

O HOLY SPIRIT, enlighten my mind that death may not be my enemy, that I may not fear it in an unseemly way for a Christian, that I many not run from death, so that when death comes and takes those dear to me, I may welcome their release from this valley of tears although I am myself deeply moved and even deprived by their departure from this world. Let me know that death reminds each of us of the infinite reality of life with you. Let me see all things in the perspective of death and everlasting life. And let me not be filled with grief either at the anticipation of my own death or the experience of the death of those dear to me. Rather, strengthen my faith, that in the midst of this changing world, I may always come closer to you, who never change and who await me and those dear to me together with the Father and the Son in life everlasting.

Groeschel, Benedict J., *Arise from Darkness*
(San Francisco, CA: Ignatius 1995) p. 130.

1. Where did Martha and Mary and Lazarus live? John 11:1

2. What does Jesus foretell in John 1:50?

3. What event is described in John 12:2-3 and John 11:2?

4. How does the mother explain the hope of resurrection in 2 Maccabees 7:27-29?

5. Compare Martha's confession of faith in John 11:27 with those in

Matthew 16:16	
Mark 8:29	
Luke 9:20	

6. How does Jesus begin His prayer in the following verses?

John 11:41 ______________________________

Matthew 11:25 ______________________________

Luke 10:21-22 ______________________________

John 17:1-3 ______________________________

7. Compare the parallel accounts of the resurrection of Lazarus and Jesus in John 20.

Lazarus	*JESUS*
John 11:31	John 20:11
John 11:38, 41	John 20:1
John 11:44	John 20:6-7
John 11:16	John 20:27-28

8. What two things happened as a result of Jesus raising Lazarus from the dead? John 11:45-47

9. Relate Jeremiah 31:10 and Isaiah 40:11 to John 11:51-52.

10. What results from Jesus' death and Resurrection? Philippians 2:8-11

11. How does Paul explain the resurrection of the dead to the Greeks? 1 Corinthians 15:42-57

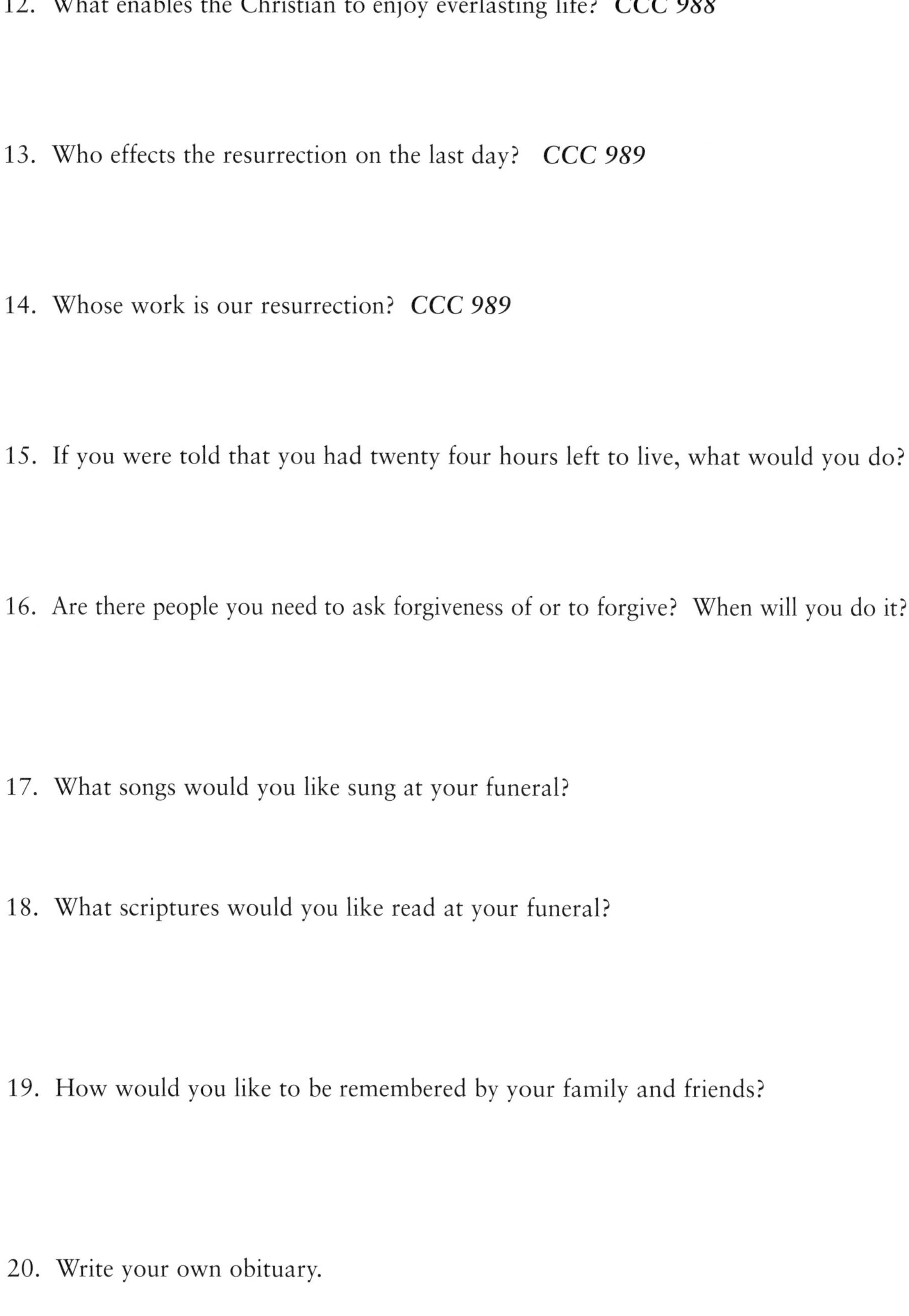

12. What enables the Christian to enjoy everlasting life? *CCC 988*

13. Who effects the resurrection on the last day? *CCC 989*

14. Whose work is our resurrection? *CCC 989*

15. If you were told that you had twenty four hours left to live, what would you do?

16. Are there people you need to ask forgiveness of or to forgive? When will you do it?

17. What songs would you like sung at your funeral?

18. What scriptures would you like read at your funeral?

19. How would you like to be remembered by your family and friends?

20. Write your own obituary.

JOHN 12

Isaiah Has Seen His Glory!

Memory Verse

"I have come as light into the world, that whoever believes in Me may not remain in darkness."
JOHN 12:46

Chapter Twelve presents the Johannine account of Palm Sunday, as Jesus enters the City of Jerusalem and is greeted by the crowds, and the follow-up to this event. As we see time and time again, each miracle or major event in this gospel is followed by a discussion. Here in John 12, the Evangelist brings in one of the Old Testament prophets to comment upon the events. St. John incorporates two quotations from Isaiah: "Who has believed what we have heard? And to whom has the arm of the Lord been revealed?" (Isaiah 53:1) and "Make the heart of this people fat, and their ears heavy, and shut their eyes; lest they see with their eyes, and hear with their ears, and understand with their hearts, and turn and be healed" (Isaiah 6:10). Then the Evangelist makes a very interesting statement of his own: "Isaiah said this because he saw his glory and spoke of him" (John 12:41). This amazing statement provides a key to the interpretation of the Gospel of John and indeed the whole New Testament.

A close relationship exists between the Book of Isaiah and all four of the gospels. In the pages of the New Testament, Isaiah is nearly the most frequently quoted Old Testament book, second only to the Book of Psalms. The Prophet Isaiah is mention by name six times in Matthew, twice in Mark, twice in Luke and four times in John–once in chapter one and three times here in chapter twelve.

John gives us an obvious clue that we can look to Isaiah for a fuller understanding of what happened on Palm Sunday. When a passage from the Old Testament is quoted in the New, the New Testament author focuses not just on the specific words quoted but on the entire context from which those words are taken. When St. John gives us two quotations from Isaiah, one right after another, he intends for us to go back to these places in the Book of Isaiah and bring that material to bear upon his narrative.

Because ancient books were copied laboriously by hand, those authors could not belabor their points the way authors could do after the invention of the printing press, and even more so now in the age of the word processor and computer. References to other authors were made with economy of means, appealing to the reader's memory and sending the reader to another book that might also be at his or her disposal.

Let us go back to the immediate context of the quotations from Isaiah and see what St. John wanted us to find there.

Let us look at the context of the first quotation. "Who has believed what we have heard? And to whom has the arm of the Lord been revealed?" (Isaiah 53:1). If we go back further to the chapter immediately preceding this one in Isaiah, we discover a statement that reads like a prophecy of Palm Sunday: "Awake, awake, put on your strength, O Zion; put on your beautiful garments, O Jerusalem, the holy city; for there shall no more come into you the uncircumcised and the unclean" (Isaiah 52:1).

Isaiah 52 and 53 are quoted extensively in the New Testament. St. Paul quotes from Chapter 52 four times (three times in Romans and once in Second Corinthians). One of the most important quotations which is partially quoted in Romans 10:15 comes from Isaiah 52: "How beautiful upon the mountains are the feet of him who brings good tidings, who publishes peace, who brings good tidings of good, who publishes salvation, who says to Zion, 'Your God reigns.' Hark, your watchmen lift up their voice, together they sing for joy; for eye to eye they see the return of the Lord to Zion. Break forth together into singing, you waste places of Jerusalem; for the Lord has comforted his people, he has redeemed Jerusalem" (Isaiah 52:7-9). The Roman liturgy uses these Isaiah prophecies during the Advent and Christmas seasons, but John alludes to them in the context of Palm Sunday. Indeed, the cries of greeting extended to Jesus by the crowds would seem to be the true fulfillment of Isaiah's vision.

Four different New Testament authors quote Isaiah 53. John quotes Isaiah 53:1. Matthew cites Isaiah 53:4. Peter recalls Isaiah 53:9 and St. Luke references Isaiah 53:12 in his Gospel and verses 7-8 in the Acts of the Apostles. This shows that the early Church used Chapters 52 and 53 of Isaiah extensively in their catechesis. Before the New Testament was written, the apostles used the texts of the Old Testament to tell the story of Jesus and explain their understanding of Him. They believed that Isaiah foresaw the coming of Jesus, and explained what would happen ahead of time. So John asserts "Isaiah said this because he saw his glory and spoke of him" (John 12:41). John implies here that Isaiah saw the events of Palms Sunday and the glory that Jesus would receive from the crowds, and described them in advance.

Now, look at the context of the second Isaiah passage that is quoted by John. "He has blinded their eyes and hardened their heart, lest they should see with their eyes and perceive with their heart, and turn for me to heal them" (John 12:40). This quotation follows immediately upon the previous one in John, but it comes from quite a different place in the book of Isaiah, much earlier in the book (Isaiah 6:9-10). Back in the original Isaiah context, it follows soon after Isaiah's great vision of the heavenly throne: "I saw the Lord sitting upon a throne, high and lifted up; and his train filled the temple. Above him stood the seraphim; each had six wings: with two he covered his face and with two he covered his feet, and with two he flew. And one called to another and said: 'Holy, holy, holy is the Lord of hosts; the whole earth is full of his glory'" (Isaiah 6:1-3).

With this allusion, John takes his commentary of Palm Sunday to a much higher level. Isaiah not only looked forward in time and saw the events of Palm Sunday, so that he described them ahead of time, he also had a transcendent vision of heavenly events, events to which nearly everyone on the face of the earth is blind. St. Paul usually gets the credit for the saying "what no eye has seen, nor ear heard" (1 Corinthians 2:9), but he was actually quoting none other than Isaiah (Isaiah 64:4). Isaiah had seen what is denied to other mortals on this side of the veil–he had seen the glory of the living God!

Therefore, it is a very powerful statement when John comments that "Isaiah said this because he saw his glory and spoke of him" (John 12:41). John states again, as he did in the Prologue to his Gospel, that "the Word was with God and the Word was God" (John 1:1). Therefore, the glory that Isaiah saw in heaven and described was indeed the glory of Jesus, not just the glory of His earthly deeds but the very glory of His quintessential being.

The references to Isaiah show that John intends the events of Palm Sunday to be interpreted on a two-fold level. First, there is the historical happening which was foreseen and described by the Old Testament prophecy. Second, there was the simultaneous transcendent meaning of this event which was also seen by the Old Testament prophet. Since this transcendent meaning belongs to eternity rather than to time, we are out of the realm of temporal sequence. So Jesus can rightly say, "Before Abraham was, I am" (John 8:58). Jesus existed before time began in His transcendent divine nature and so pre-existed Abraham, even though He was not born until long after Abraham's time. Similarly, here in chapter twelve, John intends us to understand that Jesus was in heaven with the Father at the time of Isaiah's heavenly vision, and therefore the "Holy, holy, holy!" of the angels is an eternal hymn of praise to the Son along with the Father.

Here are the two levels of meaning to Palm Sunday, then, according to John the Evangelist. The citizens of Jerusalem are singing historical praises to Jesus, as foreseen ahead of time by Isaiah (Isaiah 52:6-9),while the angels of heaven are singing eternal praises to Jesus, as seen in the transcendent vision of Isaiah (Isaiah 6:1-4). As proof that heaven is involved in the events of Palm Sunday, John reveals the heavenly Father breaking through into the discussion of events, and God speaks from the sky, saying, "I have glorified it (God's Name) and I will glorify it again" (John 12:28). Note the word "glory" used again, the glory seen by Isaiah, which is ascribed to Jesus in John 12:41. Some people in the crowd thought they heard thunder, an allusion to Psalm 29: "The God of glory thunders . . . and all in his temple say 'Glory!'" (Psalm 29:3, 9). Others believed that they heard an angel speaking. Angels, of course, do not speak on their own authority, but speak for God. Angels, too, are prophets, in that they are sent by God to proclaim good news. With the glorious events of chapter twelve, John prepares us for the "scandal of the Cross." He fortifies us with the doctrine that Jesus is God, so that we shall see a vision of God in Jesus' death upon the Cross. Remember that John was the only one of the twelve apostles actually to witness the gruesome details of Calvary—but for him the Cross is about glory. He wants to make sure that we share this faith in Jesus with him while we read on to the succeeding chapters.

Perhaps it would be efficacious at this point to pray the familiar prayer of the Church, which offers glory to God and restates for us the Divine Majesty of God and the eternal mystery of the Trinity.

TE DEUM

You are God: we praise you;
You are the Lord: we acclaim you;
You are the eternal Father:
All creation worships you.
To you all angels, all the powers of heaven
Cherubim and Seraphim sing in endless praise:
Holy, holy, holy, Lord, God of power and might,
heaven and earth are full of your glory.

The glorious company of apostles praise you.
The noble fellowship of prophets praise you.
The white-robed army of martyrs praise you.

Throughout the world the holy Church acclaims you:
Father of majesty unbounded,
your true and only Son, worthy of all worship,
and the Holy Spirit, advocate and guide.

You, Christ, are the King of Glory,
the eternal Son of the Father.
When You became man to set us free
You did not spurn the Virgin's womb.

You overcame the sting of death,
and opened the kingdom of heaven to all believers.
You are seated at God's right hand in glory.
We believe that You will come and be our judge.

Come then, Lord, and help your people,
bought with the price of Your own blood,
and bring us with your saints to everlasting glory.

1. Describe the setting for John 12.

   - When is this occurring? John 12:1 ______________________________
   - What is going on? John 12:2 ______________________________
   - Who is present? John 12:2-4 ______________________________

2. In your own words, describe the kindness shown to Jesus in John 12:3-5.

3. What does Jesus do in John 13:5-15?

4. How did St. Rose of Lima interpret Jesus' words in John 12:7-8? *CCC 2449*

5. Why did the crowd assemble and what was being planned? John 12:9-10

6. When in the Mass do the faithful say the words from John 12:13 and Revelation 4:8?

7. What does Zechariah foretell in Zechariah 9:9? What verse fulfills this prophecy?

8. How would you know that Jesus' hour is coming? John 12:23

9. Compare the main idea from the following verses.

Matthew 10:39	
Mark 8:34-36	
Luke 9:24-26	
John 12:24-26	

10. What was Jesus purpose in coming to earth? John 12:27, *CCC 606, 607*

11. How is the name of God glorified?

John 12:28-34	
Philippians 2:5-11	
CCC 434	

12. Who and what did the crowd hear? John 12:28-30

13. Can you find any Biblical evidence for hearing the voice of God? Who heard God?

Genesis 3:9-10, 13	
Genesis 7:1	
Genesis 12:1-4	
Exodus 3:4 Leviticus 1:1	
Joshua 1:1-2	
1 Samuel 3:4-10	
Mark 1:4-11	
Mark 9:2-7	
Acts 9:4-10	

14. Who is the ruler of this world that Jesus will cast out? John 12:31-33, *CCC 550*

15. How will the Messiah draw all men to Himself? John 12:32, Isaiah 53:4, 10-12

16. How does St. Paul compare present suffering with what is to come? Romans 8:18

17. Jesus came into the world as light, so that we may not remain in darkness. What do the following verses say about light and darkness?

Genesis 1:3-4	
2 Samuel 22:29	
John 3:19-21	
Ephesians 5:8-10	
1 Peter 2:9	

18. How can a person remain in darkness? 1 John 2:9-11

19. How can you get out of darkness and into the light? 1 John 1:6-9

20. Has there ever been a time in your life when you felt like you were walking out of the darkness and into the light? If you can't answer this question, perhaps it is time to go to the Sacrament of Reconciliation.

21. John 12:48 warns us that some will reject Christ and enter into judgment. Invert the preceding verse, John 12:47, to determine what we can do to avoid judgment. Then, go to Acts 2:38 and Acts 3:19 and report what St. Peter says.

JOHN 13

Jesus, the Servant of Love

Memory Verses

"You call me Teacher and Lord; and you are right, for so I am. If I then, your Lord and Teacher, have washed your feet, you also ought to wash one another's feet."

JOHN 13:13-14

"A new commandment I give to you, that you love one another; even as I have loved you, that you also love one another. By this all men will know that you are my disciples, if you have love for one another."

JOHN 13:34-35

Jesus Washes the Apostles' Feet. John 13 begins the Last Supper discourse of Jesus which continues through four chapters. John gives special attention to this important event in the life of Jesus and provides careful recounting of His words and actions. John tells us that during the supper, the devil had already put it into the heart of Judas Iscariot to betray Jesus (John 13:2).

The Gospels reveal the presence and activity of the devil throughout Jesus' life (Matthew 4:1-11, Luke 22:3, John 8:44, 12:31). Satan is "the enemy" (Matthew 13:25), "the evil one" (1 John 2:13). St. Thomas Aquinas (1225-1274 AD) points out that, in this passage, on the one hand we clearly see the malice of Judas, who fails to respond to this demonstration of love, and on the other hand great emphasis is laid on the goodness of Christ, who reaches out beyond Judas' malice by washing his feet also and by treating him as a friend right up to the moment when he betrays Him (Luke 22:48).

Jesus, aware that His earthly ministry was reaching its climax, took off His outer garments and girded with a towel, poured water into a basin to wash the disciples' feet. Peter objects to Jesus' act of humility and subservience, but ultimately relents when Jesus explains that obedience is necessary for salvation. We can't get to heaven on our own. We need Jesus. We need the Suffering Servant to wash us and bring us redemption and reconcile us to the Father.

Jesus' entire life illustrates loving service. Jesus reaches out to the poor, the rich, the crippled, the blind, the lame, the hungry, the lepers, and the outcasts with His loving touch and salvific grace. Just as Jesus washes the feet of the disciples, God washes

away original sin in the waters of baptism. Furthermore, Jesus washes away our recurrent sins in the Sacrament of Reconciliation. St. Augustine (354-430 AD) comments "When He washed the feet of the disciples He said this also: 'He that has washed has no need to wash, except his feet, and he is entirely clean.' Whence has water so great a power that it can touch the body and cleanse the heart, unless by the action of the word; and not that it is spoken, but that it is believed? For also in the word itself, the fleeting sound is one thing, the abiding power another" (St. Augustine of Hippo, *Homilies on John,* 80.3).

When considering that the disciples walked the dirty, dusty roads along with sheep and animals who relieved themselves along the way, one can imagine the foul odors and unpleasant task that Jesus chose to perform. Feet washing of guests generally would be assigned to the lowest of the servants in a household. Jesus takes the most repugnant task and then directs us to serve one another in similar ways. Jesus serves in perfect obedience to the Father's will. Jesus serves us to the point of dying on the cross, a painful, shameful death for our sins.

Thoughts on Temperature for Foot Washing

When you go to another to wash his feet, be concerned as to the temperature of the water!

Some come with boiling hot water. They are so angry, so upset, so distracted by something that has happened in the past—and so mad about it—that they come to the other person and say, "Here stick your feet in here!" Nobody wants to have his feet washed with boiling water.

Some go to the other extreme and come with ice water. They are so righteous, so holier-than-thou, so above it all. They come with this frigid, freezing water and want to wash your feet. Nobody wants to have his feet washed with ice water.

Some find a third extreme and come without any water! They try to dry-clean your feet with "a piece of their mind," just scrubbing away harshly. What they say may be true, but there is no water of love, nothing to wash the dirt gently away, but only a rigid insistence on scraping away every imperfection and the skin along with it!

There is another way—that is to come and wash one another's feet in love, in the spirit of servanthood.

From *Illustrations for Biblical Preaching,* edited by Michael P. Green, (Grand Rapids, MI: Baker Book House, 1989) 420-421.

St. Paul shows the humility and obedience of Jesus in poetic tones in his letter to the Philippians, admonishing believers to follow Christ's example. "Do nothing from selfishness or conceit, but in humility count others better than yourselves. Let each of you look not only to his own interests, but also to the interests of others. Have this mind among yourselves, which is yours in Christ Jesus, who though He was in the form of God, did not count equality with God a thing to be grasped, but emptied Himself, taking the form of a servant, being born in the likeness of men. And being found in human form He humbled Himself and became obedient unto death, even death on a cross" (Philippians 2:3-8).

Meekness, humility and servanthood run contrary to the current ethos advanced in contemporary society. Music, advertising and the media thrust out an entirely different message. "You deserve a break today." "Take care of Number One." "Don't let anyone get in your way." "Stick up for your rights." "I did it MY way." Living in a secular, materialistic culture makes living the gospel message challenging.

Jesus Models Servanthood in Love and Truth. Servanthood should not be confused with behavior that allows or enables others to persist in their sin. People who hide or ignore self-destructive or abusive behaviors are not acting in love, as Jesus did. Discernment and counsel from a priest may be required to decide how to handle difficult situations dealing with alcoholism, drug abuse, domestic violence, pornography, gambling or adultery.

Moreover, some activities might not look like service, but it fact may please God very much. A mother may serve her teen-age children by teaching them to do their own laundry, preparing them for adulthood, rather than doing it all for them. A father, who encourages his children to get part-time jobs to earn money serves them by preparing them with life skills. Other times, family members can identify opportunities to assist those in the family and in the community and be a blessing to them. Similarly, in parish life, prayer and discernment enable Christians to make good choices. The person who shows up at church every time the doors are open, but neglects family responsibilities may have disordered priorities. Jesus gave example by serving those closest to Him and then reaching out to serve others.

Jesus Predicts His Betrayals. Jesus, knowing all things, knew that his disciples were fickle. The Old Testament prophesied the betrayals that the Messiah would endure. "Strike the shepherd that the sheep may be scattered" (Zechariah 13:7) describes fittingly the behavior of the disciples at Jesus' trial and crucifixion. The Psalmist foretells the pain of betrayal that Jesus would experience from His own disciple, Judas. "Even my bosom friend in whom I trust, who ate of my bread, has lifted his heel against me" (Psalm 41:9).

Jesus knew that Judas would betray Him and in his despair and remorse, go out and hang himself (Matthew 27:3-5). Jesus also knew that Peter, the rock on whom He would build His Church, would deny Him and abandon Him. Consider the differences in the two apostles. Both denied Jesus. Both abandoned Him. Peter, however, repent-

ed of his weakness and returned to Jesus in sorrow. Peter did not wallow in self-pity and guilt. He returned to the Lord and was used mightily by God in building up the Church. The major difference between Peter and Judas is that Peter loved Jesus and had enough humility to acknowledge his error and repent of his sin. Peter learned to rely not so much on himself, but on the immense love and power of Christ.

Jesus' New Commandment. Jesus forewarns the apostles that He will be leaving them shortly. He will be glorified by God the Father and He will glorify the Father. The unfolding of the story, which is so familiar to us, recounting and retelling the passion narrative of Jesus every Lent and every Passiontide, must have been terribly confusing and upsetting to the disciples. Why would Jesus leave them? What was about to take place? How should they prepare? What must they do?

Before His passion, Jesus gave a new commandment, the hallmark of the New Covenant, "Love one another, even as I have loved you" (John 13:34). The disciples could not have imagined that for Jesus "love is strong as death" (Song of Solomon 8:6). Never before had anyone seen sacrificial love as great as the love Jesus would show in dying for mankind.

Love is the identity card of the true disciple (John 13:35). The new covenant of love is the thrust of the New Testament, just as the law and commandments identified the Old Testament. The measure of love required by this new commandment is the measure by which Jesus loves us, not how we love ourselves. Christians must serve and forgive one another even as Jesus served, forgave, and purified His disciples, knowing that they would betray and abandon Him. We cannot comprehend the challenge of this commandment until we grasp the depths of Jesus' love for us.

The commandment to love one another, encompasses all of the other commandments and prescriptions of the law and fully manifests the Father's will. In loving another, one seeks out the best for the beloved. Love has the power to build up, to transform, and to ennoble.

The early Christians were known by the love they showed for one another and the faith and courage they had in accepting even death for the Lord. Christian love continues to be manifest in sacrificial giving and serving. Hospitals, orphanages, and schools have been started by the church throughout the ages to provide love and charity to those in need. Mother Teresa exemplified Christian love in her life, which was recognized throughout the world. St. Maximilan Kolbe offered his life at the hands of the Nazis, so that a man with a wife and children could live. St. Maximilan didn't have to die. He freely offered his life. He volunteered to go to the starvation bunker in the place of a Jewish man who had been appointed to die. That man, whose life was spared was present at the canonization of St. Maximilian Kolbe in Rome! Countless other examples of Christian love and service could be recounted to build faith and provide example. What examples of contemporary Christian love and service come to your mind? In any event, no example of love is greater than the one depicted by Jesus on the crucifix.

"At the evening of life, you will be judged on your love" (St. John of the Cross, *Dichos,* 59). On judgment day, will it be more important how smart you were, how many promotions you received, how much overtime you worked, how many committees you served on or how well you loved those God put in your life?

Lord God, our strength and salvation, put in us the flame of Your love
and make our love for You grow to a perfect love
which reaches to our neighbor.

1. What command is given in Deuteronomy 6:5?

2. How can you determine the time frame of John 13? John 13:1-2

3. Describe Peter's initial reaction to Jesus' washing the disciples feet. John 13:6, 8

4. How did Peter adjust his attitude? John 13:9

5. What happens to those who serve as Jesus did? John 13:17

6. How is the disciple described in John 13:23 and who do you think this refers to?

7. What problems occurred in serving in Luke 10:38-41?

8. Can you recall a time when someone served or assisted you in some special way?

9. Share your example of the most Christ-like servant that you know.

10. Who helped Judas betray Jesus? John 13:2

11. Do you think that the devil still tries to trip up people? 1 Peter 5:8

12. How can you resist the power of the evil one in your life? James 4:7, 1 Peter 5:9

13. What is the new commandment given by Jesus? John 13:34

14. What is our goal in life? ***CCC 1822, 1823, 1829***

15. Look up the familiar passage is 1 Corinthians 13:4-7. In place of the word "love" put your name and complete the verse. Circle the words that describe you.

____________ is patient and kind.

____________ is not jealous or ____________. v4

____________ is not ____________ or ___________.

____________ does not insist on _______ ________ ______.

____________ is not ____________ or ______________; v 5

____________ does not rejoice at ________,

but rejoices in ____________. v 6

____________ bears all things, ____________ all things,

____________ all things, ____________ all things. v 7

16. Who is the most loving person you have ever met? Describe that person.

17. The fundamental task of marriage and family is to be at the service of _________. *CCC 1653*

18. What three things does the Lord require of you? Micah 6:8

19. Who do you think is referred to in Song of Solomon 4:7?

    Whose love is perfect, flawless?

20. Who is the person in your life most difficult to love and/or serve?

21. Pray and ask God to show you one practical thing that you could do in love or service for someone this week. Share with your group when you have done it.

JOHN 14

Jesus, the Way, the Truth, and the Life

Memory Verses

**"Jesus said to him,
'I am the way, and the truth, and the life;
no one comes to the Father, but by me.'"**

JOHN 14:6

**"Jesus answered him,
'If a man loves me, he will keep my word, and my Father will love him,
and we will come to him and make our home with him.'"**

JOHN 14:23

Jesus Prepares a Place for Us. After delivering the sad news that He will be betrayed by one of His own (John 13:21) and will be leaving the disciples (John 13:33), Jesus comforts them with words of warmth and tenderness. Jesus will go through death and resurrection to His Father's house and will prepare a place for believers to follow. There are many rooms in the Father's house so there need be no fear of being left out or excluded due to lack of space. John 14:2 refutes the claims of some sects that only a select few will be admitted into paradise and when that number is complete, no one else can be admitted. Catholics refer to the Father's house as Heaven.

HEAVEN ~ Eternal bliss, life with God, communion of life and love with the Trinity and all the saints in heaven. Heaven is the state of supreme and definitive happiness, the goal of the deepest longings of the human heart.

Heaven, promised by Jesus, remains the hope and longing of all human hearts. Jesus came down from heaven where He existed for all eternity with the Father. After His passion, death and Resurrection, Jesus "ascended into heaven and is seated at the right hand of the Father. He will come again in glory to judge the living and the dead, and His kingdom will have no end." Catholics proclaim this truth each Sunday at Mass in The Nicene Creed, recited aloud and in unison at the conclusion of the Liturgy of the Word. Every human being is on pilgrimage in this world, hoping and longing to spend eternity in heaven.

"What will be that glory, and how great the joy of being admitted to the sight of God! To be so honored as to receive the joy of eternal light and salvation in the presence of Christ the Lord, your God! To greet Abraham, and Isaac, and Jacob, and all the patriarchs, apostles, prophets, and martyrs! To rejoice with the just and with the friends of God in the kingdom of heaven, in the delight of the immortality that will be given! To receive there what eye has not seen nor ear heard, what has not entered into the heart of man!"

St. Cyprian of Carthage (200-258 AD) *Letter to the people of Thibar,* 58.10

St. John Damascene, also known as John Chrysorrhoas, the Golden Speaker writes "We shall rise again, therefore, our souls united again to our bodies, the latter now made incorruptible and having put corruption aside; and we shall stand before the awesome tribunal of Christ. And the devil, his demons, the antichrist, the impious and the sinners shall be consigned to everlasting fire, not material fire such as we know, but such fire as God would know. And those who have performed good actions will shine like the sun with the angels in eternal life, with our Lord Jesus Christ, seeing Him forever and being ever in His sight, and deriving increasing joy from Him, praising Him with Father and Holy Spirit in the infinite ages of ages."

St. John Damascene (645-749 AD), *The Source of Knowledge,* 3, 4, 27

PAROUSIA ~ The glorious return and appearance of our Lord and Savior Jesus Christ as judge of the living and the dead, at the end of time; the second coming of Christ, when history and all creation will achieve their fulfillment.

All people want to go to heaven, and Thomas does a big favor asking Jesus how to get there. "How can we know the way?" asks Thomas (John 14:5). Jesus responds by pointing out that He, Himself, is the way to reconciliation with God, the Father. Jesus is not just a guide to salvation; He is not simply one of many ways to the Father. Jesus is the Way that God has provided to open the gates of heaven for sinful man.

Jesus Is the Way. He is the only link between God and man, heaven and earth. He is the Fullness of Truth because by coming to this world, He shows that God is faithful to His promises, and because He teaches the truth about God. He is the Life because from all eternity He shares divine life with His Father, and because He makes us, through grace, sharers in that divine life.

A contemporary philosophy proposes that it doesn't really matter what one believes as long as he is sincere. And if there is a heaven, almost everybody will be there. After all, would a loving God send anyone to hell? And yet, God affords each human being the free will to choose heaven or hell. Humans are free to accept salvation or to reject it. Man can't build his own tower of Babel to heaven. Jesus words' provide life-giving truth and also point out the tragedy that foolish thinking and adopting the notions of this world can prove one to be sincerely wrong with disastrous consequences!

Christian hope is not in a program, nor in a method, but in a person. Jesus Himself is "the way and the truth and the life." Revealing the perfect union of Jesus with the Father are both His words and His works. (John 14:10-11)

Attempts to over-simplify the gospel result in formulae being offered to get into heaven. Well-meaning people offer assurances that all you need to be saved is to pray a certain prayer or believe certain truths. Our Holy Father, Pope John Paul II, points us to the fullness of truth in his encyclical, *Veritatis Splendor (The Splendor of Truth).*

> It is urgent to rediscover and to set forth once more the authentic reality of the Christian faith, which is not simply a set of propositions to be accepted with intellectual assent. Rather, faith is a lived knowledge of Christ, a living remembrance of His commandments, and a truth to be lived out. A word, in any event, is not truly received until it passes into action, until it is put into practice. Faith is a decision involving one's whole existence. It is an encounter, a dialogue, a communion of love and of life between the believer and Jesus Christ, the Way, and the Truth, and the Life (John 14:6). It entails an act of trusting abandonment to Christ, which enables us to live as He lived (Galatians 2:20), in profound love of God and of our brothers and sisters.
>
> Pope John Paul II, *Veritatis Splendor,* August 6, 1993, no. 88

Philip's request that Jesus show them the Father demonstrates the difficulty with which the apostles try to reconcile Jesus' unity with God the Father and the mystery of the Blessed Trinity, which remains a mystery to this day. The fact that Jesus is one with God the Father can only be accepted, by God's grace, with the gift of faith. It cannot be proven or comprehended by the most intelligent of human minds.

Jesus astonishes the apostles by foretelling that those who believe in Him will do the works of Jesus and even greater works than these. Jesus promises to do whatever is asked in His name that the Father may be glorified. Remember that Jesus acted in perfect obedience to the Father, in the Father's timing, that the Father would be glorified. Jesus doesn't offer winning lottery tickets or a tip on the fastest horse at the racetrack. Rather, Jesus offers believers an invitation to discipleship. His disciples will do the works Jesus did. They will proclaim the good news of the kingdom of God. They will heal the sick and raise the dead and share in His suffering, even to the point of martyrdom.

Jesus Promises the Holy Spirit. Jesus repeatedly calls the disciples to love and to obey. Love for God demands a willingness to walk in His ways, to obey the commandments and to do what He asks. Jesus promises those who love Him and keep His word, that He will remain with them, that the Father will come also, and Jesus and the Father will make their home with the disciple. Moreover, Jesus promises that the Father will send the Holy Spirit, the Counselor, the Paraclete in Jesus' name. Jesus has been instructing

the disciples about His intimacy with God the Father and now He invites them to share in this intimacy.

In the Old Testament, God dwelled in the midst of the people of Israel, but in this New Covenant, Jesus reveals that God wants to dwell within the soul of man. Jesus invites man to share in the intimacy that He enjoys with God the Father.

> St. Augustine reflects on this intimacy, God's presence in the soul of man. "Late have I loved you. O beauty so ancient and so new, late have I loved you! You were within me, and I was in the world outside myself. I searched for you in the world outside myself . . . You were with me, but I was not with you . . . You called me; you cried aloud to me; you broke my barrier of deafness; you shone upon me; your radiance enveloped me; you cured my blindness."
>
> St. Augustine of Hippo (354-430 AD), *Confessions,* 10.27

Jesus has been with the apostles for three years, loving them, teaching them, showing them the ways of God. Now, just prior to His passion and crucifixion, Jesus knows that the disciples will be scattered and frightened. They will run away and hide. Some of them will go back to fishing for a living. Jesus knows that they will have a hard time of it when He is gone. Any good parent prepares a child for a painful event that will come. The child asks if the doctor will give a shot. The good parent points to the time after the injection is given, when the child will be comforted with a lollipop.

God, better than the best of human parents, prepares His children for difficult times ahead. Jesus assures the disciples that He will not leave them alone. He will intercede in heaven. Jesus and the Father will dwell with them, and He will ask the Father to send the Holy Spirit. Jesus will give believers a peace that passes all understanding. The world's peace simply offers a cease fire until the next battle or war. The peace of Jesus sustains the believer in good times and bad. Jesus rejoices to return to His Father and instructs the disciples to rejoice with Him. Then, Jesus sets out for the final battle, in which He will overcome the ruler of the world, the devil, the prince of darkness.

The death of Jesus is not a temporary victory for Satan, but a sign of Christ's loving obedience to the Father. Jesus sets His face toward Calvary. He chooses to do battle with the evil one, so that man can be redeemed, and the relationship between God and his rebellious children can be restored. Jesus came down from heaven and He knew that He would return to heaven when His mission on earth was completed. Only Jesus understood the bliss of heaven. He wanted to share with us the glory of eternity in His Kingdom. Because of original sin, we could not enter heaven on our own. Mankind needed a Messiah, a Savior, a Redeemer. Jesus freely chose to be the sacrificial Lamb, who takes away the sin of the world. In doing so, Jesus shows us the greatest love the world will ever know. Jesus opened the gates of heaven for us. Jesus invites us to share in His royal inheritance. He invites us to be part of the family of God for all eternity. What wondrous love is this!

1. Find two different translations of the Bible and write John 14:2 from each of them.

2. Who can hope for heaven? ***CCC 1023***

3. What will heaven be like? ***CCC 1024, 1025***

4. Which three apostles asked questions of Jesus in John 14? Give questions and verses.

Thomas	***Lord, we don't know where you're going, how can we know the way?***	***John 14:5***

5. What do the following passages say about Truth?

Psalm 51:6	
Isaiah 45:19	
Zechariah 8:16	
John 16:13	
John 18:38	

6. Is there objective truth? How can you know? John 14:6

7. Define "truth." *CCC 2468, 2505*

8. Find the verse in John 14 that speaks directly about Jesus' oneness with the Father.

9. What can you learn from the following verses?

Matthew 7:7	
Matthew 18:19-20	
John 16:23-24	
1 John 3:21-22	

10. Why might some prayers go unanswered? 1 John 5:14-15

11. List as many references to the Holy Spirit as you can find from John 14 with verses.

12. Describe the Holy Spirit. *CCC 683, 684, 685*

13. Where do we see the Holy Spirit at work in the Church? *CCC 688*

14. List the gifts of the Holy Spirit found in Isaiah 11:2-3.

15. What gift of the Spirit from Isaiah 11:2-3 do you have in abundance?

16. What gift from Isaiah 11:2-3 would you pray to the Holy Spirit to receive?

17. What fruit of the Spirit from Galatians 5:22-23 do you have in abundance?

18. What fruit of the Spirit from Galatians 5:22-23 would you like to pray to the Holy Spirit to receive more?

19. What person do you know who best exemplifies the fruit of the Holy Spirit? Why?

Monthly Social Activity

Again this month, your small group will meet for coffee, tea, or a simple snack in someone's home. Pray for this social event and for the host or hostess. Make every effort to participate in this social activity. If this is hard for you to do, ask God for the grace to step out of in faith for His greater honor and glory.

Prepare to complete one of the following statements:

- One thing I am very grateful to God for is_______

or

- When I count my blessings, the three (3) things I am most thankful for are

____

____

____

Please make sure that *everyone* in your group shares some reflections!

JOHN 15

Jesus, the True Vine

Memory Verses

**"I am the vine, you are the branches.
He who abides in me, and I in him, he it is that bears much fruit,
for apart from me you can do nothing."**

JOHN 15:5

**"This is my Commandment, that you love one another as I have loved you.
Greater love has no man than this, that a man lay down his life for his friends.
You are my friends if you do what I command you."**

JOHN 15:12-14

Jesus, the True Vine. Jesus begins another of His "I AM" proclamations with imagery that would have been very familiar to Jews of His time. The Hebrew Scriptures present a beautiful vineyard song in Isaiah 5:1-7 and a prayer to restore God's vineyard in Psalm 80:8-20. In these passages, the vine that God brought out of Egypt, nurtured and protected refers to Israel, His chosen people. Whereas, Israel was the vine and God the vinedresser, now Jesus is the vine and His disciples are the branches, deriving life and sustenance from Him. Jesus provides the true fulfillment and completion of the Old Testament promises and longings.

From the beginning, Jesus associated His disciples with His own life, revealed the mystery of the Kingdom to them, and gave them a share in his mission, joy, and sufferings. Jesus spoke of a still more intimate communion between Him and those who would follow Him: "Abide in me, and I in you . . . I am the vine, you are the branches" (John 15:4-5). And He proclaimed a mysterious and real communion between His own life and ours. "He who eats My flesh and drinks My blood abides in me, and I in him."

The branches of the vine grow upwards, towards the life-giving sun. This is the direction of life: Upwards! Meanwhile, gravity, a natural force ordained by God, pulls us down. A certain amount of gravity is good for us, keeping our feet planted firmly on the ground, and giving us good muscle tone. Too much gravity would crush us, and too little would send us flying off into space! It is there for us to push against, to give us a boost in standing tall against the sky. The spiritual equivalent of gravity is guilt. Just as gravity pulls down our bodies, guilt tugs at our spirits. Just as we must rise each morning to slough off the drag in our bodies, so each night our consciences remind us of how we have compromised our spirits.

Guilt, too, is a natural force ordained by God, and a certain amount of guilt is a healthy thing. It alerts us when we have made mistakes that need correcting. Too much guilt would crush us, and too little would leave us without moral responsibility. Guilt reminds us of our feet of clay even while our spirits soar into the skies. Gravity and guilt are real forces that have to be dealt with. We do not overcome the force of gravity by pretending that it doesn't exist, as for example by stepping off a cliff thinking we can fly. Neither do we overcome the force of guilt by pretense. We are sinners.

The way to master such forces is by generating a superior counter-force. The counter-energy to guilt is virtue. The virtue of faith lifts our minds with godly truth. Hope lifts our wills with godly resolve. The virtue of charity lifts our hearts into God-like love. Virtue requires a strength of mind, will and heart which comes from God, by which we may live risen lives. Christianity is a religion about resurrection, about the lifting up of humanity. Our Savior said, "When I am lifted up from the earth, I will draw all men to Myself" (John 12:32). He overcame gravity in His body so that we might overcome guilt in our souls. The life-giving Spirit of Christ is pulling you upward against gravity and guilt. Stand firm, stand fast, stand tall, steadfast in the faith.

Jesus gives the blueprint for living the Christian life. The disciple abides in Jesus, and draws strength from Jesus in the Blessed Sacrament. The Christian cleaves to Jesus in the Church and draws life and protection from the church, prayer and the sacraments. Apart from Jesus, and outside of His Church, dangerous perils lurk in the darkness. Cling to Jesus for safety and life. He is our blessed assurance.

The Church Is the Field of God. Here the ancient olive tree grows whose roots were the prophets and in which the reconciliation of Jew and Gentile has been achieved. His land, like a choice vineyard, has been planted by the heavenly Sower. Christ, the true vine, gives life and fruitfulness to the branches, to us, who through the Church remain in Christ without whom we can do nothing. Stay secure in the arms of the Church.

Some suggest that only the Bible is required to live a life pleasing to God. But, the Bible doesn't offer imagery of a single flower growing alone. The Bible gives a picture of a vine, whose branches are dependent for its very life on staying connected to that vine. Apart from the vine, the branch withers and dies and is thrown into the fire to be burned. A Christian in isolation is in a very dangerous place indeed. Moreover, the Bible is silent on many issues that plague people today. Issues such as gambling, artificial insemination, and cloning, can't be adequately discerned using the Bible alone. Catholics look to the wisdom of the Magisterium in learning how to live lives which are pleasing to God and in accord with His perfect will. Jesus establishes His church, making it possible for us to cleave to Him and receive His grace.

Through the power of the Holy Spirit we take part in Christ's Passion by dying to sin, and in His Resurrection we are born to a new life. We are members of His Body, the Church, branches grafted onto the vine which is Jesus Christ.

Abiding in Christ Produces Results. The disciple bears fruit. For apart from Jesus you can do nothing. How many times do Christians get in over their heads trying to please God and produce results relying on their own strengths, their own talents and ideas, and their own efforts? God's folly is greater than man's wisdom. How often do people ask God to bless their plans, rather than asking God what He has planned? Have you ever prayed, assuming that your will and God's will were synonymous? The believer abiding in Christ and obeying the commandments experiences answered prayer (John 15:7), love (John 15:10), and joy (John 15:11). The fruitful Christian demonstrates love, joy, and holiness that cause others to want to know Jesus and live in Him. Jesus commands us to love one another and bear fruit, that the Father will be glorified. Sometimes it may be easier to love the stranger on the other side of the world than the person in one's own family, workplace, or community. Nonetheless, Jesus doesn't suggest or encourage us to love; Jesus commands us to love one another.

Do Not Love the World. Sacred Scripture uses the phrase *the world* in different conceptual constructs. Earlier in the Gospel of John, we learned that God so loved the world that He sent his only begotten Son to redeem this world (John 3:16). In Genesis, God creates the world and everything in it and finds that everything He has created is good. However, in this context, *the world* seems to refer to that kingdom which is opposed to the will of God, that kingdom which is under the dominion of the "prince of this world" referred to in John 12:31, which is Satan. Furthermore, John later cautions believers, "Do not love the world or anything in the world. If anyone loves the world, the love of the Father is not in him" (1 John 2:15).

Jesus warns that conflict is inevitable for those who choose to follow Him. Jesus was hated and persecuted in this world. He suffered the humiliation of crucifixion, the death of a condemned criminal, although He was innocent, to save us from the penalty due for our sins. Most of the apostles would be persecuted, imprisoned and ultimately martyred for their faith in Christ. Jesus does not offer health, wealth and happiness in this life, but, rather pruning and suffering in this life, and ultimately eternal bliss in the world to come.

The more productive and vibrant you are, the more you will need to be pruned. This message would have had special meaning for the members of the early Church. They would suffer from the trauma of division within the community and the pain and embarrassment of being expelled from the synagogue.

Contemporary society offers opportunities for Christians to feel at odds with the world. Some entertainment proves unsuitable for Catholics. Responsible parents discern that their children must forego certain movies or activities. Even in school, certain books are inappropriate for a given child. One popular book fetes mental illness, sodomy, adultery, murder and cannibalism. The major antagonist in the book is a fanatical Christian, suffering from mental illness! Jesus warned us about hostility from the world. He also promised that those who abide in Him would be pruned, and pruning hurts!

Infertility, loss of employment, betrayal, a difficult marriage, or the death of a loved one might be used by God to prune us. Pruning is essential because our sinful nature needs to be purified until we are conformed to the image of God in Christ. Death has new meaning for us because we are configured to the death of Christ. Although pruning hurts, it is the only way to grow and flourish. It is far better to be pruned by a loving God than to be beaten down by the world, the flesh and the devil.

Pruning hurts! In the midst of anguish, loneliness, betrayal or bereavement, one can lash out at God. Yet, cleaving to Jesus and abiding in Him provides the grace to endure the torment. Relinquishing one's hold on Jesus, leaving the Church, or abandoning the sacraments leaves one separated from that source of grace, hope and love. Bitterness and resentment can result. Whereas, abiding in Jesus can ultimately bring sense and meaning out of suffering. God can write straight with our crooked lives.

While suffering is never easy or pleasant, often that very time is the source of one's greatest intimacy with God. St. Ignatius Loyola found God while recovering from his battle wounds. Many people experience the nearness of God during their most intense experiences of pain or affliction. Look at Mary, Our Lady of Sorrows, who experienced such torment in witnessing the passion of her Son and yet persevered to witness the glory of the Resurrection and Ascension of Our Lord.

Finally, Jesus promises the Holy Spirit, the Counselor, the Spirit of Truth who will come. Jesus does not leave His disciples without hope or consolation, but promises the gift of the Holy Spirit, the indwelling of the Holy Spirit, who will never leave. Jesus is the vine, the source of life. Cling to Christ, the source of life and hope. Cleave to Jesus in good times and bad, most especially in the painful, excruciating times. He is the source of comfort and hope. For, in times of trouble, to whom else can you turn?

1. What practical thing could you do to apply this chapter to your life this week?

    _____ Pray more each day.

    _____ Speak to a priest about getting right with the Church.

    _____ Celebrate the Sacrament of Reconciliation.

    _____ Receive the Eucharist more frequently and more joyfully.

    _____ Perform an act of love for someone who is difficult for you to love.

    _____ Smile more. Demonstrate the joy of the Lord each day.

2. Complete the following "I AM" proclamations of Jesus.

I who speak to you am _____.	John 4:26
(referring to the _____________)	John 4:25
I am the ________ ____ __________.	John 6:35
I am the ____________ ___________.	John 6:51
I am the __________ of the _________.	John 8:12, John 9:5
I am the _________ ___________.	John 10:11
I and _____ __________ are one.	John 10:30
I am the ___________________ and the _________.	John 11:25
You call me ____________ and ________, and so I am.	John 13:13
I am ____ _____, ____ __________, and ____ ________.	John 14:6
I am the _______ ________.	John 15:1

3. Write your favorite verse from Psalm 80, "A Prayer to Restore God's Vineyard."

4. In "The Vineyard Song" Isaiah 5:1-7, what two questions does God ask?

5. Describe the setting and parable told in Matthew 21:33-43.

6. How are God's people referred to in 1 Corinthians 3:9?

7. How many times does the word "abide" or "abiding" appear in John 15?

   List the verses.

8. What happens to those who don't abide in Christ? John 15:6

9. How is God the Father glorified? John 15:8

10. What does the fruit refer to in John 15:2, 5, and 8? *CCC 2074*

11. What three things can you do to appropriate this verse? *CCC 2074*

12. If we keep the commandments, what two things does Jesus promise? John 15:10-11

13. In order to bear more fruit, what must be done? John 15:2

14. What does Jesus warn about in John 15:18-20?

15. Who does Jesus promise to send in John 15:26?

16. John 15:26-27 ends by preparing us to do what?

17. Was there a time in your life when God was pruning you to bear more fruit for Him? Have you ever needed to separate yourself or your child from some worldly influences?

18. Jesus speaks about abiding in His love that His joy might be in you and that your joy may be full (John 15:10-11). Have you experienced His love and His joy in your life, even in the midst of suffering or persecution?

JOHN 16

The Promise of the Holy Spirit

Memory Verses

"When the Spirit of truth comes, he will guide you into all the truth"

JOHN 6:13A

"So you have sorrow now, but I will see you again and your hearts will rejoice, and no one will take your joy from you."

JOHN 16:22

**"I have said this to you, that in me you may have peace.
In the world you will have tribulations; but be of good cheer,
I have overcome the world."**

JOHN 16:33

The Coming of the Paraclete. Jesus warns the disciples that hard times will come. Aware of His impending Passion and Death, Jesus forewarns the apostles in order to strengthen them and prepare them for grief and suffering. Not only will Jesus suffer and die, but the apostles will endure persecution as well. The intimacy with Jesus that His followers have enjoyed will be coming to an end. Jesus will leave them and cross over into the world of the dead, and ultimately He will depart from this world to return to His Father in heaven, from whence He came. However, despite His impending death and departure, Jesus offers them consolation.

Once Jesus returns to the Father, the Spirit will be sent to the believers. The Spirit is called *the Holy Spirit* who dwells in believers. There are also evil spirits who do not indwell but possess people. Although there are many different names by which the Holy Spirit is called, *Advocate, Paraclete, Counselor, Spirit of Truth,* the relationship between the Holy Spirit, Jesus and God the Father emerges in these passages. St. John gives us glimpses of this Third Person of the Blessed Trinity, who can remain elusive to many Christians. The early Church fathers can help us to gain a deeper understanding of and love for the Holy Spirit.

St. Irenaeus (140 - 202 AD) said "The Lord promised to send us the Paraclete, who would make us ready for God. Just as dry wheat without moisture cannot become one dough or one loaf, so also, we who are many cannot be made one in Christ Jesus, without the water from heaven. Just as dry earth cannot bring forth fruit unless it receives moisture, so also we, being at first a dry tree, can never bring forth fruit unto life, without the voluntary rain from above. Our bodies achieve unity through the washing

which leads to incorruption; our souls, however, through the Spirit. Both are necessary, for both lead us on to the life of God" (St. Irenaeus, *Against Heresies,* 3, 17, 2).

Many Christians experience dryness at some point in life. People try to live good lives and yet problems arise and their efforts don't bring fruit. They find they can't pull themselves up on their own strength alone. Some attempt to read Sacred Scripture with great expectations and every good intention, yet achieve little success. The words don't make sense. Nothing seems to gel. After praying to the Holy Spirit and being filled with the Holy Spirit, the Bible comes alive and a supernatural source provides understanding.

St. Athanasius (295 - 373 AD) further explains "The Spirit, then, being established in us, the Son and the Father come; and they make their dwelling in us. For the Trinity is indivisible, and its Godhead is one; and there is one God over all and through all and in all. This is the faith of the Catholic Church; for on the Trinity the Lord founded it and rooted it, when He said to His disciples, 'Go out and instruct every people, baptizing them in the name of the Father and of the Son and of the Holy Spirit' (Matthew 28:19)" (St. Athanasius, *Four Letters to Serapion of Thmuis,* 3, 6).

Ponder the Mystery. This is the faith we profess, the faith handed down to many of us by our parents and passed on from us to our children. Whatever treasures or family heirlooms we pass on to our children, nothing can be as valuable as the fullness of truth of this faith, which can open the gates to everlasting bliss in heaven.

St. Cyril of Jerusalem (337 - 352 AD) comments "The Father through the Son with the Holy Spirit gives every gift. The gifts of the Father are not this, and those of the Son that, and of the Holy Spirit the other. For there is one salvation, one power, and one faith. There is one God, the Father; one Lord, His only-begotten Son; and one Holy Spirit, the Advocate; and it is enough for us to know these things. Do not inquire curiously into His nature or substance. It is sufficient for us, in regard to our salvation, to know that there is Father, Son, and Holy Spirit" (St. Cyril, *Catechetical Lectures,* 16, 24).

The Holy Spirit empowers the believer to be and to accomplish what could never be done alone. The Holy Spirit indwells the believer and brings supernatural gifts of wisdom, fortitude, understanding, counsel, piety and fear of the Lord. Scripture comes alive and becomes understandable. Thoughts come into one's head to pray for someone or do something that may seem unusual, but later may become clear in the scope of God's plan. Late one night, a young man felt compelled to buy a bottle of milk. He drove to a poor part of town and stopped in front of a house with a light on. The man felt prompted to knock on the door of the stranger's home. A frazzled man came to the door and said "Thank God! Our baby is crying and hungry and we have no money for milk. We have been praying that God would send us milk for the baby."

On another occasion a woman was troubled in the middle of her housework and felt compelled to kneel and pray for her daughter, away at college. Later that night the

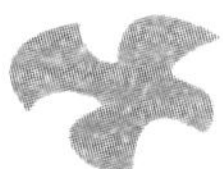

daughter called to report that at the very moment the mother was praying, the daughter had been harassed by a troubled man who was trying to harm her. She had been jogging in a secluded park. At the exact time the mother started to pray, a policeman appeared, seemingly from nowhere and rescued the young woman from the assailant.

Pondering the sacred mysteries, we rejoice when God grants us even a little glimmer of illumination into the fullness of truth. We praise and worship God in the Blessed Trinity. Guard against the pride that would lead one to believe that these mysteries will ever be fully comprehensible in this life.

St. Hilary of Poitiers (315-367 AD) says "We are all spiritual men, if the Spirit of God is in us. But this Spirit of God is the Spirit also of Christ. And since the Spirit of Christ is in us, the Spirit of Him also who raised Christ from the dead is in us, the Spirit of Him also who raised Christ from the dead will vivify our mortal bodies too, on account of His Spirit's dwelling in us. We are vivified, therefore, on account of the Spirit of Christ's dwelling in us through Him that raised Christ from the dead" (St. Hilary of Poitiers, *The Trinity*, 8, 21).

The Catholic Bishop prays for the gifts of the Holy Spirit to come down in the sacrament of Confirmation to vivify and bring the Catholic into maturity. The same gifts which came down upon Jesus can empower the mature Christian. "And the Spirit of the Lord shall rest upon him, the spirit of wisdom and understanding, the spirit of counsel and might, the spirit of knowledge and the fear of the Lord" (Isaiah 11:2).

The Holy Spirit is present to us in the Church, a communion alive in the faith of the apostles. Within the Church, the action of the Holy Spirit is manifest

- in the Sacred Scriptures which the Holy Spirit inspired,
- in the Sacred Tradition, passed on by the apostles and Church Fathers,
- in the Church's Magisterium guided by the Holy Spirit,
- in the Eucharist, where the Holy Spirit brings us into communion with Christ,
- in prayer, wherein the Holy Spirit intercedes for us,
- in charisms and ministries where the Holy Spirit builds up the Church;
- in the apostolic and missionary life of the Church,
- in the witness of saints through whom the Holy Spirit inspires holiness and continues the work of salvation.

St. John tells us the Counselor will come to "convince the world concerning sin and righteousness and judgment" (John 16:8). The sin of this world is the rejection of God and the refusal to accept and believe the provision of God the Father for sinful man. Jesus, the Righteous One is revealed by the power of the Holy Spirit, the Spirit of Truth. Satan, the ruler of this world, is judged as a deceiver, a liar and a thief. Without the Holy Spirit, we are incapable of discerning those things which look good from those things which actually are good. Satan tempts us with things that appear to be pleasing

to us, but ultimately bring about disaster. All that glitters is not gold. The Holy Spirit guides believers into the fullness of truth. And in the fullness of truth, Jesus is glorified and the Father is made known.

Moreover, the Holy Spirit convicts believers of sin. In times past, confessional lines were long and communion lines short. People acknowledged their sinfulness. The philosophy of the contemporary world is that everyone is OK. I'm OK. You're OK. Everyone is basically good. If someone makes a mistake, someone else is probably to blame. A poor childhood, weak parents, an inadequate education, something or someone else bears responsibility for any wrongdoing. In a violent and materialistic culture, it's easy to be lulled into feeling that compared to everyone else, I'm not so bad. But, God doesn't ask us to compare ourselves with everyone else. Jesus calls us to a much higher road. "You, therefore, must be perfect, as your heavenly Father is perfect" (Matthew 5:48). The Holy Spirit enables the believer to see himself clearly and repent of serious sin and also to reject what may be unnecessary or excessive guilt.

Jesus Is the Victor. How confused the disciples must have been when Jesus told them that in a little while they would see Him no longer and again in a little while they would see Him again. In hindsight, obviously Jesus was speaking about His death and His return to the Father and then His resurrection and the time of reunion with the disciples. Weeping, sorrow and lamentation would accompany Jesus' suffering and death. Ultimately, His resurrection would bring great joy to the apostles and to the whole world of believers for all time.

The childbirth analogy is poignant. Mothers and children suffer in the birthing process, but the outcome is life and joy. Jesus foretells that although sorrow will come now, ultimately hearts will rejoice and "no one will take your joy from you" (John 16:22). Emotions are fleeting in this life. Everyone experiences joys and sorrows. Jesus promises a joy that can never be taken away, everlasting joy!

The indwelling of the Holy Spirit enables the believer to discern the will of God and to pray accordingly. Jesus invites the believer to ask the Father anything and assures that God has the power and desire to make one's joy full. Moreover, Jesus promises that "the Father Himself loves you" (John 16:27). Ponder the incredible truth that God the Father loves you! God loves you with an everlasting love. He will continue loving you until the end of time. He created you. You belong to Him and He will never leave you or forsake you. "Can a woman forget her suckling child, that she should have no compassion on the son of her womb? Even these may forget, yet I will not forget you. Behold, I have graven you on the palms of My hands" (Isaiah 49:15-16). God will never forget you. He has written your name on the palm of His hand.

The disciples rejoice that they can now understand what Jesus is telling them. Nonetheless, Jesus warns that soon the disciples will be scattered and He will be left alone. Yet, Jesus can never be alone, because in the Blessed Trinity, the Father, Son and Holy Spirit are one and together. From a human perspective, the scene at the foot of

the cross shows only the apostle, John and Mary the mother of Jesus and the other Mary. From a heavenly perspective, God the Father and the Holy Spirit look down upon the sacrifice of the God-Man for the sins of mankind.

Jesus final words in John 16 provide the eternal perspective. Jesus says "I have said this to you that in Me you may have peace. In the world you have tribulation; but be of good cheer, I have overcome the world" (John 16:33). The crucifixion is not a victory for Satan. Once the disciples comprehend what has taken place in Jesus' glorification, then they will understand that Jesus has been victorious.

Every human heart longs for that peace which passes understanding, a peace which remains through good times and bad. Every human being suffers sorrows and disappointments of some kind in this world. There are hurts, betrayals, problems, obstacles and pains. The world, the flesh and the devil harass the believer. It could be discouraging, overwhelming. Yet, Jesus admonishes the believer to be of good cheer.

Jesus has overcome the world, the flesh and the devil. Jesus has conquered sin and death once and for all. The battle between good and evil is embarked upon and Satan is defeated. Jesus has overcome all the forces of evil that are pitted against Him and us. Jesus Christ is our victor!

When the Holy Spirit fell upon the apostles at Pentecost, their lives were transformed. Peter, who denied Jesus in the courtyard and ran away, was given the courage to preach to thousands and ultimately embrace martyrdom. The apostles could discern where each of them should go to share the Good News. The Holy Spirit transformed cowardice into courage, confusion into clarity for the disciples of Jesus.

God can do the same for you. God does not intend for you to walk through this life alone. The Holy Spirit can provide you with daily comfort and inspiration. How should you live your life? How and when should you pray? What should you do about relationship problems and conflicts? How and where should you earn your money and how should you spend it? What can you do to make a difference in this world? Only the Holy Spirit knows the answers to these questions. Only the Holy Spirit can guide you in your particular situation and show you the perfect will of God for your life in each and every circumstance. Jesus promised to ask the Father to send the Spirit of Truth to lead you and guide you into the fullness of truth.

Are you experiencing the presence and comfort and inspiration of the Holy Spirit in your life? Would you like to experience a greater outpouring of the Spirit of God in your life and in the depths of your soul? If so, pray and expect God to answer this prayer. Ask the members of your small group to pray for you for a fresh outpouring of the Holy Spirit in your life. Sing or pray aloud the following song to the Holy Spirit.

Spirit of the Living God, fall afresh on me.
Melt me, mold me, fill me, use me. Spirit of the Living God, fall afresh on me.

1. What was Jesus' motive for speaking all these things to the apostles? John 16:1

2. Why didn't Jesus warn them about His parting earlier? John 16:4-5

3. Read the entire chapter of John 16. Write down as many references to the Holy Spirit as you can find along with the verses.

4. See how many titles of the Holy Spirit you can find in the following verses.

Genesis 1:2	
Isaiah 11:2	
Matthew 3:16	
John 14:16	
Acts 2:4	
Galatians 3:14, Ephesians 1:13	
1 Peter 4:14	

5. Who can understand the thoughts of God? *CCC 687*

6. When does Jesus fully reveal the Holy Spirit? *CCC 728*

7. When is the Holy Spirit manifested? *CCC 731*

8. When is the Holy Trinity fully revealed? *CCC 732,* Acts 2:33-36

9. What was the purpose of the Spirit of the Lord? Isaiah 61:1-3

10. When was this purpose fulfilled and by whom? Luke 4:18-19

11. To whom is the fullness of the Spirit given? Joel 3:1-2, Ezekiel 36:25-27, *CCC 1287*

12. What is the role of the Holy Spirit in Christian prayer? *CCC 2615*

13. Write your favorite prayer to the Holy Spirit. Use any Prayer Book or *CCC 2671.*

14. List six (6) gifts of the Holy Spirit from Isaiah 11:2.

15. Describe the temple of the Holy Spirit in 1 Corinthians 6:19-20. How was it obtained? What is the response to God?

16. List some spiritual gifts given by the Holy Spirit in 1 Corinthians 12:4-10.

17. Have you ever felt prompted by the Holy Spirit to do something or pray for someone?

18. John 16:21 makes a reference to pain in childbirth. Read Genesis 3:14-16 to find out the origin of pain in childbearing.

19. What does Jesus invite us to do in John 16:24?

20. Would you like a greater outpouring of the Holy Spirit in your life?

** Share a prayer request with your small group and ask them to pray for you.

Prayer unleashes the power to change the impossible!

The Preacher and the Pope

In the fall of 1978 the Billy Graham Society sought places to hold evangelistic rallies in Eastern Europe. "In Cracow, permission to preach in the baroque splendor of St. Ann's Church had been given to me earlier by Cardinal Karol Wojtyla, with whom I was scheduled to have tea," recalls American preacher, Billy Graham. Hard-line Communist officials hoped to use the American Protestant evangelist to weaken the strong Roman Catholic Church. Reverend Graham responds "It was a naive hope; I would not have done or said anything that might be taken as anti-Catholic."

"Cardinal Wojtyla went to Warsaw October 2, thus missing the American evangelist Billy Graham, whom he had given permission to preach in St. Anne's Church. By October 3, the Primate of Poland and the archbishop of Krakow were in St. Peter's Basilica praying at the bier of John Paul I." Was it mere coincidence that as the most prominent evangelist in America was preaching in the church of the archbishop of Krakow, that same archbishop was preparing to assume the chair of St. Peter in Rome?

Later, Cardinal Wojytla, now John Paul II invited Mr. Graham to the Vatican. "As I was ushered into his quarters, Pope John Paul II greeted me, and we shook hands warmly. I found him extremely cordial and very interested in our ministry. After only a few minutes, I felt as if we had known each other for many years. He expressed great delight at the small gift I had brought him, a woodcarving of a shepherd with his sheep done by a North Carolina craftsman. We recalled together Jesus' words in John 10:14, 16. 'I am the good shepherd; I know my sheep and my sheep know me . . . I have other sheep that are not of this sheep pen. I must bring them also.' In return the pope gave me a medallion commemorating his papacy and several magnificently bound volumes."

Billy Graham, *Just As I Am* (New York, NY: Harper Collins, 1997), 571-573, 579-580

George Weigel, *Witness to Hope: The Biography of John Paul II* (New York, NY: Harper Collins, 1999), 248

JOHN 17

The Priestly Prayer of Jesus

Memory Verses

"Holy Father, keep them in thy name, which thou hast given me, that they may be one even as we are one."

JOHN 17:11B

"Sanctify them in truth; thy word is truth."

JOHN 17:17

Prayer for Glorification. For many people, imminent and impending death would be met with denial, fear and frustration, clinging desperately to this life. Not so, with Our Lord Jesus, who aware of His approaching death, prays to His Father and teaches His apostles simultaneously. It seems as if Jesus proclaims His own last will and testament as the hour of His death nears. St. Athanasius (295-373 AD) tells us that "it is plain that as the Word He knows the hour and end of all things. If He had not known the hour, He would not have said 'Father, the hour is come'(John 17:1)" (St. Athanasius, *Discourses Against the Arians,* 3, 42).

The Priestly Prayer of Jesus parallels The Lord's Prayer in several ways:
(1) Both address God as Father (John 17:1, Matthew 6:9)
(b) Both glorify God with the divine name (John 17:1, 11-12; Matthew 6:9)
(c) Both seek to do the will of God (John 17:4, Matthew 6:10)
(d) Both beg deliverance from the devil, the evil one (John 17:15, Matthew 6:13)

Like The Lord's Prayer, this prayer of Jesus reflects His oneness with the Father and His desire to move completely in the center of the Father's will. Both prayers revere the name of God (John 17:1 and Matthew 6:9). Both prayers seek protection and deliverance from Satan's powers and the forces of evil in the world (John 17:15 and Matthew 6:13). The Lord's Prayer, shorter and more succinct, provides background for this beautiful and poetic priestly prayer of Jesus.

John 17 is often described as Jesus' last will and testament. In the liturgical context, this priestly prayer, especially for ordained priests, is read at the Chrism Mass on Holy Thursday when priests renew their vows of ordination. From an ecumenical perspective, it begs God for Christian unity. Above all these interpretations, the prayer stands as Jesus' last public accounting to His Father for His mission. Jesus' work was accomplished in front of the disciples who were with Him from the beginning (John 15:27, John 1:35-51), and this accounting is made before them as witnesses.

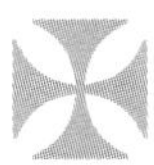

Just as the angels proclaimed "Glory to God in the highest" (Luke 2:14) at the birth of Jesus in Bethlehem, now Jesus manifests the glory of God in completing the mission entrusted to Him in reconciling the sons of Adam to the Creator. Jesus manifests for us the gift of original innocence and justice, which He possesses. This gift had been given to Adam and Eve but was forfeited in the garden by original sin which was handed down to the rest of mankind. The apostles could have prayed with David "I waited patiently for the Lord" (Psalm 40:1). Later St. Paul wrote to Titus that we were "awaiting our blessed hope, the appearing of the glory of our great God and Savior, Jesus Christ, who gave himself for us to redeem us from all iniquity and to purify for himself a people of his own who are zealous for good deeds" (Titus 2:13-14).

The glorification of Jesus has three dimensions to it.

1) It promotes the glory of the Father, because Christ, in obedience to God's redemptive decree (Philippians 2:6), makes the Father known and so brings God's saving work to completion.
2) Christ is glorified because His divinity, which He has voluntarily disguised, will eventually be manifested through His human nature which will be seen after the Resurrection invested with the very authority of God Himself over all creation (John 17:2, 5).
3) Christ, through His glorification, gives man the opportunity to attain eternal life, to know God the Father and Jesus Christ, His only Son: this in turn redounds to the glorification of the Father and of Jesus while also involving man's participation in divine glory (John 17:3).

The Navarre Bible, *The Gospels and Acts of the Apostles,* (Princeton, NJ: Scepter, 2000), 651

Jesus Prays for the Apostles. The men given by God to Jesus, the apostles, listen to these amazing words of Jesus to His Father. These twelve men, chosen by God, whom Jesus named apostles were "Simon, whom he named Peter, and Andrew his brother, and James and John, and Philip, and Bartholomew, and Thomas, and James the son of Alphaeus, and Simon, who was called the Zealot, and Judas the son of James, and Judas Iscariot, who became a traitor" (Luke 6:14-16). Interestingly, these apostles represent the common man: fishermen, tax collectors and the like. Prominent leaders, scholars of the day, diplomats, the rich and the famous seem surprisingly under-represented in this group.

Nonetheless, this group of apostles, led by Peter, became the structure that has sustained Christ's Church for 2,000 years. So that the full and living Gospel might always be preserved in the Church the apostles left bishops as their successors. The apostles handed down to the bishops their own position of teaching authority. The responsibility of giving authentic interpretation of the Word of God has been entrusted to the bishops in communion with the successor of Peter, the Pope.

We call the pope and bishops, successors of the apostles, the magisterium of the church. Since the time of St. Peter, there is an unbroken line of popes descending from Peter, who were entrusted with the sacred deposit of the faith. The responsibility of the pope and the bishops in union with him is to preserve Sacred Scripture and Tradition as it was handed down by Christ to the apostles and the early Church. While many popes and bishops have been saintly and others have been weaker human beings, nonetheless, the Holy Spirit has protected the deposit of faith intact and inerrant throughout the ages.

In January 1964, while the Second Vatican Council was in session, Pope Paul VI made a pilgrimage to the Holy Land. This was the very first visit by any of Peter's successors to the land from which Saint Peter had come. The Holy Father visited Bethlehem, Nazareth and Jerusalem, and streets named Paul VI are now in each of these cities.

On the Feast of the Epiphany, January 6, 1964 a very special meeting took place in Jerusalem between Pope Paul VI and Patriarch Athenagoras I of Constantinople. The earthly head of the Roman Catholic Church met with the highest-ranking prelate of the Eastern Churches for the first time in nearly a thousand years. When the Pope and the Patriarch sat down in the same room together, they chose to have a Bible Study! They read to each other Chapter 17 of the Gospel according to Saint John. Patriarch Athenagoras read each verse in the original New Testament Greek, and Pope Paul VI responded with the same verse in the Vulgate version translated from Greek into Latin by Saint Jerome. Verse by verse, they each read John 17 in both Greek and Latin. This was a solemn and official act of both churches, meeting in the text of the Bible.

They selected Chapter 17 of John for their text for two reasons. First, the impetus for reconciliation between the Eastern and Western Churches was very strong at this time. On the last day of the Second Vatican Council, December 8, 1965, the Pope in Rome and the Patriarch in Constantinople read simultaneous proclamations lifting the mutual excommunication between them which had been in force for almost a millennium. The meeting in Jerusalem and mutual reading of John 17, with Christ's plea for unity among his disciples, was part of the build-up to the lifting of ecclesiastical censures.

Second, the concern for holiness that Christ expresses in John 17 was a great theme of both prelates. Bishops have three functions—ruling, teaching and sanctifying—but the most important of these is sanctifying. The ruling and the teaching exist purely for the sake of the sanctification. Meeting in the same room in Jerusalem were the highest sanctifiers of East and West. They knew that the unity they wished to promote was possible only through more sanctification, not less. The Biblical text that they chose to read together makes this perfectly clear.

Jesus intercedes to the Father on behalf of His disciples.
He specifically asks the Father to give them the following blessings:

- steadfastness—keep them in Thy name (John 17:11),
- joy fulfilled in them (John 17:13),
- protection from the evil one (John 17:15),
- sanctification in truth, or holiness (John 17:17).

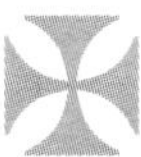

Jesus tells the apostles that He knows that one of them will betray Him. He has guarded them and none of them has been lost, "but the son of perdition, that the scripture might be fulfilled" (John 17:12). This reference to Judas Iscariot, who would betray Jesus with a kiss recalls Jesus' words earlier: "it is that the scripture may be fulfilled, 'He who ate My bread has lifted his heel against Me'" (John 13:18, Psalm 41:9). Perhaps Jesus makes this reference here to assure the apostles that He knows His betrayer and He willingly accepts the cross before Him. Jesus continues to love Judas and offers him mercy to the end, knowing the outcome and the choices that Judas will make, first to betray Christ and then to take his own life.

Jesus prays for protection for the apostles from the evil one. While acknowledging that Satan possesses the power to hurt and destroy, Jesus affirms that God's power is greater than the power of evil in the world. Later on St. John will reassure his disciples "Little children, you are of God, and have overcome them [evil spirits]; for He who is in you is greater than he who is in the world" (1 John 4:4).

Moreover, Jesus asks God to sanctify them in truth (John 17:17). St. Augustine of Hippo (354-430 AD) asks "And what else is 'in the truth' except 'in Me', since the truth is the Word that in the beginning is God?" Sanctification comes then, from clinging to Jesus Christ who is the truth and abiding in Him.

Jesus Prays for All Believers. Ultimately, Christ prays for the Church, for all believers in all ages who believe in Christ through the gospel that is preached by the apostles and their successors. Even after the crucifixion and death of Jesus Christ, His Church will flourish and the gospel will be proclaimed to the ends of the earth. After His Resurrection, Jesus promises "Lo, I am with you always, to the close of the age" (Matthew 28:20). He will never leave or forsake or abandon His children.

The Christian, the disciple of Jesus, acquires knowledge of God through living a life of faith and maintaining a personal relationship with Jesus Christ. Baptism enables sinful men to become children of God and to share in the divine nature, growing in knowledge, faith and holiness. Unfortunately, some "cradle Catholics," who were baptized as infants, remain in the cradle well into adulthood. Sanctification presupposes a growth in maturity and holiness. Prayer and the sacraments provide the means of growing in grace and intimacy with Jesus Christ.

The union of love shared between God the Father and Jesus Christ manifests itself in the Holy Spirit. Jesus invites believers to enter into and share in this divine mystery as He prays "even as thou, Father, art in me, and I in thee, that they also may be in us, so that the world may believe that thou hast sent me" (John 17:21). The unity of the Blessed Trinity proves the standard for unity in Christian marriage and the unity in the Church that the human heart longs for. Vatican II strongly recommended that we pray and work for ecumenical dialogue and Christian unity. Perhaps the best example for us has been our Holy Father, John Paul II, who without compromising the truth, has met virtually every leader of every religion in the world with love and charity.

Ecumenism for the lay person poses daunting challenges. Almost everyone has witnessed family strife due to religious differences and the pain parents endure when a child wanders into a sect or cult. Faithful Catholics strive to avoid two opposite extremes, judgmentalism and indifferentism. Jesus warns us sternly "Judge not, that you be not judged" (Matthew 7:1). Some people assume that the gift of faith that they prize so dearly has been given and understood fully by everyone. Each of us is called to account for the fullness of truth that God has blessed us with and to share it with others in love. Often in discussing matters of faith and religion, more heat is generated than light. Contentiousness must be avoided. The attitude that "No one will be saved, but me and thee, and I'm not too sure about thee" can prove disastrous.

Indifferentism, the opposite fatal flaw may be even more common. Indifferentism wrongly supposes that whatever anyone chooses to believe is fine; one religion is just as good as any other. It doesn't matter what you believe as long as you're sincere. Unfortunately, one can be sincerely wrong. Contemporary thought suggests that as long as no one is being harmed, it doesn't matter what you believe or do. Of course, this mindset ignores objective truth and inhibits striving to comprehend the fullness of truth.

What should lay Catholics do? First, know the fullness of the Catholic faith in all its beauty. Study the Bible, the *Catechism of the Catholic Church,* the encyclical letters of our Holy Father and the Christian classics. "An intelligent mind acquires knowledge, and the ear of the wise seeks knowledge" (Proverbs 18:15). Second, live the fullness of faith. Pray and frequent the sacraments. Live the beauty and fullness of your vocation. Third, pray for unity. Pray for unity in marriages, families, churches, and communities. Pray for those who have no faith and those who have abandoned the practice of their faith. Pray that God will heal the hurts that Christians have inflicted on others, often inadvertently. Always be prepared to defend the faith in love and charity. "A gentle tongue is a tree of life, but perverseness in it breaks the spirit" (Proverbs 15:4).

St. Paul encouraged the Ephesian community: "Speaking the truth in love, we are to grow up in every way into him who is the head, into Christ" (Ephesians 4:15). In order to speak the truth, one must know the truth. Speaking the truth in love, charity and kindness precludes harshness, arrogance and self-righteousness. The good wife "opens her mouth with wisdom and the teaching of kindness is on her tongue" (Proverbs 31:26). St. Peter instructs: "In your hearts reverence Christ as Lord. Always be prepared to make a defense to any one who calls you to account for the hope that is in you, yet do it with gentleness and reverence" (1 Peter 3:15).

Some err in wanting to share the faith, before they have begun to live the faith. Some try to beat others over the head with the truth, whether they are ready to hear it or not. The wise person will live the faith so humbly and so prayerfully that others will be drawn to ask: "How can I find the peace and joy that you have obtained?" Thus, the prayer of Jesus will be fulfilled "The glory which thou has given me, I have given to them, that they may be one even as we are one" (John 17:22). May the glory of God be manifest in His Church throughout the world, in each and every one of us who proclaim and confess that "Jesus Christ is Lord, to the glory of God the Father" (Philippians 2:11).

1. What physical gesture did Jesus make prior to prayer? John 17:1

2. List each verse in which you find the word "Father" in John 17. How many times?

3. Who has the power to give eternal life? John 17:2, John 10:10

4. What fulfills the petitions of "The Lord's Prayer," the Our Father? *CCC 2758*

5. Find the longest prayer in the Gospel. What does it embrace? *CCC 2746*

6. Describe a very early reference to priesthood in the Bible. Who was the priest and what did he do and say? Genesis 14:18-20

7. What did God command Moses to do in Exodus 30:30?

8. When the Lord established the Levitical priesthood, what was the inheritance of the tribe of Levi, the priests? Deuteronomy 10:8-10

9. In the Roman Catholic Church, the holy sacrifice of the Mass requires an ordained minister, a priest, to celebrate the sacrament in *persona Christi.* Why? ***CCC 1142***

10. Who can receive the Sacrament of Holy Orders in the Roman Catholic Church? ***CCC 1577, 1578***

11. Using a dictionary, the *Catechism* and your own words, define "Magisterium."

12. Where did Catholics get the idea of a Pope? Matthew 16:16-20

13. Can you find an Old Testament foreshadowing of this role? Isaiah 22:22-23

14. Who is referred to in John 17:12 and how is he called?

15. Did Jesus know who His betrayer would be? John 13:11, Psalm 41:9

16. Have you ever had an opportunity to share your faith in a positive way? Have you ever prayed for Christian unity?

17. List some of the things that Jesus prayed for you. John 17:20-25

18. Can you recall a particular priest who had a positive impact on your life or the life of your family?

19. Priests can suffer from loneliness, over-work, exhaustion, temptation and criticism. What practical thing could you do this week to support a parish priest?

    _____ Commit to daily prayer for the needs of the parish priest.

    _____ Compliment the priest on a homily that was a blessing to you.

    _____ Write a note to thank a priest who has ministered to you.

    _____ Make a holy hour to pray for vocations to the priesthood.

    _____ Bake something special for a priest, or invite him to a family dinner.

    _____ Pray for a priest, unknown to you, who may be facing discouragement.

    _____ Other ideas?

20. Write your favorite verse from John 17.

Please pray the following Prayer for Priests every day this week.

Prayer for Priests

O Jesus, I pray for your faithful and fervent priests;
for Your unfaithful and tepid priests;
for Your priests laboring at home or in distant missions;
for Your tempted priests;
for Your lonely and desolate priests;
for Your young priests and Your weary priests;
for Your dying priests;
for the souls of Your priests in purgatory.
But above all I recommend to You the priests dearest to me;
the priest who baptized me;
the priests who absolved me from my sins;
the priests who gave me Your Body
and Blood in Holy Communion;
the priests who taught and instructed me;
all the priests to whom I am indebted in so many ways.
O Jesus, keep all of Your priests close to Your Sacred Heart,
protect them from the works of the enemy,
and bless them abundantly today and in eternity.
Amen.

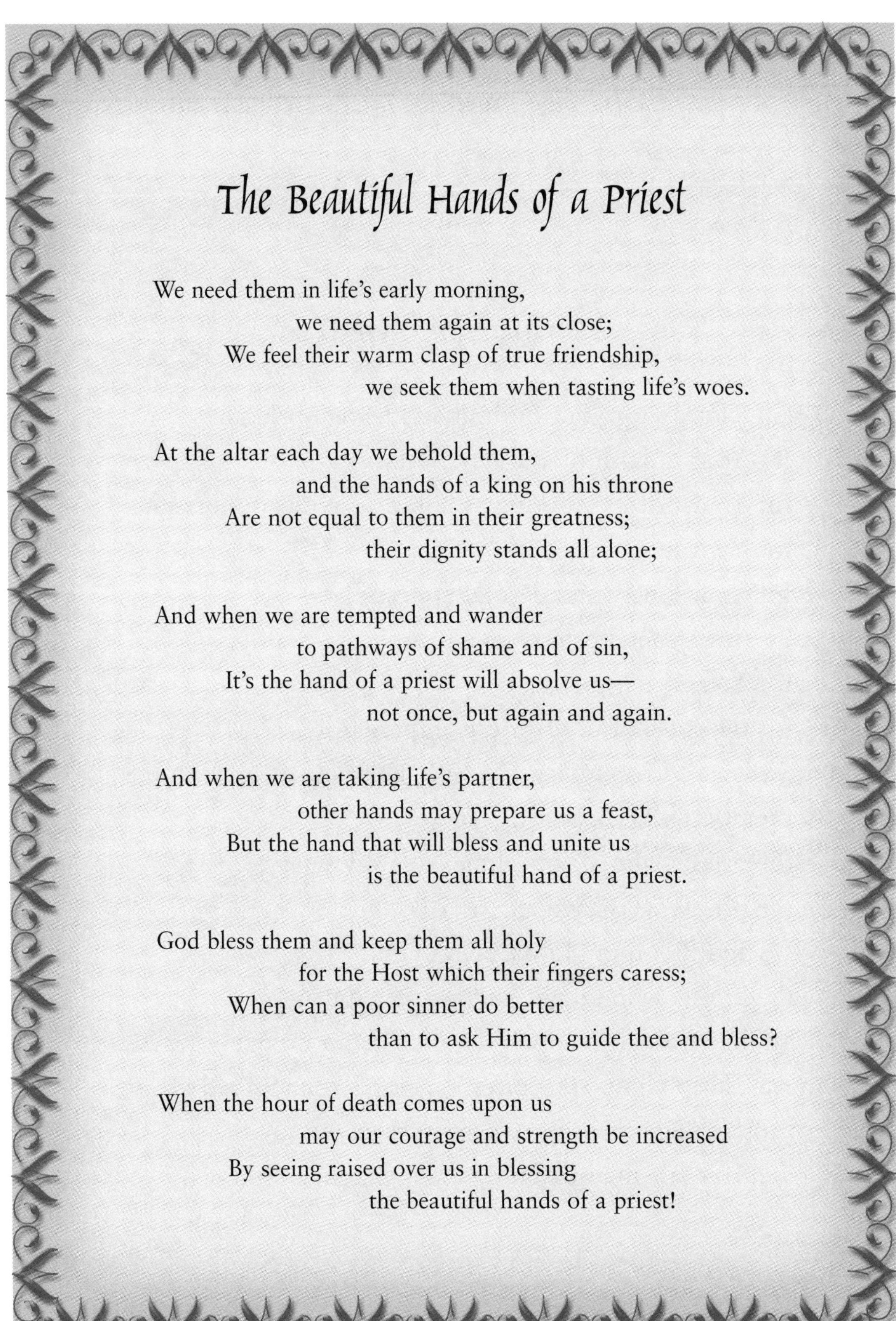

The Beautiful Hands of a Priest

We need them in life's early morning,
we need them again at its close;
We feel their warm clasp of true friendship,
we seek them when tasting life's woes.

At the altar each day we behold them,
and the hands of a king on his throne
Are not equal to them in their greatness;
their dignity stands all alone;

And when we are tempted and wander
to pathways of shame and of sin,
It's the hand of a priest will absolve us—
not once, but again and again.

And when we are taking life's partner,
other hands may prepare us a feast,
But the hand that will bless and unite us
is the beautiful hand of a priest.

God bless them and keep them all holy
for the Host which their fingers caress;
When can a poor sinner do better
than to ask Him to guide thee and bless?

When the hour of death comes upon us
may our courage and strength be increased
By seeing raised over us in blessing
the beautiful hands of a priest!

JOHN 18

The Passion of Jesus

Memory Verse

"Jesus answered, 'You say that I am a king. For this I was born and for this I have come into the world, to bear witness to the truth. Everyone who is of the truth hears my voice.'"
JOHN 18:37B

Since at least the Fifth Century AD, it has been the unvarying liturgical practice to read the Passion narrative from the Gospel of John, Chapters Eighteen and Nineteen, on Good Friday every year. So, for at least the last one thousand and five hundred Good Fridays, the Johannine Passion narrative has been read in Catholic churches everywhere.

Some time in the middle of the Eighth Century, it became customary to preface the reading with the announcement: "The Passion of Our Lord Jesus Christ according to John." The books of Gregorian Chant contain a beautiful monophonic musical setting that dates from the Ninth Century or earlier. Polyphonic musical settings began to appear in the Fifteenth Century, and eventually settings would be made by such composers as Johann Sebastian Bach in the Eighteenth Century and Arvo Part in Twentieth.

The Passion narrative begins with the account of the arrest and trial of Jesus in John 18. Here we must confront a charge which has been leveled against the Gospel of John—that John is anti-Semitic. What a distortion of the meaning and spirit of this Gospel! Above all, this is the Gospel of love. The name "John" means "The Lord is love." This is the Gospel in which Jesus says, "A new commandment I give to you, that you love one another; even as I have loved you, that you also love one another" (John 13:34). Hence the Gospel of John must be seen as completely incompatible with hatred of any kind.

By the time the Gospel of John was written down, perhaps as late as 90 - 100 A.D. many non-Jews had converted to Christianity, but they had come from the ranks of the "God-fearers" who were attracted to the positive values of Judaism without being able to accept the full burden of the Mosaic laws. Their posture toward Judaism was one of spiritual affinity and Christianity provided them with an opportunity to achieve full participation. The people in those days who hated Jews usually hated Christians, too, and probably did not recognize much difference between them.

We should note that the term "Jew" did not necessarily mean the same thing in John's time as it does today. The term "Jew" appears in only a few of the Books of the Hebrew Bible

—mainly in the late books of Ezra, Nehemiah and Esther. Jonah describes himself not as a Jew but as "a Hebrew" (Jonah 1:9). Jesus calls Nathaniel not a Jew but "a true Israelite" (John 1:47). Paul also describes himself not as a Jew but as "an Israelite" (Romans 11:1 and 2 Corinthians 11:22) and "a Hebrew" (2 Corinthians 11:22 and Philippians 3:5).

Among the four Evangelists, Matthew uses the term "Jew" only five times, Mark six times and Luke five times, while John uses the term a whopping sixty-eight times! Only the Acts of the Apostles uses the term more often than the Gospel of John, but Acts is longer than John so its frequency of use is actually less.

Many authors have said that John's criticism is directed not to the Jewish people as such, but to the Jewish leaders who failed the people in not embracing Jesus. This interpretation seems to make sense, since the crowds hailed Jesus on Palm Sunday and only turned against Him later after He had been arrested.

There is another explanation, however, which seems to fit the same facts a little better. The patriarch Jacob had twelve sons, one of whom was called Yehudah ("Judah"). This son founded one of the twelve tribes, which was called the Tribe of Yehudah, or the Tribe of Judah. When the Israelites settled in the land of the promise, this tribe settled in the hilly southern part of the Holy Land, which became known as the Portion of Yehudah, or "Judea." The people who inhabited that region, the members of the tribe of Judah, were known as Yehudi, or "Judeans," and this is the term that eventually becomes the designation "Jew." The tribe of Judah was always important, numerically larger than most of the other tribes, and it was from this tribe that David and his descendants emerged. The tribe became even more important after the northern tribes were carried away into captivity by the Assyrians.

However, the other eleven tribes did not completely disappear. The small tribe of Benjamin, which also had its portion in the South, was not carried away by the Assyrians. It was small but influential, being the tribe of King Saul and of the Prophet Jeremiah and of the Apostle Paul (Romans 11:1). Also, the tribe of Levi remained largely intact, because their most important task was staffing the Temple in Jerusalem. Even to this day, the Jewish people know who their priests are. Finally, there are individuals in the post-exilic period identified as belonging to some of the northern tribes. For example, the prophetess Anna is identified as the "daughter of Phanuel, of the tribe of Asher" (Luke 2:36). Anna lived in Judea, and was "Judean" in the purely geographical sense, but she traced her lineage to the tribe of Asher.

The four gospels are not written from a Judean but from a Galilean perspective. Jesus was raised in Galilee, called His twelve apostles there, conducted most of His public ministry there and performed most of His miracles there. When He and the apostles visited Jerusalem, they were there not as natives but as outsiders, just like pilgrims from faraway countries like Spain or Ethiopia. They spoke a different dialect of Aramaic that set them

apart from the local Jews. They belonged to the same religion, but their customs and language marked them as non-locals.

Now, there apparently was some regional antagonism between Judea and Galilee. A century before Jesus' time, a Jewish high priest had conducted in Galilee a military campaign that no doubt left residual hard feelings of the kind in which the Middle East seems to specialize. Two of the Gospels tell how Peter was subject to the suspicion of being Jesus' follower just because he was a Galilean (Mark 14:70 and Luke 22:59). Hence, in the Gospels the real opposite of the term "Jew" is not "Christian" but "Galilean." Every time the New Testament presents the term "Jew" it could just as easily be translated "Judean."

Go through John 18 and show how the term "Judean" works in each of these places.

- **John 18:12 "The *Judean* guards arrested Jesus and bound Him."** In what sense were they "Jewish" over against Jesus, who was also "Jewish"? Rather, the guards were Judean, while Jesus was a Galilean.

- **John 18:14 "It was Caiaphas who had proposed to the *Judeans* the advantage of having one man die for the people."** The people to whom Caiaphas would have proposed this were the members of the Sanhedrin. They were the leaders of the whole worldwide religion of the Hebrews, but only inhabitants of Judea were represented on the council.

- **John 18:20 "Jesus answered by saying: . . . 'I always taught in a synagogue or in the temple area where all the *Judeans* come together.'"** This accurately describes His ministry in Judea, but it does not at all describe His ministry in Galilee which frequently took place outside of sacred spaces, and it certainly does not include his two-day ministry in Samaria (John 4:40).

- **John 18:31 "'We may not put anyone to death,' the *Judeans* answered."** Judea was under direct Roman jurisdiction, so only the Romans could impose the death penalty. Galilee was ruled by a subject king, who had beheaded John the Baptist as you may recall. Hence only the Judeans were denied the option of capital punishment, not Galileans.

- **John 18:33 "Are you the King of the *Judeans*?"** No Old Testament king was ever described as "King of the Jews." David ruled as King in Judea for seven years and then as King of all Israel for thirty-three years (1 Kings 2:11). After Solomon's time there were two kingdoms, the southern "Kingdom of Judah" and the northern "Kingdom of Israel." King Herod ruled more territory than just Judea; he also ruled Samaria and Galilee. He is threatened by reports that there is a newborn "King of the Jews" (Matthew 2:2), but not because it would have challenged his jurisdiction in Samaria, only because it would have undercut his standing in Judea.

- **John 18:36 "If My kingdom were of this world, My subjects would be fighting to save Me from being handed over to the *Judeans*."** That is to say, His Galilean followers would be fighting to save Him from the Judeans who have arrested Him.

- **John 18:39 "Pilate went out against the *Judeans*."** Undoubtedly there were Jewish pilgrims from many parts of the world who were mingling with the crowd, just as on Pentecost fifty days later, but the preponderance of the crowd seems to have been Judean. The Galilean element certainly is not dictating the course of events.

- **John 18:39 "[W]ill you have me release for you the King of the *Judeans*?"** The term "King of the Judeans" appears here again. So we have looked at all nine appearances of the term translated "Jew" in our bibles in Chapter Eighteen and have shown that it makes good sense to translate it in the geographical sense as "Judean" rather than in the religious sense as "Jewish." Jesus and His twelve apostles belonged to the same race and religion as those who arrested Him. There is absolutely no basis for maintaining that any of the four gospels lay a racial or religious charge against practitioners of the Jewish religion today.

If a finger is to be pointed anywhere, it must point to ourselves, to all of us people of the whole earth, who by our sins make the death of Jesus necessary.

The people who happened to be on the scene—Romans, Judeans, and others—may be historically linked to the death of Jesus. They and we, however, are theologically linked to the death of Jesus, (with the exception of His Mother, who was Jewish! but innocent due to her sinlessness.) It is not for us who add to His suffering by each sin of ours to blame someone else for the fact of His death. That is the "blame game" which Jesus never, never indulged in. All four Gospels mention that at the moment of Jesus' arrest, the Galilean Peter cuts off the ear of a Judean slave named Malchus (John 18:10). Jesus does not encourage such behavior, but touches that Judean ear and heals it (Luke 22:51). In the very moment of being arrested, Jesus is interested not in defending Himself but only in healing those who are harming Him. We must all take refuge in that great Mercy.

1. Where did Jesus go after the Last Supper? John 18:1

2. Did Jesus know that He would suffer crucifixion and die for us? John 18:4

3. Did Jesus freely or reluctantly give up His life? *CCC 609*

4. How did Judas betray Jesus? Matthew 26:47-49

** Have you ever experienced a time in your life when you felt betrayed by a loved one? Please pray and ask Jesus to heal the hurt of that betrayal by His redeeming love.

5. How did Peter respond to Jesus' arrest? John 18:10

6. How did Jesus accept His betrayal by Judas and His arrest? John 18:11

7. What was Jesus' motivation in calmly accepting His arrest? *CCC 607*

8. Describe Peter's behavior in the following verses.

John 18:16-18	
John 18:25	
John 18:26-27	

9. How does Jesus respond to the religious authorities who question Him?

John 18:20	
John 18:21	
John 18:23	

10. Does the Church blame the Jews for the death of Jesus? *CCC 597*

11. Were ***all*** of the religious authorities opposed to Jesus? *CCC 575*

12. Name two religious authorities who were disciples of Jesus? *CCC 595, 596*

13. List four questions that Pilate presents to Jesus.

John 18:33	
John 18:35	
John 18:37	
John 18:38	

14. Define "truth." *CCC 2505*

15. How would you respond to someone saying "That may be true for you, but its not true for me"? Is there such a thing as "Objective Truth"? *CCC 2467, 2468, 2469*

16. What is the source of all truth? *CCC 2465, 2466*

17. Why did Jesus come into the world? John 18:37, *CCC 217*

18. Was Jesus' violent death an accident or the result of chance circumstances? *CCC 599*

19. Why did God permit the violence of the crucifixion? *CCC 600*

20. What is the duty of the Christian with respect to the truth? *CCC 2471, 2472*

21. Share a time when you have been called to bear witness to the truth or to act as a *witness of the Gospel.*

Monthly Social Activity

For this social activity, your small group will meet for coffee, tea, or a potluck in someone's home. Pray for this social event and for the host or hostess. Make every effort to participate in this social activity. Ask God for the grace to bring everyone in your group together for this social time for His greater honor and glory.

Prepare to complete one of the following statements:

One thing I've learned in this study of the Gospel of

John is_________________________________

or

One thing that I did in Bible Study this year that

brought me closer to God was ________________

Please make sure that *everyone* in your group *shares* some reflections!

JOHN 19

Jesus' Crucifixion and Death

Memory Verse

"When Jesus saw his mother and the disciple whom he loved standing near, he said to his mother, 'Woman, behold, your son!' Then he said to the disciple, 'Behold, your mother.' And from that hour the disciple took her to his own home."

JOHN 19:26-27

Jesus suffers scourging at the pillar and crowning with thorns. Pilate, finding no guilt in Jesus, decides to have Jesus scourged anyway. Jesus, the innocent sacrificial Lamb, remains pure and above reproach. Why would Pilate subject Jesus to flogging when he can find no crime warranting such treatment? The drama of this event unfolds with terrible irony. Jesus, majestic, and in command of His destiny, hands over His life in perfect, sacrificial love. Curious, cowardly, and indecisive, Pilate allows the feverish mob to bring condemnation on the Innocent One before him. For all of history, Pilate's injudicious conduct will be recorded and remembered.

The leaders try to force Pilate to condemn Jesus whom he twice declares to be innocent (John 18:38b, John 19:4). Pilate then forces the leaders to betray their own consciences by denying God's kingship over them. In bringing charges against Jesus and condemning Him to death, neither Pilate nor the leaders act truthfully. While the religious leaders deny that Jesus is their king, Pilate proclaims to the world in the three common languages of the time "Jesus the Nazarene, the King of the Jews."

Pilate asked Jesus "What is truth?" (John 18:38). Now, he testifies to the truth in his inscription on the cross. Truly, Jesus of Nazareth is the King of the Jews, the King of Kings and Lord of Lords. St. Paul tells us that "God has highly exalted Him and bestowed on Him the name which is above every name, that at the name of Jesus every knee should bow, in heaven and on earth and under the earth, and every tongue confess that Jesus Christ is Lord, to the glory of God the Father" (Philippians 2:9-11).

Crucifixion was the most horrific and painful form of death possible, a penalty reserved for slaves, and applied for the most serious crimes. Cicero shows how infamous a punishment it was: "That a Roman citizen should be bound is an abuse; that he should be lashed is a crime; that he be put to death is virtually parricide; what, then, shall I say, if he be hung on a cross? There is no word fit to describe a deed so horrible."

And, yet, the cross of Christ remains the precious and life-giving gift on which Jesus wins the salvation of sinners. St. Theodore the Studite explains "How precious the gift

of the cross, how splendid to contemplate! The fruit of this tree is not death but life, not darkness but light. This tree does not cast us out of paradise, but opens the way for our return."

"This was the tree on which Christ, like a king on a chariot, destroyed the devil, the Lord of death, and freed the human race from his tyranny. This was the tree upon which the Lord, like a brave warrior wounded in hands, feet and side, healed the wounds of sin that the evil serpent had inflicted on our nature. A tree once caused our death, but now a tree brings life. Once deceived by a tree, we have now repelled the cunning serpent by a tree. What an astonishing transformation! That death should become life, that decay should become immortality, that shame should become glory!"

"By the cross death was slain and Adam was restored to life. By the cross we put on Christ and cast aside our former self. By the cross we, the sheep of Christ, have been gathered into one flock, destined for the sheepfolds of heaven" (St. Theodore the Studite, *Sermon on the Adoration of the Cross,* 99).

Words fail in trying to contemplate these events, in which the Master of the Universe, the Son of God and Son of Man freely offers His life in such a painful and humiliating manner to redeem all of humanity from the deserved consequences of sin and rebellion against God. Loneliness, betrayal, hunger, thirst, nakedness, piercing flesh with thorns, whips and spear, nails pounding into hands and feet, heat, parching tongue and mouth, breathlessness and ultimate suffocation, exsanguination and death were accepted freely by Jesus, bravely and purposefully out of love for you and me.

No one has manifested this degree and quality of love in history before or after Christ. Jesus alone demonstrates sacrificial love beyond anything that has ever been seen or imagined. Jesus accepts His cross and bears it to Golgotha, the place of the skull. John Paul II asserts "Man cannot live without love... How precious must man be in the eyes of the Creator, if he gained so great a Redeemer and if God gave his only Son in order that man should not perish but have eternal life" (Pope John Paul II, *Redemptor Hominis,* March 4, 1979, no. 10.1).

The soldiers crucify Jesus and fulfill the prophecy in Psalm 22:18 by casting lots for His seamless garment. The early Church Fathers see in this seamless tunic a symbol of the unity of the Church. Throughout the ages, by divine grace, the Catholic Church remains intact. Despite rifts, splits and heresies, the integrity of the Church perseveres.

The women and the disciple Jesus loved stand nearby. There are at least three Marys at the foot of the cross and perhaps four women, if His mother's sister and Mary the wife of Clopas are two separate and distinct people. It would be unique, but not impossible for two sisters to have the same first name. One can speculate, but it cannot be known with certainty how many disciples of Jesus remain beside Him through His passion. Tradition holds that Jesus' Mother and St. John, who remained with Him at the foot of the cross, show their faithfulness to Him to the end.

Pope John Paul II explains Our Lady's faithfulness in four ways:

- her generous desire to do all that God wanted of her (Luke 1:34)
- her total acceptance of God's will (Luke 1:46)
- the consistency between her life and the commitment of faith she made
- her withstanding this test . . . to the foot of the Cross.

Pope John Paul II, *Homily in Mexico*, January 26, 1979

Mary, Our Lady of Sorrows, watches the unimaginable suffering of her Son. The Church has always venerated Mary, in her role in salvation history and her faithful and steadfast example of discipleship. "In a sense Mary as Mother became the first 'disciple' of her Son, the first to whom He seemed to say: 'Follow Me,' even before He addressed this call to the Apostles or to anyone else" (Pope John Paul II, *Redemptoris Mater*, (March 1987), no. 2.20).

The Church recognizes the dignity and vocation of women and lifts up Mary as a model and intercessor for all. Virgins can relate to her. Mothers identify with her. The motherless and lonely souls run to her for solace. And, who should be with her at the foot of the cross, but Mary Magdalene, frequently identified as a notorious sinner! The genius of Mary involves her obedience to God, in contrast with Eve's disobedience, which ultimately crushes the head of the serpent and overturns Satan's plan.

Jesus entrusts the care of His Mother to His Beloved Disciple, presumably St. John, and from that hour, John provides for the Blessed Mother. In the past few centuries some people have questioned the Perpetual Virginity of Mary, which has been a prized tenet of the Catholic Faith since the time of the Apostles. Some suggest that since the Bible speaks of brothers of the Lord there may have been other children of the Virgin Mary. This is false! No one held such a notion for the first several hundred years of Christianity. Even the reformers, Luther, Calvin and Zwingli believed that Mary remained forever a pure, intact Virgin. At this point in the Gospel, Jesus takes His responsibility as the only Son seriously when He entrusts the care of His mother to John. In Jewish culture, this would have been unthinkable if there were close relatives alive to care for her.

Jesus Knows All Things. He knows that He has accomplished the task that He came to fulfill, the Redemption of Man. On the cross, Jesus says "I thirst" (John 19:28). The duality of meaning suggests that Jesus has physical thirst and also a thirst for souls. Jesus remains thirsty for souls, who will love Him and pray to Him and grow in intimacy with Him. Jesus pronounces "It is finished" and gives up His spirit (John 19:30).

When the time comes for Jesus to fulfill the Father's plan of love, Jesus shows a glimpse of the boundless depth of His filial prayer, not only before He freely gave Himself up, but also in His last words on the cross. Jesus freely and knowingly gives up His spirit. No one takes it from Him. Jesus freely chooses to die for us to give us eternal life. Jesus dies that we might live forever. What wondrous love is this! Who can take it in? "O the depth of the riches and wisdom and knowledge of God! How unsearchable are His judgments and how inscrutable His ways!" (Romans 11:33).

Jesus Dies. Soldiers come to break Jesus' legs to hasten His death, but find their efforts are unnecessary. Perhaps the soldiers feel that they have inflicted enough suffering on an innocent victim? The soldier pierces the side of Jesus and blood and water gush forth. The blood and water, flowing from the pierced side of the crucified Jesus are types of Baptism and the Eucharist, the sacraments of new life. Hence, it is possible to be born of water and the Spirit and enter the Kingdom of God.

St. Ambrose tells us "See where you are baptized, see where Baptism comes from, if not from the cross of Christ, from His death. There is the whole mystery: He died for you. In Him you are redeemed, in Him you are saved" (St. Ambrose, *The Sacraments,* 2, 2, 6).

John 19 ends where it all began, in a garden. Adam and Eve sinned in the Garden of Eden (Genesis 3:1-24). After the Last Supper, Jesus went to the Garden of Gethsemane to pray (John 18:1) and was arrested in the garden. Now Joseph of Arimathea, a secret disciple of Jesus, and Nicodemus take away the body of Our Lord and lay it in a new tomb in the garden, where no one had ever been laid (John 19:41).

St. Augustine observed that "just as in the womb of the Virgin Mary none was conceived before Him, none after Him, so in this tomb none came before Him and none after He was buried" (St. Augustine, *Tractates on the Gospel of John,* 120, 5).

So, John 19 ends on Good Friday. The story is familiar for those who read it every year on Palm Sunday and again on Good Friday. The surprise outcome is well-known. Resurrection joy and Easter await. But, imagine what it must have been like for the first disciples. Imagine their sorrow, their confusion, their dejection. All they had given their lives to appears to be lost and failed. The humiliation of defeat weighs on them. It looks hopeless. The disciples don't know about Easter Sunday yet. The Apostles don't understand the victory of the Cross and the power of the Resurrection, yet. But, we do!

The events recorded in John 18 and 19 have been repeated so often, that they may become too familiar. The horror of the events of the Son of God dying an excruciatingly painful and humiliating death for the sins of the whole world may become dulled. In some churches the crucifix may be small or stylized to mask the shame and ugliness of the passion of Jesus Christ. But, it is the source of our salvation!

Stations of the Cross and Passion Plays have attempted to reenact the sufferings of Our Lord on Good Friday. Find a place where you can meditate on the Crucified Lord. If you want to increase your appreciation of the price Jesus paid to atone for your sins and the sins of the world, go to see a Passion Play or a movie of the Life of Christ. An especially vivid and graphic artistic presentation can be found in Mel Gibson's film, *The Passion of the Christ,* in which Jim Caviezel portrays Jesus. Whatever means help you to comprehend the magnitude of Christ's suffering may also enable you to grasp the immensity of God's great love for each of us.

1. How did Pilate judge Jesus? John 18:38, John 19:4

2. What emotion did Pilate act on? John 19:8

3. What did the soldiers do to Jesus? John 19:1-5

4. How should the Jews have dealt with blasphemy? Leviticus 24:16

5. Compare the following Old Testament and New Testament passages.

Psalm 22:18	John 19:23-2		
Psalm 69:21	John 19:29		
Numbers 9:12	John 19:33		
Zechariah 12:10	John 19:34		

6. Describe the characters and dialogue back in John 3:1-12.

7. Compare the following passages.

Numbers 21:7-9	
John 3:14-15	
Mark 15:39	

8. What can you learn from these verses?

Exodus 12:43-46	
John 19:36	
1 Corinthians 5:7	

9. Name the people standing by the cross of Jesus. How many are there? John 19:25-26

10. What is the Virgin Mary's role in the Church? ***CCC 964***

11. St. John took Mary into his home. What can you do with Mary? *CCC 2679*

12. Is Jesus Mary's only child? *CCC 501* Explain her spiritual motherhood.

13. How does Mary's role change at the foot of the cross? *CCC 2618*

** Describe the role of Marian devotion in your personal life.

14. What response can you give to Jesus' thirst? John 19:28, *CCC 2560, 2561*

15. According to St. Clement of Rome, how does conversion come about? *CCC 1432*

16. What does the water symbolize in John 19:34? *CCC 694*

17. What do the water and blood from the side of Christ pre-figure? *CCC 1225*

18. Meditate on the seven last words of Christ.

Luke 23:34	
Luke 23:43	
Luke 23:46	
John 19:26-27	
John 19:28	
Matthew 27:46 Mark 15:34	
John 19:30	

19. What do Jesus' last words on the Cross show? *CCC 2605*

20. What motivated and inspired Jesus to die for us? *CCC 606, 607, 609*

21. What do people offer to Jesus in the following verses?

Matthew 2:11	
John 12:3	
John 19:39	

22. Who buried Jesus? John 19:38-41

23. Why was Jesus buried and what does His lying in the tomb reveal? *CCC 624*

24. Did Jesus' body decay in the tomb? Psalm 16:9-10, Acts 2:26-27, CCC *627*

25. What hymn comes to mind when you think of the Passion and Death of Jesus?

** What hope do Jesus' last words give you?

JOHN 20

The Resurrection

Memory Verses

"Jesus said to him, 'Have you believed because you have seen me? Blessed are those who have not seen and yet believe.'"

JOHN 20:29

"But these are written that you may believe that Jesus is the Christ, the Son of God, and that believing you may have life in His Name."

JOHN 20:31

The Tomb is Empty! John chapter 20 recounts the most amazing, spectacular event in all of human history. The empty tomb shows Jesus' divine authority in overcoming the power of death. The actual Resurrection of Jesus' body gives evidence of more than mere immortality. All four gospel writers describe this incredible miracle (Matthew 28:1-15, Mark 16:1-18, Luke 24:1-12 and John 20:1-20).

Since the Apostle John was the only eye-witness to everything that Jesus did during the first Holy Week, the Church has chosen to read from John's Gospel on all three days of the Sacred Triduum. On Holy Thursday evening, we read from John's account of the Last Supper, with the washing of the feet which only he describes. On Good Friday, we read the Passion of Our Lord Jesus Christ according to Saint John. On Easter Sunday, we read his Resurrection Narrative (John 20).

The Easter liturgy contains a wonderful poem composed on the basis of John's Resurrection account, called "Victimae paschali laudes." It may be sung or spoken but must be included immediately before the reading of the Gospel on Easter Sunday. It may also be used throughout the octave of Easter (Easter Week). The last half of the hymn summarizes what Mary Magdalene reported to the Apostles on the first Easter morning:

Christians, to the Paschal Victim, offer your thankful praises.
A Lamb the sheep redeemeth;
Christ, who only is sinless, reconcileth sinners to the Father.
Death and life have contended in that combat stupendous,
The Prince of Life, who died, reigns immortal.
Speak Mary, declaring, what thou sawest wayfaring:
"The tomb of Christ, who is risen, the glory of Jesus' resurrection,
Bright angels attesting, the shroud and napkin resting.

Yea, Christ our hope is arisen; to Galilee He goes before you.
Christ indeed from death is risen, our new hope obtaining."
Have mercy, Victor King, ever reigning. Amen. Alleluia.
Attributed to Wipo of Burgundy (died after 1046 AD)

People have always dreaded death more than any other tragedy: crippling illness, financial ruin, natural disaster, or human betrayal. Death looms as the awe-inspiring adversary to be avoided at all costs. After all, what would it be like to not awaken in the morning? What if conversation with friends and loved ones stopped abruptly? What if you could no longer laugh or cry, hold a baby, smell flowers, or enjoy a meal?

1500 years after the death of Jesus, the British playwright, William Shakespeare reflected on the treachery of death. Hamlet, Prince of Denmark, mourning his father's untimely and underhanded death, contemplates suicide with the famous soliloquy, which begins "To be or not to be, that is the question." Humans mourn the death of loved ones and attempt to avoid or postpone death by any and all means possible.

Mary Magdalene goes to the tomb early in the morning, while it is still dark on the first day of the week, Sunday, and finds the stone moved away from the opening to the tomb. High drama mounts. Imagining that Jesus' body has been stolen, she runs to Peter to report her findings. Once again, the primacy of Peter unfolds. She does not go to James or Jude or John. She goes directly to Peter. He will know what to do.

Peter and the beloved disciple, presumably John, race to the tomb. John, probably youthful and fit, wins the race to the tomb, but defers to Peter and does not enter the tomb. John peeks in to see the burial clothes lying in the empty tomb, but waits for Peter to go into the tomb first. Peter and John represent the charisms of love and authority within the Church. Traditionally believed to be younger, John outruns Peter and reaches the tomb first. But Jesus' love is not a reckless love that flouts deference to authority. Both love and authority are of Jesus. Properly exercised, they are never in conflict.

Now, if Jesus' body had been stolen as Mary feared and the guards were bribed to report (Matthew 28:11-15), wouldn't the burial linens have vanished with the stolen corpse to its new place of repose? Furthermore, it was in Pilate's best interest and the vested interests of the scribes and Pharisees to have a dead body. Logic insists that if there were a dead body to be found, many people would have paid dearly to turn it up!

Christ's Resurrection is a real, historic fact! Overwhelming evidence proves that Jesus' body and soul were reunited and He appeared to many reliable witnesses. John S. Copley, a great British legal mind and High Chancellor of England, said "I know pretty well what evidence is, and I tell you such evidence as that for the Resurrection has never broken down yet." The empty tomb provides the greatest source of hope for those who ponder human mortality. "Death is swallowed up in victory. O death, where is thy victory? O death, where is thy sting?" (1 Corinthians 15:54-55).

The Resurrection remains the most significant event of history, verified by the sign of the empty tomb, the burial clothes and the reality of the apostles' encounters with the risen Christ. And yet, the Resurrection remains at the very heart of the mystery of faith as something that transcends and surpasses history. The risen Savior does not reveal Himself to the world, but only to His disciples, who came up with Him from Galilee to Jerusalem, and who now proclaim the Resurrection to all people.

Jesus Appears to Mary Magdalene. Was Mary Magdalene weeping for grief over the loss of her Lord, or from fear that His body had been stolen? Considering the events of the weekend, from the Passover to the Garden of Gethsemane, to the trial of Jesus and His death to His burial, one who had stayed by His side would be understandably exhausted and emotionally spent. Mary may have been the woman who had been forgiven much and loved much (Luke 7). Those who love deeply also mourn deeply the loss of the beloved. Mary perseveres in seeking the Lord. She asks about Him and promises that if He has been carried away, she will go to Him. Mary Magdalene's perseverance teaches that anyone who sincerely keeps searching for Jesus will eventually find Him. Jesus' persistence in calling His disciples "brethren" despite their fickle abandonment should fill us with hope in the midst of our own failures and infidelities.

Jesus calls Mary by her name and she recognizes Jesus when she hears His voice. Jesus said to her "Mary!" This is reminiscent of John 10:4. Jesus' sheep recognize His voice. Mary doesn't recognize Jesus at first, because His risen body appears different from the previous appearance that she was accustomed to encountering. Yet, like one of His sheep, she recognizes the Shepherd when He calls her by name. Mary responds in Hebrew "Rabboni!" which means Teacher (John 20:16).

Redemption has been won by Jesus on the cross for the sins of all of us. Jesus, by His Passion, death and Resurrection has accomplished the salvation of the world from sin and separation from God. Now Jesus will ascend to God the Father. Jesus commissions Mary to bring the good news to the disciples: "I am ascending to my Father and your Father, to my God and your God" (John 20:17). Jesus enjoys a distinctive and unique relationship with God the Father in being the Second Person of the Blessed Trinity and sharing in the Divine Nature. Jesus is the one true God, eternally coexistent with the Father. Yet, in His great love, Jesus brings fallen man, now redeemed, into the family of God and makes believers adopted children of the Father. "See what love the Father has given us, that we should be called children of God; and so we are" (1 John 3:1).

St. John portrays the complementarity of sexual roles in this Gospel. Jesus gives great honor in appearing first to the women and commissioning them to announce the good news to the disciples. God also gives great honor and precedence to Peter and the apostles in allowing Peter to enter the empty tomb first and examine the evidence for the resurrection. Each sex has a distinctive and special role in the Church and in God's plan, even though the roles are different.

On the same Sunday evening, Jesus appears to the fearful apostles. Jesus comes into the room through the locked doors and brings joy and gladness with Him, as well as peace, which the world cannot give (John 14:27). Jesus bestows on them the promised gift of the Holy Spirit (John 16:7-16). Now they are empowered to do the work that Jesus commissions them to do. Jesus gives the apostles the power to forgive sins.

The Church has always understood that Jesus Christ conferred on the apostles the authority to forgive sins, a power exercised in the sacrament of Penance. "The Lord instituted the sacrament of Penance when, after being risen from the dead, He breathed upon His disciples and said 'Receive the Holy Spirit ...' The consensus of all the Fathers has always acknowledged that by this action so sublime and words so clear the power of forgiving and retaining sins was given to the apostles and their lawful successors for reconciling the faithful who have fallen after Baptism" (Council of Trent, *On Penance,* 1).

> ***The sacrament of Reconciliation provides a sublime expression of God's love and mercy.***
> ***The Lord always awaits us with open arms.***
> ***When we repent of our sin,***
> ***He forgives us and restores to us the dignity of being children of God, which is lost through sin.***

St. Pacian of Barcelona (? 392 AD) explains "Certainly God never threatens the repentant; rather, He pardons the penitent. You will say that it is God alone who can do this. True enough; but it is likewise true that He does it through His priests, who exercise His power. What else can it mean when He says to His apostles: 'Whatever you shall bind on earth shall be bound in heaven; and whatever you shall loose on earth shall be loosed in heaven?' " (St. Pacien of Barcelona, *Letters to Sympromian,* 1, 6).

Pope Pius XII recommended frequent and regular confession as the means for growing in the spiritual life and advancing in virtue. Penance provides the opportunity to grow in true self knowledge and humility. Bad habits can be uprooted. Spiritual negligence can be addressed. The conscience is purified and graces are received.

Why can't you just confess your sins to God privately? Why confess your sins to a priest? What does the Bible say? Jesus said "If you forgive the sins of any, they are forgiven; if you retain the sins of any, they are retained" (John 20:23). How can a person know which sins are forgiven and which are retained, if he doesn't do what Jesus commanded in the Bible? Sacramental confession need not be feared or avoided. The Sacrament of Reconciliation is God's great gift and provision for sinful man.

If one has perfect contrition and cannot confess his sins to a priest, God still has the power to forgive. But, for those who have the ability to celebrate the Sacrament regularly, the priest helps to discern how to break patterns of sin and weakness. Sometimes

people are poor judges of their own behavior. They can be too hard on themselves or too lenient. The Holy Spirit anoints the priest with special grace to help the penitent discern how to see himself clearly and experience God's love and mercy.

Thomas Doubts. Was it mere coincidence that Thomas was not with the other apostles when Jesus walked through the doors to them? Or did God plan this remarkable drama so that doubting hearts for years to come could find comfort and hope?

"Surely you do not think," St. Gregory the Great (540-604 AD) comments, "that it was pure accident that that chosen disciple was missing; who on his return was told about the appearance and on hearing about it doubted; doubting, so that he might touch and believe by touching? It was not an accident; God arranged that it should happen. His clemency acted in this wonderful way so that through the doubting disciple touching the wound in his Master's body, our own wounds of incredulity might be healed" (St. Gregory the Great, *Homilies on the Gospels,* 26, 7).

Next Sunday, the disciples were in the house and Thomas was with them. The doors were locked, and Jesus came again and stood before them and offered His peace. When Jesus summoned Thomas to put his finger in His nail prints and his hand in Jesus' wounded side, Thomas answers with the marvelous profession of faith "My Lord and my God!" (John 20:28). Thomas provides an ejaculation for Christians to repeat over the centuries in awe over Jesus' Real Presence in the Eucharist. My Lord and my God!

Christ admonishes doubting Thomas. "Have you believed because you have seen Me? Blessed are those who have not seen and yet believe" (John 20:29). Jesus blesses the Christians throughout the ages, who struggle with doubt and disbelief and yet strive to choose to trust in Him.

> Starve your doubts.
> Feed your Faith!

The writer of the letter to the Hebrews explains that "Now faith is the assurance of things hoped for, the conviction of things not seen . . . And without faith it is impossible to please him" (Hebrews 11:1, 6). The entire chapter of Hebrews 11 chronicles the heroes of faith who believed God, even when they didn't understand what He was doing or why, even in the midst of struggle, suffering, confusion and persecution.

St. John explains his objective in writing this Gospel at the conclusion of John chapter 20. Despite the numerous signs and miracles that Jesus performed in the presence of the disciples, which were not written down, these signs and wonders were recorded "that you may believe that Jesus is the Christ, (the Messiah,) the Son of God, and that believing you may have life in His name" (John 20:31). The empty tomb promises that death does not hold the final word. Jesus has conquered sin and death! Jesus rose from the dead. He lives forever. The hope of the Christian is to die in Christ and thus to live forever in heaven with Him. The beatific vision allows the repentant sinner the opportunity to see the face of God and live!

1. What do the following Old Testaments passages anticipate or foretell?

Psalm 16:9-11	
Isaiah 52:13	
Hosea 6:1-2	

2. What did Jesus foretell in the following Gospel passages?

Matthew 16:21	
Mark 8:31	
Luke 9:22	
John 2:19-22	

3. Describe Mary Magdalene as portrayed in these passages. Luke 8:1-3, John 19:25

4. Who was the first person to examine the evidence of the Resurrection? Luke 24:1-12, John 20:6-8

5. After Jesus Christ died and rose from the dead, to whom did He appear?

VERSE	PERSON	PLACE	TIME
Mark 16:9-11	*Mary Magdalene & other women*	*Garden in Jerusalem*	*Easter Sunday morning, very early*
Luke 24:34-43 John 20:19-20			
John 20:26-29			
Luke 24:13-32			
John 21:1-14			
1 Corinthians 15:7			

6. What is the first element of evidence of the Resurrection? *CCC 640*

7. On the basis of whose testimony do Christians proclaim "The Lord has risen indeed!"? *CCC 641*

8. Although the Resurrection, is an historical event verified by evidence and testimony, still it remains

____. *CCC 647-648*

9 To whom did Jesus ascend on Easter Sunday? John 20:17

10. What did Jesus give the apostles in John 20:22?

11. What did Jesus give to the apostles in John 20:23?

12. Who has the power to forgive sins and to whom does he give this power? ***CCC 1441, CCC 1444-1446***

13. In the Old Testament, was confession of sin a private affair between a person and God? Leviticus 5:14-26

14. In the New Testament, is the confession of sin a private affair between the sinner and God? James 5:16

15. Ideally how often should a good Catholic go to Confession? ***CCC 1457-1458***

16. Is there any sin too great for God to forgive? ***CCC 982***

17. Some people hold to the doctrine of "sola scriptura," to suggest that the Bible alone is the sole authority in matters of faith. Catholics do not believe this notion first proposed in the 16th century. Why not? 2 Thessalonians 2:15

18. Is everything that Jesus did recounted in the Bible? John 20:30

19. What is the pillar and foundation of the truth? 1 Timothy 3:15

20. Why do Catholics go to Mass on Sunday? ***CCC 2174***

** Have you ever felt like Thomas in John 20:25? What prayer from the Bible could you pray in times of doubt? Mark 9:24

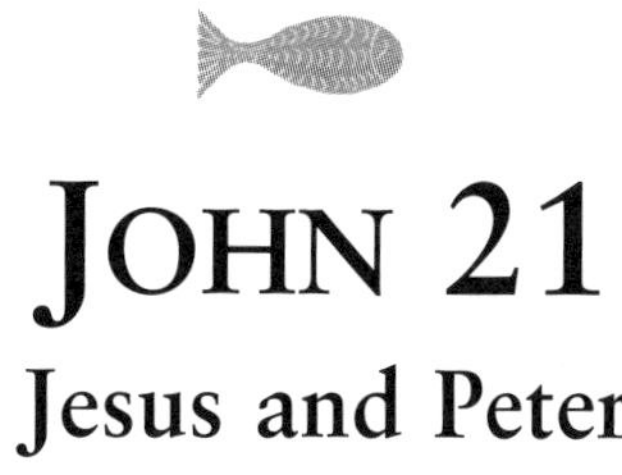

JOHN 21

Jesus and Peter

Memory Verse

"There are also many other things which Jesus did, were every one of them to be written, I suppose that the world itself could not contain the books that would be written."

JOHN 21:25

John seems to have completed his narrative in Chapter 20 and here an epilogue appears. Some biblical scholars suggest that John 21 was written by the evangelist or by one of his disciples later to highlight the primacy of Peter and underscore his authority as head of the universal Church and perhaps to explain why the beloved disciple had suffered death. However, no ancient manuscripts of the Gospel of John have ever been discovered without the inclusion of Chapter 21. And, the Christian community would be considerably poorer without this beautiful chapter.

Remember the beginning of the Gospel which we have studied together through the course of this book? "In the beginning was the Word, and the Word was with God, and the Word was God. He was in the beginning with God" (John 1:1-2). We know that the beginning of a book is important, but the ending is also important. Let us pay attention to how this same Gospel brings itself to a close. Chapter 20 ends with what seemed like a conclusion to the whole book, but then Chapter 21 continues and ends with another conclusion, the real one. Compare the two conclusions:

Now Jesus did many other signs in the presence of the disciples, which are not written in this book; but these are written that you may believe that Jesus is the Christ, the Son of God, and that believing you may have life in his name. (John 20:30-31)	But there are also many other things which Jesus did; were every one of them to be written, I suppose that the world itself could not contain the books that would be written. (John 21:25)

These two endings look very similar, and indeed both of them state clearly that the Johannine Tradition is bigger than the Johannine Gospel. John knows the other miracles that appear in Matthew, Mark and Luke—and he knows other miracles still that never found their way into any of the accounts. The Apostle John and his community knew many more miracles than the ones selected for use in this written record. Because books had to be copied by hand in those days, it was necessary to practice economy of style, and keep books as concise as possible. For that reason, the written New

Testament is only a fraction of the entire inspired preaching of the Apostles. The Gospel of John selects just a few miracles from the treasury known to the early Church, because they illustrate the major aspects of Christ's identity. We later readers cling to the texts that transmit these truths to us, but we must take heed to John's conclusion—the Gospel itself is not an end but a beginning, and it is our beginning.

The Disciples Catch a Miraculous Draught of Fish. Peter, Thomas, Nathanael, James, John, and two other disciples demonstrate close brotherhood in staying together at the Sea of Tiberias, obediently waiting for the Lord. Peter, taking the initiative, decides to go fishing and the others follow him. Despite fishing through the night, they catch nothing. Without Jesus, little of value can be accomplished. To act apart from Jesus is futile. Only in and through Jesus can believers bear plentiful fruit that will last. Jesus appears at dawn on the shore, but the disciples cannot immediately recognize Him.

The beloved disciple, presumably John said to Peter, "It is the Lord" (John 21:7). Now, "John" is a very beautiful name, shared by several persons in the New Testament: the Baptist, the Evangelist, the father of Peter, and one of the other disciples, called John Mark. It has taken many forms in different languages—Giovanni (Italian), Juan (Spanish), Jean (French), Johann (German and Finnish), Jan (Dutch, Polish, Slovak), and Sean (Irish). In the New Testament Greek it is "Ioannes," which is very close to the original Hebrew "Yohannan," which means "The Lord loves" or "The Lord is love." When John writes that "God is love" (1 John 4:16), which is the theme of his writings, he is using his own name as a key to decode the whole meaning of revelation.

John the Evangelist never mentions himself by name in the entire Gospel, though he does mention John the Baptist and John, the father of Peter. John refers to the Apostles as "The Twelve" (John 6:67, 6:70, 6:71, 20:24 and Revelation 21:14), but never gives a list of all of their names as the other evangelists do. In the Book of Revelation, the author refers to himself as "I, John" on several occasions at the beginning and at the end of the book (Revelation 1:9, 21:2 and 22:8).

In the Gospel of John, the evangelist refers to himself only as "the disciple whom Jesus loved" on four occasions toward the end of the book (John 13:23, 19:26, 21:7 and 21:20). Tradition unanimously identifies this disciple "whom Jesus loved" as John, who avoids mentioning his own name out of humility. Some scholars have called into question this identification. They demand a standard of proof that ancient people would never have expected. In fact, the phrase "the one whom Jesus loved" is another paraphrase of the name "John," which means "the one whom the Lord loves." In the original Hebrew, "Jesus loves" and "The Lord loves" sound very much alike, even more so than in the Greek. The evangelist may have avoided mentioning his own name, but he could not have been more clear in his purpose. He is not only identifying himself as the one loved by Jesus, he is identifying Jesus as the Lord!

"Love, love is farsighted. Love is the first to appreciate kindness. The adolescent apostle, who felt a deep and firm affection for Jesus, because he loved Christ with all the

purity and tenderness of a heart that had never been corrupted, exclaimed: 'It is the Lord!' When Simon Peter heard that it was the Lord, he put on his clothes and sprang into the sea (John 21:7). Peter personifies faith. Full of marvelous daring, he leaps into the sea. With a love like John's and a faith like Peter's, what is there that can stop us?" (St. Josemaría Escrivá, *Friends of God,* [Princeton, NJ: Scepter, 1981], 265).

Vibrant, active Christian faith demands the balance of faith and love. Faith without love becomes rigid and overbearing. Love without faith lacks the character of constancy. The effective disciple seeks to grow in both faith and in love.

Jesus, ever the servant, builds a fire to cook breakfast for His hungry friends. Interestingly this charcoal fire recalls the scene in John 18:18 when Peter was warming himself around a charcoal fire, denying Jesus three times on the night before the Savior's death. Peter's triple denial of Christ (John 18:17, 25-26, Luke 22:31-34) will now be answered by a triple affirmation of Peter's love for Jesus (John 21:15-17) and Peter's acceptance of the commission to care for and tend the flock of Christ.

What can we make of this surprisingly large catch of fish? St. Jerome proposed that the number 153 represented the various kinds of fish in the sea, indicating universality. The number 153 could also symbolize the number of churches at the time of the writing of this account: 150 in the diaspora plus three in Judea, Samaria, and Galilee. Whatever symbolism was intended by the evangelist and the Holy Spirit, the vast number in the unbroken net speaks to abundance and unity.

Imagine the joy of the disciples seeing Jesus, alive on the shore, preparing another meal for them. Just as the disciples recognized Jesus on the way to Emmaus in the breaking of the bread (Luke 24:13-33), here the disciples recognize Jesus as He feeds them once again. As with the multiplication of the loaves and fishes, when Jesus fed thousands, He again provides abundantly. Jesus supplies lavishly. He doesn't skimp.

Mystical imagery abounds in this gospel account. To ponder and meditate on the Gospel of John for a lifetime, one could not exhaust the richness entailed herein.

St. Thomas Aquinas in his *Commentary on St. John* interprets the mystical meaning of this scene of the boat on the Sea of Tiberius in this way.

> ***"The boat is the Church, whose unity is symbolized by the net which is not torn; the sea is the world, Peter in the boat stands for the supreme authority in the Church, the number of the fish signifies the number of the elect."***

Jesus Feeds Peter. Jesus feeds Peter before He commissions and empowers Peter to shepherd the Church. The shame and humiliation Peter must have felt after having denied our Lord three times on the eve of the crucifixion underscores this passage. Yet,

Our Lord would not include this embarrassing incident for the world to read without sufficient reason to bless and instruct Christians for all time. Is there an application in Peter's denial of Christ and then his repentance and affirmation of love for Christ that could help people of this day and time? Perhaps Peter's example will encourage weak sinners in their efforts to rise from sin to new life by the power of the Holy Spirit and enable others to do the same. The merciful love of God pours grace upon sinners, inviting them to repent and return to Him again and again.

Peter denied Jesus three times and repented. The Lord's gaze of infinite mercy drew tears of repentance from Peter. After the Resurrection, Peter made a threefold affirmation of love for Jesus. Peter's second conversion involves the community, as the Lord calls the whole Church to "Repent!" St. Ambrose spoke of two conversions in the Church, water and tears: the water of Baptism and the tears of repentance.

Hence, Peter demonstrates the need to turn back to Christ again and again after sinning and separating from God. Some people believe that once a person makes a commitment to Christ, a confession of faith, salvation is assured and nothing else is required. However, Peter's example in this Bible account proves the need for continued repentance and a continual conversion of the heart toward union with God.

Why did Jesus single out Simon Peter after breakfast for His inquisition? James and Andrew, Philip and Bartholomew had also abandoned Jesus in His hour of need. No one remained with Jesus at the foot of the cross except the beloved disciple and the women. Humanly speaking, one could expect Jesus to chastise Peter and take away his position of leadership among the apostles. Wouldn't it make sense to give the primacy to John, who showed love and courage in staying near Jesus until His death? And yet, God's ways are not the ways humans might think to be fair or best. Jesus feeds the apostles and then commands Peter to feed others.

The Church has always understood this passage in John's Gospel as Jesus directly and publicly conferring upon Peter the prime authority and responsibility for leading the Church. Jesus established the primacy of Peter. The papacy is not the result of human custom, preference or legislation. Rather, the papacy provides an unbroken line of shepherds, some 264 in all, as of this writing, from Peter, who was martyred around 67 AD to John Paul II. In the first 200 years of Christianity, every single Pope but one was martyred. Many of the successors of St. Peter have been saints, some have been less exemplary. Yet the line of apostolic succession remains unbroken.

The Fathers of the Church have always understood, and the First and Second Vatican Councils have reiterated, that the primacy of Peter is a grace conferred by Jesus upon Peter and his successors, the popes, in order to guard and protect the deposit of faith, to define sound doctrine and to guard and protect the unity of the Church. It may help to look over the successors of Peter, the popes, and to pray for our current Holy Father and those that God will appoint in the future to shepherd the Church for our children and grandchildren in generations to come.

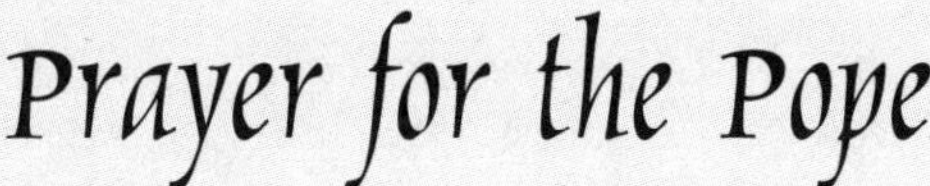

Prayer for the Pope

God, our Father, we ask You to look with mercy and love on
Your servant, Pope ___________ whom You have chosen
to govern Your Church and shepherd Your people.
May he, through word and through example,
direct, sustain and encourage the people in his care
so that with them
he may share everlasting life in Your kingdom.

May the Lord preserve our Holy Father, ___________.
May He give him life
and protect him in this life
and reserve for him the reward of the just.   Amen.

A History of Popes

1. St. Peter (- 67 A.D.)
2. St. Linus (67-76)
3. St. Cletus (76-88)
4. St. Clement (88-97)
5. St. Evaristus (97-105)
6. St. Alexander (105-115)
7. St. Sixtus (115-125)
8. St. Telephorus (125-136)
9. St. Hyginus (136-140)
10. St. Pius I (140-155)
11. St. Anicetus (155-166)
12. St. Sotter (166-175)
13. St. Eleutherius (175-189)
14. St. Victor I (189-199)
15. St. Zephyrinus (199-217)
16. St. Callistus (217-222)
17. St. Urban I (230-235)
18. St. Pontian (230-235)
19. St. Anterius (235-236)
20. St. Fabian (236-250)
21. St. Cornelius (251-253)
22. St. Lucius (253-254)
23. St. Stephen (254-257)
24. St. Sextus II (257-258)
25. St. Dionysius (259-268)
26. St. Felix (269-274)
27. St. Eutychian (275-283)
28. St. Gaius (283-296)
29. St. Marcellinus (296-304)
30. St. Marcellinus I (308-309)
31. St. Eusebius (309-309)
32. St. Melchiades (311-314)
33. St. Silvester (314-335)
34. St. Mark (336-336)
35. St. Julius (337-352)
36. St. Liberius (352-366)
37. St.Damascus (366-384)
38. St. Siricius (384-399)
39. St. Anastasius I (399-401)
40. St. Innocent I (401-417)
41. St. Zosimus (417-418)
42. St. Boniface I (418-422)
43. St. Celestine (422-432)
44. St. Sixtus III (432-440)
45. St. Leo (440-461)
46. St. Hilarus (461-468)
47. St. Simplicus (468-483)
48. St. Felix III (483-492)
49. St. Gelasius I (492-496)
50. St. Anastasius II (496-498)
51. St. Symmachus (498-514)
52. St. Hormisdas (514-523)
53. St. John I (523-526)
54 St. Felix IV (526-530)
55. St. Boniface (530-532)
56. St. John II (533-535)
57. St. Agapitus I (535-536)
58. St. Silverius (536-537)
59. Virgilius (537-555)
60. Pelagius (556-561)
61. John III (561-574)
62. Benedict I (575-590)
63. Pelagius II (579-590)
64. St. Gregory I (590-604)
65. Sabinian (604-606)
66. Boniface III (607-607)
67. Boniface IV (608-615)
68. St. Adeodatus I (615-618)
69. Boniface V (619-625)
70. Honorius I (625-638)
71. Severinus (640)
72. John IV (640-642)
73. Theodore I (642-649)
74. St. Martin I (649-655)
75. St. Eugene I (654-657)
76. St. Vitalian (657-672)
77. Adeodatus II (672-676)
78. Donus (676-678)
79. St. Agatho (678-681)
80. St. Leo II (682-683)
81. St. Benedict II (684-685)
82. John V (685-686)
83. Conon (686-687)
84. St. Sergius I (687-701)
85. John VI (701-705)
86. John VII (705-707)
87. Sissinius (708-708)
88. Constantine (708-715)
89. St. Gregory II (715-731)
90. St. Gregory III (731-741)
91. St. Zacharias (741-752)
92. Stephen II (752-757)
93. St. Paul I (757-767)
94. Stephen III (768-772)
95. Hadrian I (772-795)
96. St. Leo III (795-816)
97. Stephen IV (816-817)
98. St. Paschal I (817-824)
99. Eugene II (824-827)
100. Valenine (827-827)
101. Gregory B (827-844)
102. Sergius II (844-847)
103. St. Leo IV (847-855)
104. Benedict III (855-858)
105. St. Nicholas I (858-867)
106. Hadrian II (867-872)
107. John VIII (872-882)
108. Marinus I (882-884)
109. St. Hadrian III (884-885)
110. Stephen V (885-891)
111. Formosus (891-896)
112. Boniface VI (896-896)
113. Stephen VI (896-897)
114. Romanus (897-897)
115. Theodroe II (897-897)
116. John IX (898-900)
117. Benedict IV (900-903)
118. Leo V (903-903)
119. Sergius III (904-911)
120. Anastasius III (911-913)
121. Lando (913-914)
122. John X (914-928)
123. Leo VI (928-928)
124. Stephen VII (928-931)
125. John XI (931-935)
126. Leo VII (936-939)

127. Stephen VIII (939-942)
128. Marinus II (942-946)
129. Agapitus II (946-955)
130. John XII (955-964)
131. Leo VIII (963-965)
132. Benedict V (964-966)
133. John XIII (965-972)
134. Benedict VI (973-974)
135. Benedict VII (974-(83)
136. John XIV (983-984)
137. John XV (985-996)
138. Gregory V (996-999)
139. Silvester II (999-1003)
140. John XVII (1003-1003)
141. John XVIII (1004-1012)
142. Sergius IV (1009-1012)
143. Benedict VIII(1012-1024)
144. John XIX (1024-1032)
145. Benedict IX (1032-1044)
146. Silvester III (1045-1045)
147. Benedict IX (1032-1044)
148. Gregory VI (1045-1046)
149. Clement II (1046-1047)
150. Benedict IX (1047-1048)
151. Damascus II (1048)
152. St. Leo IX (1049-1054)
153. Victor II (1055-1057)
154. Stephen IX (1057-1058)
155. Nicholas II (1059-1061)
156. Alexander II (1061-1073)
157. St.Gregory VII(1073-1085)
158. Bl. Victor III (1086-1087)
159. Bl. Urban II (1088-1099)
160. Paschal II (1099-1118)
161. Gelasius II (1118-1119)
162. Callistus II (1119-1124)
163. Honorius II (1124-1130)
164. Innocent II (1130-1143)
165. Celestine II (1143-1144)
166. Lucius (1144-1145)
167. Bl. Eugene III (1145-1153)
168. Anastasius IV(1153-1154)
169. Hadrian IV (1154-1159)
170. Alexander IIi (1159-1181)
171. Lucius III (1181-1185)
172. Urban III (1185-1187)
173. Gregory VIII (1187-1187)
174. Clement III (1187-1191)
175. Celestine III (1191-1198)
176. Innocent III (1198-1216)
177. Honorius III (1216-1227)
178. Gregory IX (1227-1241)
179. Celestine IV (1241-1241)
180. Innocent IV (1243-1254)
181. Alexander IV (1245-1261)
182. Urban IV (1261-1264)
183. Clement IV (1265-1268)
184. Bl. Gregory X (1271-1276)
185. Bl. Innocent V (1276-1276)
186. Hadrian V (1276-1276)
187. John XXI (1276-1277)
188. Nicholas III (1277-1280)
189. Martin IV (1277-1280)
190. Honorius IV (1285-1287)
191. Nicholas IV (1288-1292)
192. St. Celestine (1294-1294)
193. Boniface VIII (1295-1303)
194. Bl. Benedict XI(1303-1304)
195. Clement V (1305-1314)
196. John XXII (1316-1334)
197. Benedict XII (1334-1342)
198. Clement VI (1342-1352)
199. Innocent VI (1352-1362)
200. Bl. Urban V (1362-1370)
201. Gregory XI (1362-1370)
202. Urban VI (1378-1389)
203. Boniface IX (1389-1404)
204. Innocent VII (1404-1406)
205. Gregory XII (1406-1415)
206. Martin V (1417-1431)
207. Eugene IV (1431-1447)
208. Nicholas V (1447-1455)
209. Callistus III (1455-1458)
210. Pius II (1458-1464)
211. Paul II (1464-1471)
212. Sixtus IV (1471-1484)
213. Innocent VII (1484-1492)
214. Alexander VI (1492-1503)
215. Pius III (1503)
216. Julius II (1503-1513)
217. Leo X (1513-1521)
218. Hadrian VI (1522-1523)
219. Clement VII (1523-1534)
220. Paul III (1534-1549)
221. Julius III (1550-1555)
222. Marcellus II (1555)
223. Paul IV (1555-1559)
224. Pius IV (1560-1565)
225. St. Pius V (1566-1572)
226. Gregory XIII (1572-1585)
227. Sixtus V (1585-1590)
228. Urban VII (1590)
229. Gregory XIV (1590-1591)
230. Innocent IX (1591-1591)
231. Clement VIII (1592-1605)
232. Leo XI (1605)
233. Paul V (1605-1621)
234. Gregory XV (1621-1644)
235. Urban VIII (1623-1644)
236. Innocent X (1644-1655)
237. Alexander VII (1655-1667)
238. Clement IX (1667-1669)
239. Clement X (1670-1676)
240. Bl Innocent XI (1676-1689)
241. Alexander VIII (1689-1691)
242. Innocent XII (1691-1700)
243. Clement XI (1700-1721)
244. Innocent XIII (1721-1724)
245. Benedict XIII (1724-1730)
246. Clement XII (1730-1740)
247. Benedict XIV (1740-1758)
248. Clement XIII (1758-1769)
249. Clement XIV (1769-1774)
250. Pius VI (1775-1799)
251. Pius VII (1800-1823)
252. Leo XII (1823-1829)
253. Pius VIII (1829-1846)
254. Gregory XVI (1834-1846)
255. Pius IX (1846-1878)
256. Leo XIII (1878-1903)
257. St. Pius X (1903-1914)
258. Benedict XV (1914-1922)
259. Pius XI (1922-1939)
260. Pius XII (1939-1958)
261. Bl. John XXIII (1958-1963)
262. Paul VI (1963-1978)
263. John Paul I (1978)
264. John Paul II (1978-)

In studying the list of successors of St. Peter, many saints and holy men come to light. Jesus handed Peter the keys to the kingdom of heaven. He promised that He would remain with us until the end of time. And so He will. The study of the Gospel of John ends with depictions of the beloved disciple, St. John, and St. Peter. This gospel was probably written around the year 85-90 AD well after the death of St. Peter. The Bible, as known today was not yet complete and compiled in the format that people now enjoy. Yet Christianity had been birthed and the world had been ransomed for God. Man has been reconciled to God through the life and death of Jesus Christ.

This gospel reveals saints and sinners, blessings and miracles, fidelity and betrayals, suffering and ultimately Resurrection joy and the promise of everlasting life. St. John, beloved of the Lord, provides a model of the ideal follower of Jesus. John experienced the mercy and love of God. John believes in Jesus and along with Peter trusts that Jesus is the Christ, the Son of God. After experiencing the mercy and love of God, the apostles are empowered by the Holy Spirit to go out and spread the good news. In doing so, they love others as Jesus has loved them. May each of us commit to opening our hearts to experience the mercy and love of God, trust in Jesus and love others as He commanded. May people recognize Christians by the love they see and be drawn to the Source of all love. May God give us the courage to share what He has given us.

1. How does Jesus show that He is present in His risen humanity, not a ghost? *CCC 645*

2. What term does Jesus use in addressing His disciples? John 21:5

3. How does the beloved disciple identify Jesus in John 21:7?

   What does this title mean? *CCC 448*

4. Can you find a similar background setting in John 18:18 and John 21:9?

5. How did the disciples come to recognize Jesus? John 21:12-13

6. What three questions and three commands did Jesus give to Peter?

John 21:15		
John 21:16		
John 21:17		

7. What is the most important thing you do to show Jesus you love Him?

8. In your own words, define what Jesus is preparing Peter for in John 21:18-19.

9. Meditate on the two word invitation that Jesus gives in John 21:19.

10. Catholics see St. Peter as the rock upon whom Jesus built His Church, the first among the apostles. Give three titles for the Pope found in the Glossary of the Catechism under Peter (Saint). *CCC* ***Glossary*** "Peter (Saint)"

    ____

    ____

    ____

11. Define the mission entrusted to St. Peter. *CCC 552*

12. The "Magisterium" of the Church, the pope and bishops in union with him has existed since the time of Christ for what purpose? *CCC 2032*

13. Where do we get Christian moral teaching? *CCC 2033*

14. How are the Roman Pontiff and the bishops' teachings different from any other good Christian who teaches sound Christian doctrine? *CCC 2034*

15. Where did Peter get his authority? Matthew 16:17-19

16. What is the significance of the key? Isaiah 22:22-23

17. Peter's name is mentioned 191 times in the Bible, more than all of the rest of apostles put together. What do these passages show?

Acts 1:15	
Acts 2:14-36	
Acts 5:1-11	
Acts 5:14-15	
Acts 5:29	
Acts 9:37-40	
Acts 15:7-12	

18. Do Catholics believe that everything in the Bible is true? *CCC 107*

19. How should a Catholic read the Sacred Scripture? *CCC 113*

20. Are there truths which are not contained in the Bible? John 21:25

21. Who determines which interpretation of a Bible passage is authentic? *CCC 85*

22. How can you be sure you're not misinterpreting a Bible passage? *CCC 87*

23. What is your favorite chapter or verse in the Gospel of John?

24. What one thing did you learn or see in a new light in your study of John?

25. Did you gain any fresh insight looking into the Catechism of the Catholic Church?

26. What is the best thing that Bible Study has done for you?

*** Will you commit to pray every day for the successor of St. Peter, Our Holy Father, the Pope?

*** Will you pray about inviting someone to join you in Bible Study next time?

Appendix

Humanae Vitae

God's Loving Design

8. Married love particularly reveals its true nature and nobility when we realize that it takes its origin from God, who is love, the Father from whom every family in heaven and on earth is named.

Marriage, then, is far from being the effect of chance or the result of the blind evolution of natural forces. It is in reality the wise and provident institution of God the Creator, whose purpose was to effect in man His loving design. As a consequence, husband and wife, through that mutual gift of themselves, which is specific and exclusive to them alone, develop that union of two persons in which they perfect one another, cooperating with God in the generation and rearing of new lives.

The marriage of those who have been baptized is, in addition, invested with the dignity of a sacramental sign of grace, for it represents the union of Christ and His Church.

Married Love

9. In the light of these facts the characteristic features and exigencies of married love are clearly indicated, and it is of the highest importance to evaluate them exactly. This love is above all *fully human,* a compound of sense and spirit. It is not, then, merely a question of natural instinct or emotional drive. It is also, and above all, *an act of the free will,* whose trust is such that it is meant not only to survive the joys and sorrows of daily life, but also to grow, so that husband and wife become in a way one heart and one soul, and together attain their human fulfillment.

It is a love which is *total*—that very special form of personal friendship in which husband and wife generously share everything, allowing no unreasonable exceptions and not thinking solely of their own convenience. Whoever really loves his partner loves not only for what he receives, but loves that partner for the partner's own sake, content to be able to enrich the other with the gift of himself.

Married love is also *faithful and exclusive* of all other, and this until death. This is how husband and wife understood it on the day on which, fully aware of what they were doing, they freely vowed themselves to one another in marriage. Though this fidelity of husband and wife sometimes presents difficulties, no one has the right to assert that it is impossible; it is, on the contrary, always honorable and meritorious. The example of countless married couples proves not only that fidelity is in accord with the nature of marriage, but also that it is the source of profound and enduring happiness.

Finally, this love is *fruitful.* It is not confined wholly to the loving interchange of husband and wife; it also contrives to go beyond this to bring new life into being. Marriage and conjugal love are by their nature ordained toward the procreation and education of children. Children are really the supreme gift of marriage and contribute in the highest degree to their parents' welfare.

Responsible Parenthood

10. Married love, therefore, requires of husband and wife the full awareness of their obligations in the matter of responsible parenthood, which today, rightly enough, is much insisted upon, but which at the same time should be rightly understood. Thus, we do well to consider responsible parenthood in the light of its varied legitimate and interrelated aspects.

With regard to the biological processes, responsible parenthood means an awareness of, and respect for, their proper functions. In the procreative faculty the human mind discerns biological laws that apply to the human person.

With regard to man's innate drives and emotions, responsible parenthood means that man's reason and will must exert control over them.

With regard to physical, economic, psychological and social conditions, responsible parenthood is exercised by those who prudently and generously decide to have more children, and by those who, for serious reasons and with due respect to moral precepts, decide not to have additional children for either a certain or an indefinite period of time.

Responsible parenthood, as we use the term here, has one further essential aspect of paramount importance. It concerns the objective moral order which was established by God, and of which a right conscience is the true interpreter. In a word, the exercise of responsible parenthood requires that husband and wife, keeping a right order of priorities, recognize their own duties toward God, themselves, their families and human society.

From this it follows that they are not free to act as they choose in the service of transmitting life, as if it were wholly up to them to decide what is the right course to follow. On the contrary, they are bound to ensure that what they do corresponds to the will of God the Creator. The very nature of marriage and its use makes His will clear, while the constant teaching of the Church spells it out.

Observing the Natural Law

11. The sexual activity, in which husband and wife are intimately and chastely united with one another, through which human life is transmitted, is, as the recent Council recalled, "noble and worthy." It does not, moreover, cease to be legitimate even when, for reasons independent of their will, it is foreseen to be infertile. For its natural adaptation to the expression and strengthening of the union of husband and wife is not thereby suppressed. The fact is, as experience shows, that new life is not the result of each and every act of sexual intercourse. God has wisely ordered laws of nature and the incidence of fertility in such a way that successive births are already naturally spaced through the inherent operation of these laws. The Church, nevertheless, in urging men to the observance of the precepts of the natural law, which it interprets by its constant doctrine, teaches that each and every marital act must of necessity retain its intrinsic relationship to the procreation of human life.

Union and Procreation

12. This particular doctrine, often expounded by the magisterium of the Church, is based on the inseparable connection, established by God, which man on his own initiative may not break, between the unitive significance and the procreative significance which are both inherent to the marriage act.

The reason is that the fundamental nature of the marriage act, while uniting husband and wife in the closest intimacy, also renders them capable of generating new life—and this as a result of laws written into the actual nature of man and of woman. And if each of these essential qualities, the unitive and the procreative, is preserved, the use of marriage fully retains its sense of true mutual love and its ordination to the supreme responsibility of parenthood to which man is called. We believe that our contemporaries are particularly capable of seeing that this teaching is in harmony with human reason.

Faithfulness's Design

13. Men rightly observe that a conjugal act imposed on one's partner without regard to his or her condition or personal and reasonable wishes in the matter, is no true act of love, and therefore offends the moral order in its particular application to the intimate relationship of husband and wife. If they further reflect, they must also recognize that an act of mutual love which impairs the capacity to transmit life which God the Creator, through specific laws, has built into it, frustrates His design which constitutes the norm of marriage, and contradicts the will of the Author of life. Hence to use this divine gift while depriving it, even if only partially, of its meaning and purpose, is equally repugnant to the nature of man and of woman, and is consequently in opposition to the plan of God and His holy will. But to experience the gift of married love while respecting the laws of conception is to acknowledge that one is not the master of the sources of life but rather the minister of the design established by the Creator. Just as man does not have unlimited dominion over his body in general, so also, and with more particular reason, he has no such dominion over his specifically sexual faculties, for these are concerned by their very nature with the generation of life, of which God is the source. "Human life is sacred—all men must recognize that fact," Our predecessor Pope John XXIII recalled. "From its very inception it reveals the creating hand of God."

Unlawful Birth Control Methods

14. Therefore We base Our words on the first principles of a human and Christian doctrine of marriage when We are obliged once more to declare that the direct interruption of the generative process already begun and, above all, all direct abortion, even for therapeutic reasons, are to be absolutely excluded as lawful means of regulating the number of children. Equally to be condemned, as the magisterium of the Church has affirmed on many occasions, is direct sterilization, whether of the man or of the woman, whether permanent or temporary.

Similarly excluded is any action which either before, at the moment of, or after sexual intercourse, is specifically intended to prevent procreation—whether as an end or as a means.

Neither is it valid to argue, as a justification for sexual intercourse which is deliberately contraceptive, that a lesser evil is to be preferred to a greater one, or that such intercourse would merge with procreative acts of past and future to form a single entity, and so be qualified by exactly the same moral goodness as these. Though it is true that sometimes it is lawful to tolerate a lesser moral evil in order to avoid a greater evil or in order to promote a greater good, it is never lawful, even for the gravest reasons, to do evil that good may come of it—in other words, to intend directly something which of its very nature contradicts the moral order, and which must therefore be judged unworthy of man, even though the intention is to protect or promote the welfare of an individual, of a family or of society in general. Consequently, it is a serious error to think that a whole married life of otherwise normal relations can justify sexual intercourse which is deliberately contraceptive and so intrinsically wrong.

Recourse to Infertile Periods

16. Now as We noted earlier, some people today raise the objection against this particular doctrine of the Church concerning the moral laws governing marriage, that human intelligence has both the right and responsibility to control those forces of irrational nature which come within its ambit and to direct them toward ends beneficial to man. Others ask on the same point whether it is not reasonable in so many cases to use artificial birth control if by so doing the harmony and peace of a family are better served and more suitable conditions are provided for the education of children already born. To this question We must give a clear reply. The Church is the first to praise and commend the application of human intelligence to an activity in which a rational creature such as man is so closely associated with his Creator. But she affirms that this must be done within the limits of the order of reality established by God.

If therefore there are well-grounded reasons for spacing births, arising from the physical or psychological condition of husband or wife, or from external circumstances, the Church teaches that married people may then take advantage of the natural cycles immanent in the reproductive system and engage in marital intercourse only during those times that are infertile, thus controlling birth in a way which does not in the least offend the moral principles which We have just explained.

Neither the Church nor her doctrine is inconsistent when she considers it lawful for married people to take advantage of the infertile period but condemns as always unlawful the use of means which directly prevent conception, even when the reasons given for the later practice may appear to be upright and serious. In reality, these two cases are completely different. In the former the married couple rightly use a faculty provided them by nature. In the latter they obstruct the natural development of the generative process. It cannot be denied that in each case the married couple, for acceptable reasons, are both perfectly clear in their intention to avoid children and wish to make sure that none will result. But it is equally true that it is exclusively in the former case that husband and wife are ready to abstain from intercourse during the fertile period as often as for reasonable motives the birth of another child is not desirable. And when the infertile period recurs, they use their married intimacy to express their mutual love and safeguard their fidelity toward one another. In doing this they certainly give proof of a true and authentic love.

Consequences of Artificial Methods

17. Responsible men can become more deeply convinced of the truth of the doctrine laid down by the Church on this issue if they reflect on the consequences of methods and plans for artificial birth control. Let them first consider how easily this course of action could open wide the way for marital infidelity and a general lowering of moral standards. Not much experience is needed to be fully aware of human weakness and to understand that human beings—and especially the young, who are so exposed to temptation—need incentives to keep the moral law, and it is an evil thing to make it easy for them to break that law. Another effect that gives cause for alarm is that a man who grows accustomed to the use of contraceptive methods may forget the reverence due to a woman, and, disregarding her physical and emotional equilibrium, reduce her to being a mere instrument for the satisfaction of his own desires, no longer considering her as his partner whom he should surround with care and affection.

Finally, careful consideration should be given to the danger of this power passing into the hands of those public authorities who care little for the precepts of the moral law. Who will blame a government which in its attempt to resolve the problems affecting an entire country resorts to the same measures as are regarded as lawful by married people in the solution of a particular family difficulty? Who will prevent public authorities from favoring those contraceptive methods which they consider more effective? Should they regard this as necessary, they may even impose their use on everyone. It could well happen, therefore, that when people, either individually or in family or social life, experience the inherent difficulties of the divine law and are determined to avoid them, they may give into the hands of public authorities the power to intervene in the most personal and intimate responsibility of husband and wife.

Limits to Man's Power

Consequently, unless we are willing that the responsibility of procreating life should be left to the arbitrary decision of men, we must accept that there are certain limits, beyond which it is wrong to go, to the power of man over his own body and its natural functions—limits, let it be said, which no one, whether as a private individual or as a public authority, can lawfully exceed. These limits are expressly imposed because of the reverence due to the whole human organism and its natural functions, in the light of the principles We stated earlier, and in accordance with a correct understanding of the "principle of totality" enunciated by Our predecessor Pope Pius XII.

Concern of the Church

18. It is to be anticipated that perhaps not everyone will easily accept this particular teaching. There is too much clamorous outcry against the voice of the Church, and this is intensified by modern means of communication. But it comes as no surprise to the Church that she, no less than her divine Founder, is destined to be a "sign of contra-

diction." She does not, because of this, evade the duty imposed on her of proclaiming humbly but firmly the entire moral law, both natural and evangelical.

Since the Church did not make either of these laws, she cannot be their arbiter—only their guardian and interpreter. It could never be right for her to declare lawful what is in fact unlawful, since that, by its very nature, is always opposed to the true good of man.

In preserving intact the whole moral law of marriage, the Church is convinced that she is contributing to the creation of a truly human civilization. She urges man not to betray his personal responsibilities by putting all his faith in technical expedients. In this way she defends the dignity of husband and wife. This course of action shows that the Church, loyal to the example and teaching of the divine Savior, is sincere and unselfish in her regard for men whom she strives to help even now during this earthly pilgrimage "to share God's life as sons of the living God, the Father of all men."

III. PASTORAL DIRECTIVES

19. Our words would not be an adequate expression of the thought and solicitude of the Church, Mother and Teacher of all peoples, if, after having recalled men to the observance and respect of the divine law regarding matrimony, they did not also support mankind in the honest regulation of birth amid the difficult conditions which today afflict families and peoples. The Church, in fact, cannot act differently toward men than did the Redeemer. She knows their weaknesses, she has compassion on the multitude, she welcomes sinners. But at the same time she cannot do otherwise than teach the law. For it is in fact the law of human life restored to its native truth and guided by the Spirit of God.

Observing the Divine Law

20. The teaching of the Church regarding the proper regulation of birth is a promulgation of the law of God Himself. And yet there is no doubt that to many it will appear not merely difficult but even impossible to observe. Now it is true that like all good things which are outstanding for their nobility and for the benefits which they confer on men, so this law demands from individual men and women, from families and from human society, a resolute purpose and great endurance. Indeed it cannot be observed unless God comes to their help with the grace by which the goodwill of men is sustained and strengthened. But to those who consider this matter diligently it will indeed be evident that this endurance enhances man's dignity and confers benefits on human society.

Value of Self-Discipline

21. The right and lawful ordering of birth demands, first of all, that spouses fully recognize and value the true blessings of family life and that they acquire complete mastery over themselves and their emotions. For if with the aid of reason and of free will they are to control their natural drives, there can be no doubt at all of the need for self-denial. Only then will the expression of love, essential to married life, conform to right order. This is especially clear in the practice of periodic continence. Self-discipline of this kind is a shining witness to the chastity of husband and wife and, far from being

a hindrance to their love of one another, transforms it by giving it a more truly human character. And if this self-discipline does demand that they persevere in their purpose and efforts, it has at the same time the salutary effect of enabling husband and wife to develop to their personalities and to be enriched with spiritual blessings. For it brings to family life abundant fruits of tranquility and peace. It helps in solving difficulties of other kinds. It fosters in husband and wife thoughtfulness and loving consideration for one another. It helps them to repel inordinate self-love, which is the opposite of charity. It arouses in them a consciousness of their responsibilities. And finally, it confers upon parents a deeper and more effective influence in the education of their children. As their children grow up, they develop a right sense of values and achieve a serene and harmonious use of their mental and physical powers.

Promotion of Chastity

22. We take this opportunity to address those who are engaged in education and all those whose right and duty it is to provide for the common good of human society. We would call their attention to the need to create an atmosphere favorable to the growth of chastity so that true liberty may prevail over license and the norms of the moral law may be fully safeguarded.

Everything therefore in the modern means of social communication which arouses men's baser passions and encourages low moral standards, as well as every obscenity in the written word and every form of indecency on the stage and screen, should be condemned publicly and unanimously by all those who have at heart the advance of civilization and the safeguarding of the outstanding values of the human spirit. It is quite absurd to defend this kind of depravity in the name of art or culture or by pleading the liberty which may be allowed in this field by the public authorities.

To Christian Couples

25. And now We turn in a special way to Our own sons and daughters, to those most of all whom God calls to serve Him in the state of marriage. While the Church does indeed hand on to her children the inviolable conditions laid down by God's law, she is also the herald of salvation and through the sacraments she flings wide open the channels of grace through which man is made a new creature responding in charity and true freedom to the design of his Creator and Savior, experiencing too the sweetness of the yoke of Christ.

In humble obedience then to her voice, let Christian husbands and wives be mindful of their vocation to the Christian life, a vocation which, deriving from their Baptism, has been confirmed anew and made more explicit by the Sacrament of Matrimony. For by this sacrament they are strengthened and, one might almost say, consecrated to the faithful fulfillment of their duties. Thus will they realize to the full their calling and bear witness as becomes them, to Christ before the world. For the Lord has entrusted to them the task of making visible to men and women the holiness and joy of the law which united inseparably their love for one another and the cooperation they give to God's love, God who is the Author of human life.

We have no wish at all to pass over in silence the difficulties, at times very great, which beset the lives of Christian married couples. For them, as indeed for every one of us, "the gate is narrow and the way is hard, that leads to life." Nevertheless it is precisely the hope of that life which, like a brightly burning torch, lights up their journey, as, strong in spirit, they strive to live "sober, upright and godly lives in this world," knowing for sure that "the form of this world is passing away."

Recourse to God

For this reason husbands and wives should take up the burden appointed to them, willingly, in the strength of faith and of that hope which "does not disappoint us, because God's love has been poured into our hearts through the Holy Spirit who has been given to us. Then let them implore the help of God with unremitting prayer and, most of all, let them draw grace and charity from that unfailing fount which is the Eucharist. If, however, sin still exercises its hold over them, they are not to lose heart. Rather must they, humble and persevering, have recourse to the mercy of God, abundantly bestowed in the Sacrament of Penance. In this way, for sure, they will be able to reach that perfection of married life which the Apostle sets out in these words: "Husbands, love your wives, as Christ loved the Church ... Even so husbands should love their wives as their own bodies. He who loves his wife loves himself. For no man ever hates his own flesh, but nourishes and cherishes it, as Christ does the Church ... This is a great mystery, and I mean in reference to Christ and the Church; however, let each one of you love his wife as himself, and let the wife see that she respects her husband."

Family Apostolate

26. Among the fruits that ripen if the law of God be resolutely obeyed, the most precious is certainly this, that married couples themselves will often desire to communicate their own experience to others. Thus it comes about that in the fullness of the lay vocation will be included a novel and outstanding form of the apostolate by which, like ministering to like, married couples themselves by the leadership they offer will become apostles to other married couples. And surely among all the forms of the Christian apostolate it is hard to think of one more opportune for the present time.

Husbands and wives, therefore, when deeply distressed by reason of the difficulties of their life, must find stamped in the heart and voice of their priest the likeness of the voice and the love of our Redeemer.

So speak with full confidence, beloved sons, convinced that while the Holy Spirit of God is present to the magisterium proclaiming sound doctrine, He also illumines from within the hearts of the faithful and invites their assent. Teach married couples the necessary way of prayer and prepare them to approach more often with great faith the Sacraments of the Eucharist and of Penance. Let them never lose heart because of their weakness.

Pope Paul IV, *Humanae Vitae*, (July 25, 1968) nos. 8-14, 16-22, 25-26, *emphasis added.*

Objectives

As a result of participating in this learning experience, children will improve their ability to

- teach and learn new moving games,
- move to meet the objective of a game, and
- appreciate and understand the origin of a variety of moving games.

Equipment

Individual games have different equipment requirements. The following equipment is needed for the games suggested in this lesson: handkerchiefs, beanbags, long ropes, and small objects to represent bones.

Organization

Throughout this lesson children will work in groups of four or five.

Description

This interdisciplinary lesson requires cooperation with the students' other teachers. The class is divided into groups of four or five students. Each group chooses a different geographic area from a list of areas, which could include Egypt, China, Scandinavia, the Arctic region, Nigeria, and Brazil. Students are given time to research their geographic areas. This lesson would ideally be a culminating experience after the different geographic areas have been studied.

Each group is given descriptions of several games that are commonly played in their chosen country or region. The group selects one game, then reads the directions, and begins to play the game. When the groups are ready, one group teaches their game to the others. In teaching the game, the group in charge should identify the national or regional origin of the game, describe characteristics of the country or region, and explain why they believe the game is so popular in its native country or region. Next, the group will demonstrate the game and explain all rules and procedures. (It is important that you closely monitor as the group teaches; students might need help focusing on the most important aspects of the game. Time efficiency in giving directions is essential.) All the students then play the game within their group.

Many games are played in their native countries in large groups. In an educational setting, however, it is more appropriate for students to play in small groups to increase individual participation and activity time.

The following are examples of games from different nationalities (Hunt, 1964).

Scandinavia

The games of Scandinavia usually focus on friendly play and competition. Most of the games are representative of a history of a physically strenuous past.

Stealing the Bone

Players

Any number

Equipment

A small object to represent a bone

Activity

Hunting, chasing, dodging, running

Appeal

Competition, skill

"Doggie Doan," who is "It," sits with his or her eyes closed in the center of the circle of players. The bone is placed behind Doggie Doan. The circle players skip as they say,

> You'd better watch the bone,
> Doggie Doan, Doggie Doan,
> I'll take it away for my own, for my own
> When I've snatched it and away I've gone.

The player nearest the bone the second time the word *own* is sung snatches it and runs. Doggie Doan chases this player. If the player with the bone returns to his or her place without being tagged, the player who is Doggie Doan is still "It." If the runner is tagged, he or she is Doggie Doan for the next game.

Nigeria

A common characteristic of chasing games from Nigeria is that the player who is caught is expected to accept a playful beating from the one he or she has been caught by.

Jumping the Beanbag

Players

Any number

Equipment

Beanbag, long rope

Activity

Jumping

One player is "It." He or she stands in the center of a circle formed by the other players. "It" holds a beanbag that is tied to the end of a rope, and swings and gradually lets out the rope until the other players have to jump to avoid being hit by the bag. When a player fails to jump and is hit by the bag, he or she is out of the game. As the players decrease in number, the speed of the bag increases. The last player in the circle is the winner.

Brazil

Some of the popular games of Brazil are singing games played in a circle.

Coelho na Toca (co-EL-yo na TO-ca)

Players

Any number in groups of three

Equipment

None

Activity

Hunting, running

One player is chosen to be "It," or the rabbit without a house. The other players are in groups of three. Two of these players form a house by holding hands. The third player is inside the house and is also called a rabbit.

At a signal, all rabbits run to another house. The rabbit without a house tries to find a home. The rabbit left outside then waits for or gives the signal and tries to become a *coelho na toca*, or rabbit in the burrow.

Assessment Suggestion

Have group members explain the rules of their game. After all games have been taught, have students name the games, their geographic origins, and their rules.

Look For

- Encourage students to work well together to learn, play, and teach their game.
- Make sure that students make good connections between the characteristics of the people of their geographic area and the games.

How Can I Change This?

- Focus on only one country or geographic area. Each group of students could find a different game for the specific country or area. Students might spend an entire lesson learning and playing games from Nigeria, for example.
- Instead of providing a list of games from which the students can select, have students do the research to find the games themselves. It would be helpful to work with the media arts teacher to ensure that adequate resources are available.
- This same lesson could be done using dance or popular leisure activities.

Teachable Moment

At the end of the lesson, make two lists, a games list and a countries list. As a review, ask students to match the game with the country.

Heave, Hurl, Fling

Suggested Grade Level

Intermediate (4 and 5)

Interdisciplinary Teaching Model

Partnership

Few themes offer the richness of the Olympic experience for pulling together the efforts of all the teachers in the school. We suggest that, if not the whole school, at least the teachers of all subjects at a particular grade level unite around an Olympic theme. Teachers are encouraged to get a copy of the suggested references as a springboard for generating ideas on integrating language arts, mathematics, science, social studies, art, music, and physical education.

Social Studies, Mathematics, Language, Science, Art, and Music

Themes of the Olympics with a partnership of all of the disciplines. Suggested Web site references: United States Olympic Committee (2008) and Beijing 2008 Olympic Games (2008).

Physical Education

Throwing events from track and field in this example (but any Olympic sport can be used)

Objectives

As a result of participating in this learning experience, children will improve their ability to

- use the muscles of the arms, shoulder girdle, back, and abdomen to develop muscle strength;
- throw a variety of objects using different styles of producing force;
- understand the history and the spirit of the Olympics; and
- comprehend relationships among disciplines when studying information related to a theme.

Equipment

One each: playground ball, basketball, Frisbee, hula hoop, and javelin (6- to 8-foot-long, 1-inch-wide [2- to 2.4-meter-long, 2.5-centimeter-wide] PVC tubing with taped handles in the middle for balance and grip); two traffic cones or markers for each pair of students

Organization

The children work in pairs, lined up along the sideline of a basketball court or football field with plenty of space between pairs. The active partner stands at the line. The marking or retrieving partner stands behind the performer. For safety purposes, a signal is used for simultaneous retrieval of objects.

Description

▶ The following introduction to the history of the Olympic Games could take place at a convocation of all teachers and children in the gymnasium or cafeteria.

"Good morning, girls and boys. We are about to begin a new unit of work in which all teachers in our school [or grade level] will combine their efforts to help you learn about the Olympic experience. Did you know that the Olympics were held in the United States—in Los Angeles (1984) and in Atlanta (1996)? The Atlanta Olympics were special because they celebrated the 100th anniversary of the modern Olympic Games. In 1896 Baron Pierre de Coubertin initiated the modern Olympic Games in France. He was inspired by the concept that 'the important thing in the Olympic Games is not to win but to take part; the important thing in life is not the triumph but the struggle. The essential thing is not to have conquered but to have fought well. To spread these precepts (beliefs) is to build up a stronger and more valiant and, above all, more scrupulous and more generous humanity.' Since that time the Olympics have been held every four years.

"The Greeks began the Olympics in 776 B.C. with a single foot race of 200 meters. The winner of the race got to carry a torch to the altar in Olympia to initiate a celebration of sacrifice by neighboring communities. The distance of 200 meters, then called a *stadion,* is still significant today, as track races are held in multiples of the stadion measure. In fact, football or soccer fields with oval tracks built around the outside and with seating for spectators are called stadiums after the Greek word. For the first 13 Olympiads, the stadion (200-meter) run was the only contest.

"Gradually, the Olympics became more popular and events were added. Chariot races around a hippodrome (800-meter track), horse races, pentathlon (discus, standing long jump, javelin, 200-meter sprint, and wrestling), boxing, and *pankration* (judo) are examples. The Olympic Games gained strength because of the ideals or beliefs they embodied, and they remained popular for over a thousand years, unchanged by fashion or political and cultural forces.

"The word *athlete* comes from the Greek word *athlon,* which means competitor. To the ancient Greeks an athlete was someone who entered a contest for any sort of prize. Competing was what counted. In fact, interest in measuring and recording individual

feats does not appear to have been important. Eventually there were many classes in which to compete. If you were not going to measure yourself against the sprinters or boxers, you could try poetry, dance, speech making, or music. The ancient Greeks did not separate physical competitions from competitions in other forms of skill. In fact, they believed in the concept of a sound mind in a sound body. Olympia was not merely a mecca for athletics, but also a human proving ground for the Greek ideal of strong, able, beauty-loving, and wise citizens (Umminger, 1963).

"It is because of these high ideals that the Greek civilization was a dominant force in history for hundreds of years. As you will learn in the next several weeks, the contributions made by the ancient Greeks continue to influence what we learn today. For example, modern medicine is influenced by the work of Hippocrates; philosophy, by that of Plato, Socrates, and Aristotle; math, by that of Euclid and Pythagoras; and literature, by that of Homer.

"We can learn some important lessons in history through our study of the Olympic Games and the ancient Greek culture. It was only when the influence of politicians and the wealthy was permitted to make itself felt that corruption crept in and athletes began to think of themselves as professionals. (Do you see any parallels occurring in politics or sport today that illustrate corrupting forces?) Athletes began to think not of the olive branch but of cash prizes to be earned for victory.

"The decline of the Olympic Games was slow. The official end of the unbroken series of Games was in A.D. 393 under the Christian ruler Theodosius I, who banned the Games. They occasionally recurred until A.D. 529, when Justinian I reissued and enforced the ban. It was at this time that the Greek civilization in its classical form officially came to an end.

"As we work together in the next few weeks, we are going to hold our own Olympics of sorts. Not only will you learn about the contributions of the Greek civilization to literature, philosophy, math, science, history, art, and music, but also each class will choose a modern country to study and adopt. Then, as a fitting end to our studies, we will conduct our own version of the Olympic Games. We will have events of all sorts, and everyone will compete in the ideal of the Olympic spirit."

- All teachers should collaborate to develop assignments or projects in language, mathematics, science, social studies, art, and music to make this a true partnership project of the whole school or grade level.

"*Citius, altius, fortius*—does anyone know what that means? [Show a picture or statue of The Discus Thrower or Winged Victory.] It is the Olympic motto and means 'swifter, higher, stronger.' Over the next few weeks we are going to learn about competing in the Greek tradition to enter a contest and to do our best. There will be many events, and everyone will be able to select a contest in which he or she can excel.

"We know from studying the history of the Olympics that the pentathlon was one of the early events. It consisted of five contests: Two were throwing, and the other three were jumping, running, and wrestling. Eventually we will get to running and jumping contests, and we may even get to bicycle races around the track to symbolize chariot races, but first we are going to focus on throwing events.

"The ancient Greeks did not have metal balls called shot puts or metal and wooden discs to throw. In all probability they used stones of different weights and shapes. And they probably used different styles of throwing in different events. Today we are going to use basketballs, soccer balls, playground balls, hula hoops, and javelins (PVC tubing) that we will heave, hurl, and fling for distance from a line. As we do that, we will simultaneously be working on the fitness concept of arm and shoulder strength because it takes a lot of strength to throw well.

"When I say 'go,' I want you each to get a partner with whom you feel you can cooperate and line up on the sideline of the football field [basketball court], one in front of the other. The first partner will be the performer and should be at the line. The other partner is the retriever and should be 3 to 5 meters [10 to 16 feet] behind the performer for safety. Also for safety, each set of partners should be about 3 to 5 meters apart. Go. . . . Good. You did that quickly. Now when I say 'go,' I want the retrieving partner to get one basketball [soccer ball, playground ball] and two markers and bring them back to the other partner at the line. What are we going to do when you hear the word 'go'? Right, Susan. The retrieving partner gets one ball and two markers and returns to the line beside his or her partner. Go. Quickly now. Good work. I like it when everyone pays attention to directions.

"Our first throwing event will be a form of throwing called heaving. We define heaving actions with our arms in several ways. First, we will sit with our backs to the line. Our legs will be bent and spread apart. We will hold the ball in our hands at or near the floor. Then, with a powerful heaving action, we will lift the ball up and over our heads, releasing it at about 45 degrees to project the ball as far as possible. [Demonstrate.] The observing partners will stand safely in front of the throwers. They will observe where the ball lands, and on my signal they will mark the spot with a marker and retrieve the ball. Does everyone understand? How do you get a good heaving action? [Lift with power quickly, then release at 45-degree angle.] Observers, go to your places and get a marker ready. Heavers, ready. Go. . . . Retrieve. Change. Observers, in your place with a marker. Heavers, ready. Go. . . . Retrieve. I am noticing that several of you are having trouble with the release. You are either letting go of the ball too early so that it goes up toward the ceiling [demonstrate incorrect form], or you are holding on to the ball too long so that it lands on the floor too soon [demonstrate incorrect form]. Remember to release the ball at 45 degrees [demonstrate correct form]. First heavers and observers in your places. Observers, watch where the ball lands. If it is farther this time, move the marker to the new position. Otherwise, leave the marker alone. Then, on my signal, you will all retrieve your balls. . . . Second heavers and observers ready. Go. . . . Retrievers, remember to mark only throws that are farther and to get your ball. [Repeat once more for a total of three throws.] Measure and record the distance of the farthest throw on a recording sheet that has been provided.

"Next we will stand up with our backs to the line. We will heave using the same motion as we did while sitting. [Demonstrate.] Lift and release at 45 degrees. Each thrower gets three heaves using the same procedure. Observers, mark and record the farthest effort. Ready, go. . . . Stop. Everyone close ranks by staying on the line, but gather toward the middle of the line. Quickly! One, two, three. Good. I like it when you respond fast so we don't waste time.

"Our next heaving effort will involve facing the line. Watch me. You will straddle your legs some. You will hold the ball with both hands and swing it down and back between your knees. Then, you will lift forward and up forcefully and release the ball [figure 6.6]. [Demonstrate.] What do you think will be the best angle of release to get the farthest distance? [45 degrees.] You're learning application of a concept from math and science. Everyone spread back out. First heavers and observers ready. Go. [Repeat until everyone has had three turns.] Mark, measure, and record the best effort. Stop. Come in again.

"This last heaving action was very similar to one used in the Scottish Highland Games, in which strong individuals balanced a long pole or a tree trunk in their arms and heaved it, sending it toppling end over end as far as they could. That is called 'tossing the caber.'

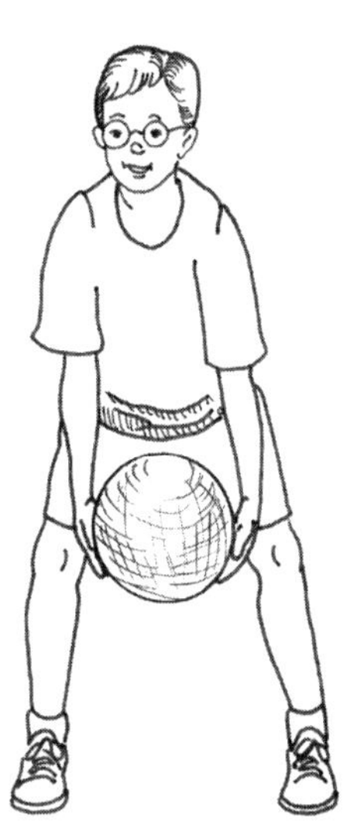

Figure 6.6 A child heaves a ball.

"Our next heaving action will be very similar to the shot-put action. Watch again. You will stand with your side to the line. You will place the ball under the side of your chin against your neck. The ball will be supported by your throwing or heaving hand. The elbow will be out away from the body. Next, you crouch down. [Demonstrate.] Without a ball, everyone do that much. Cradle, elbow out, crouch. [Check students' form.] Okay, stop and watch again. After the crouch, the body will begin its heaving action. Led by the elbow of the nonthrowing arm, the body will turn, lift, and heave as forcefully as it can. The action of the arm is a push or lift, not a throw. Make sure you lift the ball up and away from your chin at a 45-degree angle as you push the ball as far as possible. When you finish the turning action, you should be standing on the leg of your heaving arm with that side of your body closest to the line. You have rotated 180 degrees. [Demonstrate.] Remember, ready position, turn, lift, heave. Everyone go back to your position. First heavers and observers ready. Go. [Repeat until everyone has had five turns. Watch carefully for heaving actions. Do not allow children to throw the ball.] Mark, measure, and record the best effort. Stop. Come in again.

"Next, we are going to think about the concept of a hurling action. Like heaving, hurling is a forceful throwing action. But for our purposes we will define a hurl as a forward, overhand action. We can do this with one or two hands on the ball. Thus, we sometimes call a baseball pitcher a hurler. We can also think of a soccer throw-in as a style of hurling. First, we'll try a two-handed hurl. Watch. Place the ball in both of your hands and bring it back over your head. You face the line and step forward. As you step, you forcefully hurl the ball forward. Back, step, hurl. [Demonstrate.] Everyone, go with your partner back to your space. First hurler ready. Observers stand back. Go. Retrieve. Second hurler, go. Retrieve. I see some people standing still when they are hurling. For this action it doesn't make a difference which foot you use, but you must remember to step. This helps establish momentum. Also, remember to hurl up at a 45-degree angle. Three more times each. Retrievers, adjust markers to mark the best effort. Then measure the best score. Go. . . . Stop. Come in.

"The second hurling action will be an overhand throwing pattern that you already know. However, we are going to throw javelins (PVC tubing). [Softball throw for distance could be substituted.] First, a point about safety. When retrieving a javelin, lift it at the end and walk it up to vertical. Grab the handle and always carry it in a vertical position. [Demonstrate.] We don't want anyone getting poked or stabbed. Stand at least 10 feet [3 meters] behind your throwing partner to give him or her plenty of room. Remember, safety is important. If I see anyone being unsafe, you'll be asked to sit out.

"For the javelin hurling action, face the line. Hold the javelin back over your head, arm straight. Hold the javelin between your thumb and base of your fingers or between your pointer and middle fingers supported with your thumb. Do not cup your fingers or hold it like a baseball. [Demonstrate.] Next, step forward with the opposite foot. Then bring the arm through, leading overhead with the elbow. Arm back, step, hurl.

[Demonstrate.] Everyone, go back to your space with your partner. As before, take turns, five tries each. Measure and record the best score. Retrieve only on my signal. Ready, go. . . . Stop. Come in.

"Last, we're going to try a flinging action. Like heaving and hurling, flinging is a forceful throwing action. For our purposes we will define a fling as a sidearm motion. Thus, throwing a discus is a fling. As a substitute, we are going to use hula hoops. Watch. You will place the hoop in your dominant hand between your thumb and the base of your fingers. Again, be careful not to cup your fingers tightly around the hoop. [Demonstrate.] Stand with the nonthrowing arm close to the line. Place your feet shoulder-width apart. Twist or coil your body back, and get lower into a crouch. Begin to forcefully uncoil (fling) by leading with the free elbow. Your flinging arm should be relatively straight and should trail the leading action of the arm and chest. Play "crack the whip" with the hoop arm as you release the hoop in an upward, sideways arc. Follow through as your body spins around at the line by landing on the foot on the same side as the flinging arm. Coil, elbow lead, spin, fling, recover. [Demonstrate.] Go back to your space at the line with your partner. As before, five flings each. Take turns. Retrieve only on signal. Mark and record your best effort. First person ready. Go. . . . Stop. I'm noticing several errors. If you are flinging your hoop out to one side or the other, you are letting go too early or too late. If your hoop wobbles through the air, try to make your sideways arc smoother and release the hoop smoothly from between your thumb and palm. Also, make your flinging action at a rising 45-degree arc to get the most distance. Ready again, go. . . . Stop. Come in.

"We have tried several styles of heaving, hurling, and flinging today. Now as we end the class, we are going to set up two stations for each action along the line. I want you to look at your score sheets and choose one of the actions you liked best or the one that produced your best score. Go to that station and practice that event several more times, and see if you can get an even better score. Mark and record your performances. Ready, go. . . . Stop. Let's collect all the balls, hoops, javelins, and markers and put them in their proper box. Then sit down in front of me. Go.

"Today we began work on an Olympics unit. We started with throwing actions called heaving, hurling, and flinging. What Olympic events do we know that use these actions? Catherine? Yes, javelin. Steve? [Shot put.] Lauren? [Hammer throw.] Benjamin? [Caber.] Well, that is an interesting point. I mentioned that the Scottish toss the caber, but that is a sport unique to their country. In order to be an Olympic event, a sport must be sanctioned by the Olympic governing body and practiced in many countries. Each time the Olympics are held, the host country gets to choose three activities or sports as exhibition events. Then all the countries get to vote on whether to include these events in competition. That is how events are added to the Olympic Games. As we continue our Olympic unit, we will continue to practice the throwing events. We will also add running and jumping events and several sports. At the same time you will be learning about the Olympics, the Greek culture, the contributions of the Greeks throughout the ages, and other countries in all of your classes. We will finish our unit with our very own Olympics at our school. Remember, you are all *athlons,* or contestants. Do your best. Be true to the Olympic motto: *Citius, altius, fortius* (swifter, higher, stronger).

Assessment Suggestions

- Develop a mechanics checklist for each type of throw. Have students evaluate each other.
- Have students measure their throws and work toward improving throwing distance.

Look For

- Place an emphasis on the use of good technique by having the children model your demonstrations and use the learning cues that stress process characteristics. Some children (particularly the stronger ones) will be able to use their strength to achieve the best product results (distance) while using poor form. This will only hurt them over time. For example, when heaving using the shot-put style, some children will take the ball away from their chin and just throw it overhand. While they may get a good distance score, they are not developing good technique. Over time they will hurt their arms; and when they heave real weights, distance scores will also suffer.
- Encourage all children to challenge themselves. Each child should try to improve his or her own score. That is what it means to be a competitor, an *athlon.*

How Can I Change This?

- Include the use of a real (8-pound, or 3.6-kilogram) shot put, discus, javelin, hammer, or even a heavy medicine ball.
- Focus other classes in this Olympic unit on jumping events, for example, the high jump, standing long jump, running long jump, triple jump.
- Focus other classes in this Olympic unit on running events, for example, the 50-meter sprint, 100-meter sprint, 200-meter sprint, 4 × 100-meter sprint, 800-meter run.
- Develop some novelty events, such as a gladiator run in armor (cardboard), chariot race around the track on bicycles, and three-legged run with a partner.
- Investigate games from other countries. Learn them and include them as contests in your Olympics.

Teachable Moments

- Emphasize interdisciplinary work throughout this unit. The initial focus may be on the richness of the early Greek culture and its many contributions to art and architecture, government, philosophy, literature, science, and math.
- As classes adopt a country, attention may focus more on modern society. Children can research facts about a given country's flag, anthem, population, economy, government, sports, and so on.
- Develop specific interdisciplinary projects with classroom teachers. For example, record metric scores for throws, jumps, or runs in physical education. Calculate average scores and plot or graph increases in performance over trials or days. In language arts, children can select and research a favorite Olympic sport individually or in groups. They should find out the equipment used, training needed, clothing worn, countries that compete in this sport, and the current Olympic champion. They could write a report about their findings or develop a cartoon strip to depict their results. Finally, they should do some training in the sport to improve their performance.

Hogmanay

Suggested Grade Level

Intermediate (3 through 5)

Interdisciplinary Teaching Model

Partnership

You and the social studies, visual arts, and music teachers can agree to focus on using the idea of rituals as a stimulus for study in the respective disciplines. The students draw pictures or create a sculpture in their visual arts class. They listen to and sing music appropriate for the selected ritual. In physical education they create a dance that focuses on the selected ritual.

Social Studies

Learning about the history of Scotland, John Knox and the Reformation, and Hogmanay as a New Year celebration

Visual Arts

Drawing and sculpting pieces of art to represent a ritual

Music

Appreciating and singing music associated with a ritual

Physical Education

Creating a dance emphasizing activities that occur during a ritual

Objectives

As a result of participating in this lesson, students will

- discover some of the Scottish history surrounding the celebration of the coming of a new year;
- learn to draw or sculpt scenes or figures that represent participation is a selected ritual;
- listen to Scottish bagpipe music and sing songs associated with a selected ritual; and
- create a dance sequence with a beginning, middle, and end that represents activities that occur during a selected ritual.

Equipment

A drawing or a piece of sculpture from the visual arts class and words and music to "Auld Lang Syne" from the music class

Organization

Individuals, partners, and small groups

Description

Social Studies

Hogmanay's roots go back to the pagan practice of sun and fire worship. This evolved into the ancient Roman winter festival of Saturnalia, in which people celebrated the end of one year and the beginning of the next. The Vikings celebrated Yule, which became the 12 days of Christmas. In Scotland the winter festival went underground when John

Knox, leading the Scottish Reformation, banned worldly pleasures such as celebrating and having a good time, with the idea that search of the life hereafter was what was important. At the end of the 17th century the winter festival reemerged as Hogmanay. Some believe that the name is a derivation from the Gaelic "oge maidne" or "new morning." Others believe that it is derived from the Anglo-Saxon "Haleg monath" or "Holy Month" or from the Norman French word "hoguinane" or "gift at New Year."

Modern-day celebrations of Hogmanay include rituals such as parading a flaming fireball through the streets of a city to water's edge (lake or river) and throwing the flaming ball into the water. The flame and fire symbolize many things such as bringing the light of knowledge from one year to the next, lighting the way into the next uncharted year or century, and putting behind you the darkness of the past while carrying forward the sacred flame of hope and enlightenment. Another ritual is first footing or visiting other people's homes and bringing them presents such as coal, cakes, or money to wish them prosperity for the New Year. (For more information about Hogmanay, see http://en.wikipedia.org/wiki/Hogmanay and www.rampantscotland.com/know/blknow12.htm; http://hogmanay.net; McLaughlin, 2005; or do a Google search on rituals.)

Art

The art teacher can talk to the children about the rituals of parading, fireballing, and first footing. The children can then draw or sculpt appropriate pieces of art based on their interpretation of the Hogmanay festival.

Music

The music teacher can introduce the children to bagpipe music and the special song called "Auld Lang Syne" sung on New Year's Eve. "Auld Lang Syne" is a traditional song adapted from a poem of Robert Burns (1759-1796), the Scottish national poet. These are the words to the song:

Verse 1

Should auld acquaintance be forgot,
And never brought to mind?
Should auld acquaintance be forgot,
And auld lang syne?

Chorus

For auld lang syne, my dear,
For auld lang syne,
We'll take a cup of kindness yet,
For auld lang syne!

Verse 2

And surely ye'll be your pint-stowp,
And surely I'll be mine.
And we'll take a cup o kindness yet,
For auld lang syne!

Verse 3

We twa hae run about the braes,
And pou'd the gowans fine,
But we've wander'd monie a weary fit,
Sin auld lang syne.

Verse 4

We twa hae paidl'd in the burn
Frae morning sun till dine,
But seas between us braid hae roar'd
Sin auld lang syne.

Verse 5

Athe there's a hand my trusty fiere,
And gie's a hand o thine
And we'll tak a right guid-willie waught,
For auld lang syne.

Meanings

auld lang syne—times gone by
be—pay for
braes—hills
braid—broad
burn—stream
dine—dinner time
fiere—friend
fit—foot
gowans—daisies
guid-willie waught—goodwill drink
monie—many
morning sun—noon
paidl't—paddled
pint-stowp—pint tankard
pou'd—pulled
twa—two

Physical Education

"During the next several lessons we are going to be developing a dance based on the concept of rituals. I have picked a ritual that perhaps no one in this class knows about. It is called Hogmanay, and it is from Scotland. Let's begin by warming up to some of my Scottish bagpipe music. You'll find that this first selection is rather slow and droning. We'll stretch our bodies to this music."

- Do a top-down stretching series of exercises starting with the head and neck, progressing to the shoulders, then the trunk and legs.

"Now I am going to put on some Scottish country dancing music that is rather lively. I want you to spring or jig up and down to the rhythm of the music. Jump or hop in a lively manner to the beat of the music. Put your arms up in the air in different ways—one arm up, other arm up, both arms up. Travel around the floor as you jump or hop. Try different directions and pathways. Okay, stop. That sure got our hearts beating. Good warm-up. Let's come in here close to the music and sit down. We are going to talk about rituals just a bit.

"Rituals are like routines that we commonly do. We do them the same way each time. They give meaning to our lives. Rituals in all societies play a significant role in

the process of life. We celebrate birth, baptism, communion, birthdays, graduation, marriage, and death. The changing of seasons, religious holidays, and national days of significance are also celebrated with rituals. To start our lesson I have chosen the festival of Hogmanay from Scotland. Has anyone ever heard of that? [Some guesses.] Well, you have a clue from our warm-up today. It is associated with the country of Scotland. I have been talking with your teachers and we have decided that we will work together for a short time as we study Scotland and the concept of rituals.

"Hogmanay is a winter, changing-of-the-seasons, New Year festival. In the classroom and in art and music classes you will study some of the history of the Scots and the festival of Hogmanay. In physical education I have chosen to concentrate on three rituals from Hogmanay. The first is fireballing, the second is the ancient 'Ba' game, and the third is first stepping.

"In the city of Stonehaven, Scotland, citizens light fireballs on 5-foot-long wire ropes. They parade down their main street solemnly toward the sea. When they get there, they spread out and swirl the flaming balls around their heads before hurling them Olympic hammer style far out into the water. The ceremonial meaning of this ritual is connected to the fireballs as a representation of the life-giving sun or a shooting star, the flaming out of the old year, the consumer of evil spirits, or the bringer of health and happiness in the New Year. Let's start our sequence by going through the movements associated with fireballing. Make believe that you are carrying a flaming ball attached to a long wire. Parade solemnly about the room. Be aware of your spacing and try to stay spread out. Okay, you have reached the water's edge. Now you are going to spin round and round vigorously like a hammer thrower [demonstrate the action]. Let the fireball go and watch it fly into the water. Make believe you are the fireball and fly in an arc through space. Sink into the water—a dying flame. Create a shape on the floor. Let's practice that again—parade, stop, spin, watch, fly, sink, shape on the floor. Stop. Come in. Sit down.

"The second part of our ritual sequence is the 'Ba' game, played on Ne'er Day (New Year's Day). It is from the city of Kirkwall in the Orkney Islands, Scotland. Citizens of the town are divided into two teams—Uppies and Doonies. They push and wrestle back and forth, kicking a cork ball, propelling it inch by inch through the streets, until one team reaches its goal. We will do the second part of our dance with a partner. Choose a partner and sit beside your partner. Make sure that you are spread out on the floor using good space. You choose who is the Uppie and who is the Doonie. I expect to see two soccer-type players going back and forth—advancing and retreating. First, one player dominates, advancing the ball while the other retreats. Then, the other player advances while the other retreats. Stay close together. Fake each other out. Who scores? The Uppie or the Doonie? [Another scenario you could consider as an alternative is corner kick, break away, kick on goal, block, GOAL!!!] Go. Practice this part several times.

"Let's put part 1 and part 2 together. Remember who your partner is. First, spread out as individuals. Part 1: Fireballing—parade, stop, spin, watch, fly, sink, shape on the floor. Get up and be lively. This is a joyous occasion. We are celebrating the coming of the New Year. High five several people as you gradually find your partner. Shake hands and wish them luck. Part 2: Advance, retreat, fake, score. Practice several times. Okay. Stop. Come in. Sit down.

"Finally, we will do the first-footing part of our sequence. First footing in Scotland is a tradition celebrated widely around the country. It refers to the custom of being the first to step over the doorstep of someone's home after the bells have rung out the old year. A light burning in an open window has long been an invitation to come calling. That means going to visit a neighbor and bringing a gift. A lump of coal might represent a source of heat throughout the year. A cake might represent plentiful food throughout the year. And, according to Viking tradition, blondes, redheads, or anyone who is flat-

footed (this would mean that the gift giver was a Viking who was feared by the Scots) would send the household racing for the hills.

"You will do this first-footing part as partners and travel around the space greeting three other sets of partners. This simply means that each set of partners stays together throughout the first-footing part of the dance. While "Auld Lang Syne" is being sung, partners walk about and greet two other sets of partners, when they meet the third set of partners they choose to present a gift and be friendly or to run away in fear that the partners are Vikings. Let's begin walking with our partners. Greet two other sets of partners. Move on to a third set of partners carrying a gift. Now comes the fun part. Decide whether you are thankful for the present or whether one of your new friends is blonde or red-headed with flat feet; a Viking who you, as a Scot, would fear. In that case you would flee for the hills. You can quickly turn and run away and freeze in a frightened shape. Discuss with your partner how many running steps you want to take and the frozen shape you will use. Let's practice. Start singing "Auld Lang Syne." Move about and greet the first set of neighbors. Move on and greet the second set of neighbors. Move on to the third set and present your gift. Be thankful and friendly or run for the hills. If you choose to run for the hills, run and freeze in your shape. If you choose to accept a gift, freeze in a shape that is connected to the friendly set of partners. The dance is over when everyone in the class is frozen.

"Okay. Now we are going to perform our whole ritual dance. What is part 1? Yes. It is fireballing. What were the cues? Good. Parade, spin, watch, fly, sink, shape on the floor. What about part 2, the 'Ba' game? What were the cues? Advance, retreat, fake, score. Good memories. Then comes part 3, first footing. Sing "Auld Lang Syne" and meet one set of partners, second set of partners, present gift to third set of partners, be thankful or run for the hills. Let's practice the whole sequence several times. Great work. Let's show our dances to [art teacher, music teacher, and classroom teacher], who have agreed to come to the final dance presentation.

Assessment Suggestions

- On you own or along with the other teachers involved in the learning experience, use the cues for all three parts of the dance to see whether all components were present.
- Students can answer the following questions in writing. Why are rituals important? What are some other rituals?—name three. What is significant about the ritual of Hogmanay? Of the three parts we chose to represent Hogmanay, which one did you like the best? Why? If you were to change the dance, how would you change it and why?

Look For

- Make sure that the students interpret fireballing, the 'Ba' game, and first footing in creative or expressive ways and that they do not just produce literal translations of hammer throwing, kicking a ball, and greeting someone.
- Insist on quality aspects of flow and transition as students move from one part of the dance to the next. During the dance you should be able to see, for example, proud marching through the streets; wild and furious hurling of the flaming ball into the sea; vigorous give-and-take during game play; and slow, sustained, purposeful meeting and greeting.
- Make sure that the students beginning and ending poses depict an appropriate part of the ritual of Hogmanay – a proud Scottish person, carrying a flaming ball, a pose of appreciation, frantically fleeing, etc. (still or statue-like, perhaps representing the students' artwork) for the dance.

Grade Level

K through 6
Have the children physically act out the happy and sad emotions related to school. Prompt students for situations that make them happy (when you do well on a paper, when you kick a ball high on the playground, when your teacher tells you that you are special, when your friend asks you to sit with her at lunch) and sad (when you miss the bus, when you don't do as well as you had hoped on a test, when your best friend eats lunch with someone else, when you get in trouble for something that you did not do).

Moving Through the School Day—Now and Then

Social Studies

Parts of the school day

Physical Education

Creating and performing movement sequences

Grade Level

K through 3
Have students perform a movement sequence representing the parts of the school day, such as arriving at school, going to class, doing class work, going to a particular class, having lunch in the cafeteria, going out for recess, checking books out of the media center, and getting ready to go home.

Then have students create a movement sequence of the parts of the school day that their great-grandparents might have experienced (if possible, they can ask grandparents or great-grandparents for information), such as arriving at school after a long walk or a horse-and-buggy ride, going to class with students of all ages, eating a lunch brought from home, getting firewood or coal to help keep the schoolroom warm, going out for recess, getting ready to leave at the end of the day, and walking home.

Meet My Family

Social Studies

Family

Physical Education

Creating and performing movement sequences

Grade Level

K through 3
Ask students to make a movement sequence that portrays the members of their (nuclear) family. They should start with the youngest members and move through the oldest. Can

a partner tell how many people are in their family? Next ask them to make a movement sequence that shows favorite activities of each of their family members; for example, a student's mother might like to jog; his or her father might enjoy working in the yard; his or her sister might spend lots of time reading. Have students, in groups of three, try to figure the family members and activities for each movement sequence.

Watch Me Change

Social Studies

People growing and changing

Physical Education

Creating and performing movement sequences

Grade Level

K through 2

"All the people we know are growing and changing. Make a movement sequence that represents the changes that you have made from the time you were born until today. You can think about drinking from a bottle, learning to sit up, learning to roll over, learning to stand, learning to walk, learning to drink from a cup, learning to throw and kick a ball, learning to ride a tricycle or bicycle."

CITIZENSHIP

Working With My Friends

Social Studies

Working with friends

Physical Education

Creating and performing movement sequences

Grade Level

K through 3

"Physically show ways that you can work well and poorly with friends, such as sharing or not sharing equipment, helping or not helping when your friend has many things to carry, taking or not taking turns."

Let's Play by the Rules

Social Studies

Importance of rules

Physical Education

Game play

Grade Level

K through 3

Have the children participate in a tag game such as Stoop Tag or Freeze Tag. Make sure that everyone is active and not eliminated. Talk about the rules in the game and how we have rules at school, at home, and in our communities. Discuss the need for rules in these settings.

Invent a Game

Social Studies

Rules and laws governing behavior

Physical Education

Manipulative activities and game play

Grade Level

4 through 6

Provide the children with specific equipment and a scenario for game play (e.g., ball and bat, four-person striking game; racket and ball, two people, hit over a net; two vs. two, hitting a target). Explain that all games originated as inventions. For example, James Naismith invented the game of basketball when he desired an indoor game during the winter months. He nailed peach baskets to the wall of an overhead indoor track and the rules began to evolve.

Ask the children to make up a game. Have them try out some rules, play the game, see what works and what needs changing, adapt the rules, and write the rules on paper. Have them teach their game to another set of players. Discuss the role of rules in a game. Talk about rules at school, at home, and in the community. Discuss the need for rules in these settings. "Are all rules fair? What rules might be changed to be more fair?"

I Am Important in My Community

Social Studies

Caring for your community

Physical Education

Creating and performing movement sequences

Grade Level

K through 3

"You want to help take care of your community. Show through movement things that you can do to help take care of your community, such as throwing paper in the garbage can, turning the lights out when you leave the room, planting flowers at the city park. Show your partner five different actions, and have your partner show his or her five actions. Select the five best of your and your partner's actions. Make a movement sequence to show the five actions. Now use the same procedure to show ways that you can be unhelpful in taking care of your community."

Statue of Liberty

Social Studies

Citizenship

Physical Education

Body shapes, balance, and strength

Grade Level

3 through 6

"The Statue of Liberty has welcomed immigrants to the United States for more than 100 years. The Statue of Liberty provided the first glimpse of America for many immigrants as they made their way to Ellis Island. On the base of the statue are the words, 'I lift my lamp beside the golden door.' After studying about the Statue of Liberty and looking at pictures of the statue, pretend that you are a statue designer. You are going to design other Statues of Liberty and create new citizenship messages to be written on the bases of the statues. Explore making your body into different statues. Model for a partner your two best statue designs. Explain exactly what your statue represents, and tell how your message relates to good citizenship. Have your partner critique your statue." Have the students make changes and show their best design to a group or to the class.

I Get By With a Little Help From My Friends

Social Studies

Helping others

Physical Education

Creating and performing movement sequences

Grade Level

K through 3

"In families, schools, and communities we need to help others. For example, you might cooperate to carry a heavy load (gymnastics mats, bench, or other apparatus). You might work with a friend, sibling, or parent to rake leaves and stuff them into a trash bag to be carried away by the city or municipality. You might volunteer to participate in a neighborhood, park, or river cleanup effort with your family, scouting group, or church. With a partner, make a movement sequence that represents ways that you can help each other. Next, make a sequence in which you are not being helpful to each other. Talk about which way makes you feel better."

It All Depends on You and Me

Social Studies

Depending on others

Physical Education

Creating and performing movement sequences

Grade Level

K through 6

We depend on others and they depend on us. We especially depend on others for the food that we eat. Have students make a movement sequence that represents the people on whom they depend for the orange juice they have at breakfast. The sequence could include planting the orange tree, watering and pruning the tree, picking the oranges, driving the truck full of oranges to the packing plant, cleaning the fruit, operating the machine that squeezes the oranges for juice, bottling the juice, driving the juice to the store, and unpacking the juice and placing it on shelves. Other sequences might represent the cotton cycle from planting to manufacturing into a shirt, the wool cycle from raising sheep to manufacturing into a sweater, or the steel cycle from mining ore to making a car. Students could research the steps and then make up a movement sequence.

You Can Depend on Me

Social Studies

Depending on others

Physical Education

Creating and performing movement sequences

Grade Level

K through 4

"We depend on others for all types of services in our community. Think about a job in your community on which you depend. Physically show what a person in that job does, and ask a partner to guess the work that you are doing. Explain to your partner how you depend on the job that you demonstrated. Then, with your partner, find another pair of partners and show your jobs to one another."

I Like to Obey Rules

Social Studies

Obeying laws

Physical Education

Creating and performing movement sequences

Grade Level

K through 2

"We must obey traffic laws—laws for driving or walking on public roads. I have set up a traffic area, and you must follow the signs." Set up various pathways and traffic signs. Have students move through the course under control.

I'm a Safe Driver

Social Studies

Obeying laws

Physical Education

Creating and performing movement sequences

Grade Level

K through 2

"We must obey traffic lights in order to travel safely. Line up across the starting line. You will move or stop movement according to the color that I hold up. When you see green, you may move fast, but under control. When you see yellow, you should move slowly and cautiously. When I hold up red, you must stop. Always move safely. No one wants to get a ticket or be in a wreck."

CHARACTER EDUCATION

Courage Anyone?

Social Studies

Courage conquering fear

Physical Education

Developing a movement sequence to show something one is afraid of, a strategy to overcome that fear, and how one might feel once that fear is conquered.

Grade Level

2 and 3

Read *Courage* by Waber (2002) to the children. Talk about everyday occurrences that make children and adults fearful. What is it that some children are afraid of—getting lost, the dark, heights, going off a diving board? Talk about strategies that might help overcome those fears and how one would feel about being no longer fearful of a particular situation. "Make up a movement sequence that includes actions to show what you are fearful of, how you plan to overcome the fear, and how you will feel after you successfully conquer that fear."

Let's Get Together!

Social Studies

Friendship, cooperation, and persistence

Physical Education

Designing a gymnastics sequence with a partner

Grade Level

3 through 5

Read *Angelina and Alice* by Holabird (1987) to the children. Talk about the fact that Angelina and Alice had different levels of talent in gymnastics. Yet, by working hard together as partners and cooperating, they developed a sequence they were both proud of. They worked together to bring out the best in each other. Best of all, they became good friends!

Assign the children partners they might not normally work with. Have the partners create a gymnastics sequence that you or they design—balance, roll, balance; travel, balance on equipment, move off the equipment, final balance. Emphasize that you will be watching how well each set of partners cooperates and works hard together. Encourage them to be persistent, work out their differences, and compromise. At the end ask them to express orally or in writing how it felt to work with someone they didn't know very well.

TRANSPORTATION

The Wheels on the Bus Go Round and Round

Social Studies

Transportation to school

Physical Education

Expressive movement to music

Grade Level

K through 2

"We will learn the song 'The Wheels on the Bus Go Round and Round' and use whole-body movements to act out the song. For example, when you sing, 'The wheels on the bus go round and round,' make big circles with your arms or feet or do rolls. . . . Now we'll talk about riding a bus and other forms of transportation to and from school." (You can also emphasize the need for safety in transportation.)

Let's Travel to School

Social Studies

Transportation to school

Physical Education

Creating and performing movement sequences

Grade Level

K through 3

"Show through movement ways in which you are transported to school. Think about the type of transportation that you chose. What is the speed of your type of transportation? What is the size of your mode of transportation? Does size affect speed? Could you transport yourself to school? Show a partner three ways you might transport yourself to school." (Students might show skateboarding; walking; riding a bicycle, unicycle, or tricycle; using roller skates or in-line skates; hopping on a pogo stick.)

Transportation in My Community

Social Studies

Transportation in the community

Physical Education

Expressive movement

Grade Level

K through 2

"Show through movement four different types of trucks in your community. You might show a garbage truck, a moving van, an ice cream truck, a cement mixer, or a mail truck. Be sure that your movement actually matches the movement of the truck. Does the truck move fast or slow? Does it start and stop frequently? Is the truck large or small? Now show through movement four different types of movement of trucks from outside your community (urban, rural, suburban). Do the trucks primarily seen outside your community move differently from the ones in your community?"

So Many Jobs at School

Social Studies

Jobs at school

Physical Education

Creating and performing movement sequences

Grade Level

K through 3

"Make a movement sequence that represents the different jobs at school, such as the cooks in the cafeteria, the janitor, the bus driver, the nurse, the teacher, the principal. Link at least three different job actions that the person you have chosen might do. See whether a partner can guess your job."

So Many Jobs at Home

Social Studies

Jobs at home

Physical Education

Creating and performing movement sequences

Grade Level

K through 3

"Show through movement some of the tasks that are done at home, such as washing dishes, mowing the lawn, cleaning windows, cooking, writing checks to pay bills. Show a partner your task and see whether he or she can guess the task. . . . Now link two movements that represent different tasks at home. . . . Now link three movements. . . . Can your partner guess all three of your tasks? Did you and your partner show any of the same tasks?"

So Many Jobs in Our Community

Social Studies

Jobs in the community

Physical Education

Creating and performing movement sequences

Grade Level

K through 4

"There are many different jobs in our communities. Pick the job you like best, and make a movement sequence of tasks that you might perform at that job. Include three different actions that would be performed in your job." Have students see whether the other students in the class can guess their job.

Working on the Night Shift

Social Studies

Jobs in the community

Physical Education

Expressive movement

Grade Level

K through 3

"Some jobs in our communities are performed at night. Each of you will physically show three jobs that might be performed at night, for example, printing a newspaper, taking care of people as a nurse in a hospital, or driving a mail truck. In a group of three, show your jobs and have the others in your group guess what these jobs are." Have the groups choose the three most interesting jobs and show them to the class.

Working From Country to City

Social Studies

Jobs in city and country

Physical Education

Creating and performing movement sequences

Grade Level

K through 4

"People in the city can have different jobs than people who live in the country. Work with a partner. One of you will show through movement three different city jobs and the other will show three country jobs." Then have the partners switch roles and each come up with three different jobs.

YOUR STATE

Traveling Through Your State

Social Studies

State geography

Physical Education

Traveling and balancing

Grade Level

3 and 4

Draw or paint a map of your state on the gym floor or outdoor playground. Use shoe polish, chalk, or tape for easy cleanup, or use paint if you want the map to be permanent. Include county lines and features such as major rivers, lakes, mountains and other prominent land characteristics, or the ocean. Then have students identify the names and locations of cities in the state and create balance positions in various cities. "Travel in different ways from one city to another, stopping to balance in five different cities. Can you name each of the cities? Can you remember your route (mapping) and repeat it? Jump over the rivers or streams. Can you name the bodies of water? Swim (use arm actions to show different types of strokes) across the lakes. Where there are mountains, use appropriate climbing actions to show how difficult it is to go up and down a mountain."

Features of Your State

Social Studies

Special features of the state

Physical Education

Movement actions representing activities special to the state

Grade Level

3 and 4

This activity focuses on the features that make a state unique. After identifying special features that characterize your state, think about the types of movement activities the children could perform to highlight these features. In class, give the students information about special state characteristics and then have them do activities reflective of those characteristics. In this description we use South Carolina as an example.

South Carolina is divided into three areas, called the Piedmont or Upstate, which has mountains; the Sand Hills, which has rolling terrain; and the Low Country, which borders the ocean. In the Upstate, people do a special type of dance called mountain clogging. In the Low Country near Myrtle Beach, people do a dance called the shag, which has been designated the state dance. People also do the Charleston as a dance. The children could be taught each of these dances.

In the Low Country, people do a lot of shrimping with cast nets. In the mountain streams they do a lot of trout fishing. In the many lakes and reservoirs in the Sand Hills, people do a lot of bass fishing. The children could be taken fishing or could make up a movement sequence to symbolize flinging the shrimp nets and hauling them in, or the casting, reeling, and netting actions used to catch a fish.

Traveling to Different Parts of Your State

Social Studies

Traveling to different parts of the state

Physical Education

Physical fitness

Grade Level

K through 6

"You are going to pretend to travel to different cities in our state. On the fitness path outside the school [or inside the gymnasium], you will walk or run for designated time periods [during class time, recess, before or after school]. Each 10-minute time period represents a mile in your travel across the state. Pick a city and travel to it. Once you arrive at your designated city, you will study the area and discover more about your own state. How many different cities can you visit over the year? How many miles can you cover? In addition to the fitness benefit, in cooperation with the classroom teacher, have the children research information about the city or area. This could be done by reading books and magazines or using computer search. For example, Hurley in northern Wisconsin is famous for logging, Lake Mills in central Wisconsin is the location of the Glacial Drumlin Trail, Platteville in Southern Wisconsin is largely flat and a great place for agriculture. It doesn't matter when they get to their cities. This can be an ongoing project or assignment that they complete by the end of the semester or year."

HISTORY

Hello, I Am From Ireland

Social Studies

The immigrant experience

Physical Education

Creating and performing movement sequences

Grade Level

K through 4

"An immigrant is a person who moves permanently from one country to another. With a partner, make a movement sequence that represents the experience of an immigrant

coming to the United States. The immigrant is your age and is coming from a country of your choice in the year 1900. Be sure to research the immigrant experience from the time of leaving the homeland to the time of settling in the United States. Begin the movement sequence in a shape that represents your country of origin. Next, use traveling movements to show the journey to the United States. End the sequence in a shape that represents how the immigrant feels about his or her arrival in the United States."

Please Meet Harriet Tubman

Social Studies

The Underground Railroad, oppression and freedom, Harriet Tubman

Physical Education

Creating and performing movement sequences

Grade Level

K through 6

"Harriet Tubman in the late 1800s was a 'conductor' on the Underground Railroad. She helped more than 300 enslaved people get to freedom. In groups of three, make a movement sequence that represents Harriet Tubman helping two enslaved people to make their escape. Remember that most of their travel was done at night."

Take a Walk on the Moon

Social Studies

Looking to the future

Physical Education

Creating and performing movement sequences

Grade Level

K through 6

"On July 20, 1969, Neil Armstrong became the first person to take a step on the moon. He said of his step, 'That's one small step for man, one giant leap for mankind.' Develop a movement sequence showing what you think it would have been like to take that first step off the spacecraft and onto the moon's surface. Then take more steps on the moon. Next, pretend that you are exploring a new planet for the first time. Develop a movement sequence for a new planet that has a very soft, spongy surface."

The New Deal

Social Studies

U.S. history

Physical Education

Creating and performing movement sequences

Grade Level

4 through 6

"In 1932, Franklin D. Roosevelt was elected president of the United States. This was during the time of the Great Depression, when many people were out of work. He established the New Deal, through which millions of jobs were created for unemployed workers. Many of these workers planted trees and built dams and roads. Develop a movement sequence that shows how an unemployed worker might feel about being offered a good job. Begin your sequence by showing a person who is poor and out of work; then show him or her hearing about the potential job, being offered the job, and finally beginning the new job."

Famous Athletes

Social Studies

Study the life of a famous athlete

Physical Education

Participating in the sport of the selected athlete

Grade Level

4 through 6

Select a number of famous athletes from the past, such as Babe Didrikson, Nadia Comaneci, Jim Thorpe, Wilma Rudolph, Jesse Owens, Bob Beamon, Bronko Nagurski, Amos Alonzo Stagg, Babe Ruth, Jackie Robinson, Lou Gehrig, Bill Russell, Wilt Chamberlain, Bob Cousy, Walt Bellamy, Gordie Howe, Sonja Henie, or Peggy Fleming. Have the students do some research on an athlete of their choice. Have them learn about the athlete's life. What did the athlete accomplish? Did the athlete have to overcome any obstacles in striving for success? Have students participate in their athlete's sport or make up a movement sequence that represents their athlete in training and competition.

Carrying the Olympic Flame

Social Studies

History of the Olympics

Physical Education

Creating and performing movement sequences

Grade Level

2 through 4

"Many of you have seen the Olympic flame at the Olympic Games. Some of you might have seen the torch bearer running up to light the Olympic flame. Usually many people are involved in transporting the flame across the country to the Olympic site. In groups of three, design a movement sequence that represents running with the torch, arriving at the Olympic site, and lighting the Olympic flame."

Move Like an Olympian

Social Studies

History of the Olympics

Physical Education

Creating and performing a movement sequence

Grade Level

3 through 6

"Athletes can participate in many different activities at the Olympic Games. Choose your favorite activity and develop a movement sequence that represents that activity. Your sequence should have an interesting beginning, a middle part that includes several actions, and an interesting ending. Show your sequence to a partner and see if he or she can determine what your activity is. Next, teach your sequence to your partner and also learn your partner's routine."

MAPPING AND GLOBE SKILLS

Maps of Pathways

Social Studies

Mapping skills

Physical Education

Traveling over pathways

Grade Level

3 through 6

"You are going to draw a map. I will give you and a friend three traffic cones and two short ropes. You can make different pathway shapes, such as straight, zigzag, or circular shapes, with your equipment. Then travel along your pathway in different ways (walk forward, jump from side to side, hop backward). Next, draw your pathway on the paper. Be sure to include all three cones and the two short ropes in your map."

Moving in Different Directions

Social Studies

Mapping skills

Physical Education

Traveling in different directions

Grade Level

1 through 6

Students should learn movement concepts such as right, left, far, near, up, and down. Design movement activities to help teach and reinforce these concepts, for example, "Slide to the left, now to the right, and back to the left" or "Stand near a partner; now use a locomotor movement to move far from your partner."

Butterfly Time Line

Social Studies

Using a time line

Physical Education

Creating and performing a movement sequence

Grade Level

3 through 6

"Time lines show the order in which things happened. Draw a time line of a butterfly's life from egg, larva, and chrysalis (cocoon) through the butterfly stage. Then design a movement sequence that reflects your butterfly time line."

Kicking Line Graph

Social Studies

Constructing a line graph

Physical Education

Kicking

Grade Level

3 through 6

"Working in groups of four, record the number of times out of 10 tries that each person in your group is able to kick a ball to a large target on the wall. Everyone can kick at the same time and record his or her own scores. Construct a line graph that represents your scores. You can place students' names at the bottom of the graph and the numbers ranging from 0 to 10 on the left side of the graph."

Exercise Time Line

Social Studies

Using a time line

Physical Education

Physical activity and fitness, cognitive focus

Grade Level

3 through 6

"Make a time line of the months of the year. Mark the months when you are able to exercise comfortably outside in shorts. Mark the months when you exercise inside. Mark the months when you have physical education at school. Mark the months when you participate in some kind of sporting activity, in dance lessons, or in gymnastics lessons."

Cardinal and Intermediate Directions

Social Studies

Moving in cardinal and intermediate directions

Physical Education

Performing motor skills

Grade Level

4 through 6

"In order to use maps effectively, you must be able to determine direction. The cardinal directions are north, south, east, and west. The intermediate directions lie halfway between the cardinal directions. They are northeast, southeast, southwest, and northwest. Follow my directions as I have you move in certain ways in different directions." It is important to use good start and stop signals for this activity. Begin with the cardinal directions. Once students are all oriented in the same direction, they can, for example, skip south, run north, leap east, bear-walk west. The intermediate directions can be added when students are ready.

Orienteering

Social Studies

Learning to use a map and compass

Physical Education

Traveling actions and fitness

Grade Level

4 through 6

Get or make a map of the school. Set it to scale if possible. Use scouting compasses. Teach the children about azimuths or points on a compass: 0 degrees bearing is north; 90 degrees bearing is east; 180 degrees bearing is south; 270 degrees bearing is west. Hide certain articles in the outdoor play area (small trinkets, pencils, washers, nuts and bolts, etc.). You could also hide spelling words or math problems. Give students directions, for example, walk or hop 20 paces or 20 yards [18 meters] at a bearing of 110 degrees. "What did you find? . . . Now jump 30 yards [27 meters] at a bearing of 300 degrees. What did you find?" Depending on how many compasses you have, you could pair students up and have them start at different places so that they are all active at once.

Scaling the USA

Social Studies

Using a map scale

Physical Education

Performing motor skills

Grade Level

3 through 6

This activity requires that a large map of the United States be painted, drawn, or projected from an overhead projector on a floor surface. Perhaps your class could volunteer to paint the map on the blacktop surface at your school. The students, with your help, should determine an approximate scale for the map. The scale can then be gauged to individual students' strides. If working in feet or yards, a child can measure his or her stride length to approximate distances. Have students walk to and from certain destinations, count the number of steps, and multiply by the length of their stride. For example, if a child's stride is 2 feet and each foot equals 50 miles, then in one stride the child travels 100 scale miles.

NATIONAL IDENTITY AND CULTURE

Cultural Games

Social Studies

Cultures and games

Physical Education

Participating in games

Grade Level

2 through 6

"People from different cultures have special games that they play. Ask your relatives to tell you about games that might represent your culture. Show the game to your class and have everyone play."

Play in Different Cultures

Social Studies

Play in different cultures

Physical Education

Locomotor, nonlocomotor, and manipulative skills

Grade Level

2 through 6

"Ask your grandparents, older aunts and uncles, or older people in your neighborhood what they did for play when they were your age. Describe and then show these activities to your classmates. Have them participate in the activity."

Did You Get My Message?

Social Studies

Communicating with those from a different culture

Physical Education

Expressive movement

Grade Level

2 through 6

"We sometimes need to communicate with those who speak a different language. Pretend that your partner does not speak your language. Try to communicate a message without using words. You may use only body language to send your message. After your turn, give your partner a chance." (Possible messages: "I want you to play a game with me"; "I am lost, I don't know where my family is"; "I have a dog and a cat at home.")

Irish Eyes Are Smiling

Social Studies

Dance of selected cultures

Physical Education

Learning selected folk dances

Grade Level

K through 6

For this activity, collaborate with the social studies teacher. What country are the children studying? Select a folk dance from that country and teach it to the children. In this description we use Ireland as an example.

Show the children clips from *Riverdance,* Michael Flatley's film. Talk about the history of Ireland; the green, white, and orange flag representing Catholics, Protestants, and lasting peace between them; St. Patrick; kissing the Blarney stone; the economy and geography of Ireland, and some of the famous people of Irish descent (Pierce Brosnan, actor; Minnie Driver, actress; Sinead O'Connor, singer; James Galway, musician). Teach the children about jigs and reels. Teach them selected Irish folk dances—"Irish Mixer" (Phyllis Weikart's Rhythmically Moving Series) and "Siege of Ennis" (Christy Lane's *Multicultural Folk Dance Guide,* Vol. 2).

Do You Know Swahili?

Social Studies

Dance of selected cultures

Physical Education

Learning selected folk dances

Grade Level

K through 6

Collaborate with the social studies teacher. What continent are the children studying? Select a folk dance from that continent and teach it to the children. Here we use Africa as an example.

Use the books written by Tom Feelings (*Moja Means One* and *Jambo Means Hello*) to teach Swahili words to the children, for example, *watoto* (children), *mama* (mother), *baba* (father), *schule* (school), *ngoma* (dance or celebration). Words for numbers are *moja, mbili, tatu, nne, tanu, sita, saba, nane.* Teach the children about inventions of Africans and African Americans, such as the ironing board, refrigerator, golf tee, pencil sharpener, mechanical corn harvester, egg beater, automatic traffic signal, automatic shoe-making machine, and automatic lubrication system for railroad cars.

Use a globe to locate Africa. Identify the countries within Africa. What do their flags look like? What goods do they produce? What is the climate like? Investigate the history and traditions. Teach selected dances from Africa to the children ("Bele Kawe" and "Jambo" from Phyllis Weikart's Rhythmically Moving Series or "The High Life" from Christy Lane's *Multicultural Folk Dance Guide,* Vol. 1).

Activities From Around the World

Social Studies

Activities from other cultures

Physical Education

Locomotor, nonlocomotor, and manipulative skills

Grade Level

K through 6

It is fun to learn about activities from other countries. Arrange for an immigrant or a person who is very knowledgeable about a country that you are studying to come to class. Ask the person to demonstrate games, dances, or leisure-time activities to the class. Have students participate in these activities.

I Love the USA

Social Studies

Celebrating living in the United States

Physical Education

Creative dance with music

Grade Level

3 through 6

Select a patriotic song, such as "My Country 'Tis of Thee," "This Land Is Your Land, This Land Is My Land," or "The Star-Spangled Banner." Have children, with a partner, create a dance that represents the song, then present their dance with the music to a small group or to the class.

Sing a New Song, Dance a New Dance

Social Studies

Celebrate other nationalities

Physical Education

Creative dance with music

Grade Level

3 through 6

"Select a patriotic song from a country that you are studying in social studies. Find out the English translation, if necessary, and create a dance that represents the song. You and a partner can present your dance with the music for a small group or to the class."

Global Jump Rope

Social Studies

Cultural groups and exercise

Physical Education

Jumping rope

Grade Level

K through 6

"People in many cultures jump rope. Double-dutch was first played in the Netherlands. In China, children jump a rubber rope, which you might call a Chinese jump rope. In the United States we often jump a turned rope to jump rope chants. Let's form three different stations: one for double-dutch, one for Chinese jump rope, and one for self-turned jump rope to chants. Practice at each station. Which station did you like best?"

Exercise Is for Everyone

Social Studies

Cultural groups and exercise

Physical Education

Physical fitness

Grade Level

2 through 6

It is interesting to examine exercise around the world. Choose a culture and discover the types of exercise that are popular in that culture. For example, the Chinese participate in an activity called tai chi. Be prepared to demonstrate and have the class participate in your activity.

Birthday Traditions

Social Studies

Celebrating holidays

Physical Education

Creating and performing a movement sequence

Grade Level

K through 6

"Discuss how your family celebrates birthdays. Do you have a special cake, play games, or dance? Now make a movement sequence that demonstrates one of your special traditions."

The Johnny Appleseed Apple Dance

Social Studies

Celebrating holidays

Physical Education

Creating and performing a movement sequence

Grade Level

K through 6

Johnny Appleseed is often associated with Arbor Day, a day that celebrates planting trees. Johnny Appleseed lived in the late 1700s and early 1800s and traveled around planting apple trees and giving seeds to others for planting. Have students create an "Apple Dance" that reflects the actions of Johnny Appleseed.

Dances From Around the World

Social Studies

Dances from around the world

Physical Education

Cultural or folk dance

Grade Level

K through 6

Have the children learn folk dances based on a theme that is common to a variety of cultures. Themes could be occupations, agriculture, animals, weddings or celebrations; they could also be gender specific. Have the students compare and contrast how the dance movements and formations are similar and different.

GEOGRAPHY

Moving Through the Seasons

Social Studies

Activities during different seasons

Physical Education

Creating and performing a movement sequence

Grade Level

K through 6

"You participate in different activities during each of the four seasons. Show us some of the activities that you do in the spring, summer, fall, and winter. Then we'll discuss how the seasons affect what we do."

Let's Travel in February

Social Studies

Climates in the United States

Physical Education

Creating and performing a movement sequence

Grade Level

3 through 6

"The temperature of a region or state plays an important role in the climate. You are going to take an imaginary trip through the United States during February. Take a good look at the big map of the United States. You will travel in a straight line from Florida to Washington State. With a partner, make a movement sequence that represents how the temperature changes affect your journey."

Temperature Jump

Social Studies

Climate in the United States

Physical Education

Physical fitness

Grade Level

K through 6

"This task is divided into two sections. First, you will make a bar graph of the average monthly temperature in selected cities across the United States during the last year. For example, you might choose International Falls, Minnesota; Miami, Florida; Honolulu, Hawaii; Anchorage, Alaska; Boston, Massachusetts; Kansas City, Kansas; Las Vegas, Nevada; Los Angeles, California; Chicago, Illinois; and Seattle, Washington. Also include the city you live in. Make a separate chart for each city. Include all 12 months. Compare the bar graphs. What is the range of temperatures?—what is the very highest and the very lowest? What is the range of temperatures for each city? Which city has the largest and which has the smallest range?

Second, choose a city. Then, for each degree Fahrenheit of temperature, you will jump a self-turned rope one time. Begin with January: If the average temperature is 32, then take 32 jumps. Do this for each month. Discuss when you jumped the most and why, and if, there was a gradual increase and decrease in temperature through the year. Next, come up with your own physical activity for each month."

Move Around the World

Social Studies

Moving around the United States (or state or world)

Physical Education

Physical fitness

Grade Level

K through 6

This activity requires that a large map of the United States be painted, drawn, or projected from an overhead projector on a floor surface. Perhaps your class could volunteer to paint the map on the blacktop surface at your school. With the map students can do all sorts of fun activities. For example, they can create a balance shape in a state and name its capital, then travel to another state, create a different balance shape, and name its capital. An exercise routine could include activities such as running and standing on states that begin with an *M* and doing 20 curl-ups there, bear-walking to a state that borders on the Atlantic Ocean, skipping to the last five states that joined the Union, crab-walking to states that produce wheat, or sliding to states that border on another country.

These large maps present possibilities for many movement activities. You can select the activities yourself, or students can help. Students could each write an activity on an index card; the cards could be placed in a box and drawn at random.

Shape the States

Social Studies

Making the shapes of the states

Physical Education

Expressive movement

Grade Level

3 through 6

Have students work with one or more partners to form the shape of designated states with their bodies. "See how closely your bodies can match the shape of the state. Now make your shape on a different level."

Ongoing Strategies for the Physical Education Classroom

- Include place of origin when teaching games or sports. For example, when teaching badminton skills, mention that the sport originated in India and England.
- Discuss current events in physical education, dance, or sport at the beginning of class. Examples are events such as the World Series, World Cup, NCAA

Championships, National Physical Education and Sport Week or National Dance Week, and Super Bowl. Other possibilities include national news about players or teams; local news about a player who attends the school; announcements of a community race or walk occurring in the near future, Jump Rope for Heart or Hoops for Heart events, or cultural festivals.

- Use the names of geographic locations for bases, rock wall climbs, goals.
- Discuss how technology has changed equipment and access to information.
- Use world languages taught in the school for counting, identifying different movements, and team names.
- Include music for warm-ups, skill practice, or dance that represents different cultures or time periods.
- Use bulletin boards to display pictures of people of different cultural backgrounds, gender, disabilities, and ages.
- Post rules for games, social responsibility, and behavior.

Summary

Many ideas for integrating movement and social studies are presented in this chapter. You can use these ideas in integrated lessons, and you may want to expand on the ideas according to your own goals for the lesson. You should be especially conscious of requiring quality movement from students. Students need to understand that the purpose of their movement generally is to communicate a concept. A challenge in each lesson should be to perfect movement as much as possible.

Integrating Physical Education With the Arts

As teachers begin their day they frequently spend a few minutes informally chatting about their plans for the day. One informal meeting between the physical education teacher and art teacher ended in an interdisciplinary project titled "The Moving Museum." The art teacher was focused on teaching the meaning and design of African masks while the physical education teacher was planning a creative dance unit. During the art classes, students wrote about personal characteristics that expressed their identity and created masks using various materials. Students brought their writing and masks to the physical education class and cooperated in small groups to create 1-minute movement sequences that communicated the meaning of their masks. Each group was assigned a performance station in the gym. Students from other classes were invited to view the mini-performances as they switched to a different station every minute. "The Moving Museum" integrated dance, visual art, writing, African mask aesthetics, and personal meaning making.

The arts—music, theater arts, dance, and visual arts—are embedded in our daily life (figure 7.1). They provide means of expression that go beyond ordinary speaking and writing. They can express intimate thoughts and feelings. They are a unique record of diverse cultures and the ways in which cultures have developed over time. The arts provide distinctive ways of understanding human beings and nature. The arts are creative modes through which all people can enrich their lives by both self-expression and response to the expressions of others (College Board, 1983). Dance is also considered one of the arts and is a content area within physical education. It is included as an essential part of the physical education discipline in this book.

Most students have some exposure to the arts during their formal education. These experiences are as varied as the content presented. Some students may simply observe art as an illustration in a picture book; others may participate in a sequential music program; and still others are involved on a daily basis through arts magnet schools. Learning through and in the arts engages the imagination, fosters flexible ways of thinking, develops disciplined effort, and builds self-confidence. Art experiences will permanently enhance the quality of a student's life, whether he or she continues artistic activity as an avocation or a career or maintains an appreciation of the arts as an observer or audience member.

The arts are characterized by three artistic processes: creating, performing or interpreting, and responding to one's own art or the art of others. The arts provide important lessons in communication and offer a means for students to record and express their feelings, ideas, and observations about life. Through the arts, students gain a greater self-awareness and a deeper understanding of the world in which they live.

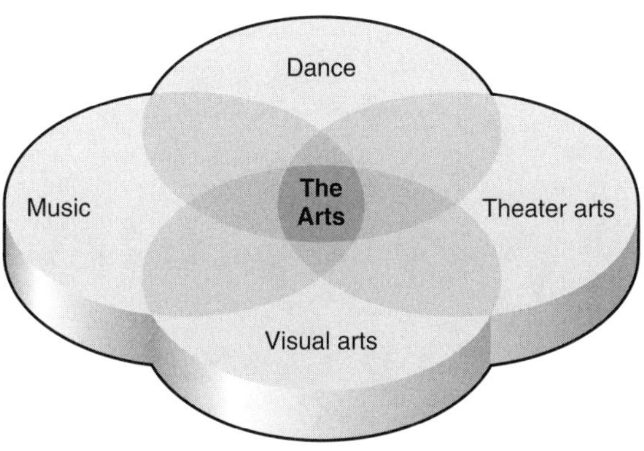

Figure 7.1 The arts community of music, theater arts, dance, and visual arts.

This chapter addresses the integration of music, theater arts, and visual arts with physical education. The content for the music, theater arts, and visual arts disciplines, included in the scope and sequence sections of this chapter, is defined by the *National Standards for Arts Education* (Consortium of National Arts Education Associations, 1994). Additional information gathered from various state standards documents,

curriculum guides, and program activities is included in this chapter. You may find a slightly different approach or version in your state or school district, one that has undoubtedly been designed to address your local perspectives and needs.

According to Elliot Eisner (1998), the development of literacy and the use of one symbol system bear on the development and use of literacy in other symbol systems. Eisner's words are particularly applicable to the integration of the arts and physical education. Children discover new ways to learn, communicate, interact, create, understand, and perform when they experience the concepts and skills learned in music, theater arts, and visual arts programs through movement.

Music is a basic expression of human culture and is perhaps the discipline most integrated with physical education. It comprises singing, performing on instruments, composing and arranging music, reading and notation, and listening and evaluating. Music naturally accompanies dancing and is frequently used to provide a rhythm for jump rope routines, warm-up exercises, or simply bouncing a ball.

The theater arts enable students to learn about themselves and others, about actions and consequences, and about customs and beliefs. It is a complex discipline that encompasses many different areas, including acting, directing, playwriting, and set designing. Acting and directing can be easily integrated with physical education, while playwriting and set designing can be related indirectly. Sport themes can be used as the inspiration for an improvised or scripted scene, or movement can be used to convey a message, as actors do with their bodies.

Education in the visual arts includes a wide range of media, techniques, and processes. Personal experiences are translated into visual form, from which the child can discover clues about him- or herself. The child can be actively involved in drawing, painting, sculpture, design, architecture, film, video, and folk arts. When developing learning experiences that integrate the visual arts and physical education, you can focus on the elements of art and principles of design, the different types of media, and the historical and cultural context. You can discuss how changes in design elements have affected the development of sport equipment (e.g., color of balls, shapes of sticks, clothing fashions), fill a fitness bulletin board with students' drawings and paintings, or create a dance about how a sculpture might move in space.

Scope and Sequence for Music

"MUSIC IS ONE OF THE GREAT PLEASURES OF LIFE. IT HAS THE POWER TO COMMAND OUR ATTENTION AND INSPIRE US. IT SPEAKS TO OUR SPIRIT AND TO OUR INNER FEELINGS. IT PROVOKES THOUGHTS ABOUT THE MYSTERIES OF LIFE, SUCH AS WHY WE EXIST, THE VASTNESS OF THE UNIVERSE, AND OUR PURPOSE ON EARTH. MUSIC REACHES DEEP INTO OUR NATURE TO CONSOLE US, TO REASSURE US, AND TO HELP US EXPRESS WHO AND WHAT WE ARE AS HUMAN BEINGS"

Fowler, 1994, p. 5

The matrix in table 7.1 indicates the grades in which specific music skills and concepts are presented. Skills and concepts introduced during the primary grades are continued during the intermediate grades at higher levels and with more complexity.

PRIMARY-GRADE MUSIC SKILLS AND CONCEPTS

Students in the primary grades are learning to enjoy and explore a variety of music. Their early hands-on experiences allow them to gain musical skills and knowledge

Table 7.1

Scope and Sequence of Music Concepts Taught in Elementary Schools

CONCEPT	GRADE						
Music	K	1	2	3	4	5	6
Singing independently and with others	×	×	×	×	×	×	×
Performing on instruments	×	×	×	×	×	×	×
Improvising melodies, variations, and accompaniment	×	×	×	×	×	×	×
Composing and arranging music	×	×	×	×	×	×	×
Reading and notating music	×	×	×	×	×	×	×
Listening to, analyzing, and describing music	×	×	×	×	×	×	×
Evaluating music and musical performances	×	×	×	×	×	×	×
Making connections between music, the other arts, and other curricular areas	×	×	×	×	×	×	×
Understanding music in relation to history and culture	×	×	×	×	×	×	×

while singing, playing instruments, creating music, and moving to music. Learning to read and notate music is introduced, along with opportunities to explore music independently and with others. As students listen to a variety of music from various cultures and different time periods, they begin to identify common musical elements and characteristics and the role that music plays in their lives. They understand how to use music as a means of individual expression and are developing the ability to listen to the creations of other people with respect, curiosity, and pleasure.

INTERMEDIATE-GRADE MUSIC SKILLS AND CONCEPTS

Students at the intermediate level build on the skills they developed in the primary grades. They can generally sing a melodic line with accurate use of pitch and rhythm and some expressive quality. Instruction in playing instruments becomes more complex with the study of keyboard, band, and orchestral instruments. The students can compose and improvise simple melodies and rhythms that demonstrate their understanding of the structure of music. Through their own performances, they attempt to communicate ideas and feelings and to recognize ideas and feelings in the performances of others. They enjoy listening to a wider variety of music and can discuss their personal response to it.

Scope and Sequence for Theater Arts

THEATRE IS . . . A STUDY OF LIFE. IT IS THE STUDY OF THINGS THAT MOTIVATE PEOPLE TO DO THE THINGS THEY DO AND LIVE AS THEY DO.

Baker and Wagner, 1977, p. 24

Table 7.2

Scope and Sequence of Theater Arts Concepts Taught in Elementary Schools

CONCEPT	GRADE						
Theater arts	**K**	**1**	**2**	**3**	**4**	**5**	**6**
Making and writing plays	×	×	×	×	×	×	×
Acting in formal or informal presentations	×	×	×	×	×	×	×
Designing and arranging environments for informal and formal presentations	×	×	×	×	×	×	×
Directing by planning improvised and scripted scenes	×	×	×	×	×	×	×
Researching information to support improvised and scripted scenes	×	×	×	×	×	×	×
Comparing and integrating art forms	×	×	×	×	×	×	×
Analyzing and explaining personal preferences and constructing meanings from dramatizations and theater, film, television, and electronic media productions	×	×	×	×	×	×	×
Relating theater arts to cultures, times, and places	×	×	×	×	×	×	×

The matrix in table 7.2 indicates the grades in which specific theater arts skills and concepts are presented. Skills and concepts introduced during the primary grades are continued during the intermediate grades at higher levels and with more complexity.

PRIMARY-GRADE THEATER ARTS SKILLS AND CONCEPTS

Young children eagerly engage in theater arts activities through acting out favorite stories, creating original situations from life experiences, and imagining themselves in fantasy worlds. Frequently, they create events and costumes, assign roles, and develop dialogue individually or with one or two other children. As a socializing activity and a means of learning, the children explore the skills and knowledge related to acting, writing, designing, and researching and begin to develop an aesthetic awareness necessary for analyzing and critiquing.

INTERMEDIATE-GRADE THEATER ARTS SKILLS AND CONCEPTS

At the intermediate level, students begin to develop scripts and scenarios that involve characters and environments and improvise dialogue to tell a story. They use movement and vocal expression to define characters and design scenery, props, costumes, lighting, and sound to communicate the locale and mood. Intermediate-grade students are able to identify and use the elements that make a dramatic work successful and to provide rationale for their personal choices in their creative and performing work. Collaborative initiatives develop during this period. These efforts bring all the elements of theater together to produce an improvised or scripted presentation on a stage or for a film, television, or other electronic media. When students create a dramatic work,

they are able to use perspectives from various cultures, time periods, and places to project their own understanding of life.

Scope and Sequence for Visual Arts

THE VISUAL ARTS INTERPRET AND REFLECT LIFE. THROUGH STUDYING ART, CHILDREN GAIN VALUABLE INSIGHTS ABOUT THE WORLD ALONG WITH KNOWLEDGE AND SKILLS THEY CAN USE THROUGHOUT THEIR LIVES.

National Art Education Association, 1991, p. 1

The matrix in table 7.3 indicates the grades in which specific visual arts skills and concepts are presented. Skills and concepts introduced during the primary grades are continued during the intermediate grades at higher levels and with more complexity.

Table 7.3

Scope and Sequence of Visual Arts Concepts Taught in Elementary Schools

CONCEPT	GRADE						
Visual arts	**K**	**1**	**2**	**3**	**4**	**5**	**6**
Understanding and applying media techniques and processes	×	×	×	×	×	×	×
Using knowledge of structures and functions	×	×	×	×	×	×	×
Choosing and evaluating a range of subject matter, symbols, and ideas	×	×	×	×	×	×	×
Understanding the visual arts in relation to history and cultures	×	×	×	×	×	×	×
Reflecting on and analyzing the characteristics and merits of one's own work and the work of others	×	×	×	×	×	×	×
Making connections between visual arts and other disciplines	×	×	×	×	×	×	×

PRIMARY-GRADE VISUAL ARTS SKILLS AND CONCEPTS

In the primary grades, children enjoy experimenting with many different art materials. The school environment may be the first place where children receive visual arts instruction and learn to make choices that enhance communication of their ideas. Creating is the key to this instruction. Skills of observation, eye-hand coordination, and manipulation of various tools are developing. Children begin to understand the purpose of visual arts in their lives and the role the visual arts play in different cultures.

INTERMEDIATE-GRADE VISUAL ARTS SKILLS AND CONCEPTS

Students in the intermediate grades continue to explore various art media, techniques, and processes. Visual expressions become more individualistic and imaginative. The students continue to formulate their own understandings and criteria for making critical judgments related to structure and function, content, techniques, and purpose. Through increased exposure to artworks from a variety of historical periods and cultures, students gain a deeper awareness of their own values and the values of other people. They begin to understand that art is influenced not only by aesthetic ideas but also by many societal customs and beliefs.

Learning Experiences

Each of the four learning experiences (table 7.4) demonstrates one of the interdisciplinary teaching models presented in chapter 1. The learning experiences have been designed to include skills and concepts from physical education and music, theater arts, and visual arts. For each learning experience we provide a name, suggested grade level, interdisciplinary teaching model, objectives, equipment, organization, complete description of the lesson, and assessment suggestions. In addition, tips on what to look for in student responses, suggestions for how you can change or modify the lesson, and ideas for teachable moments are offered to provide further insights into each learning experience.

Table 7.4

Music, Theater Arts, and Visual Arts Learning Experience Index

Skills and concepts	Name	Suggested grade level	Interdisciplinary teaching model
Theater arts: acting as circus animals and performers Physical education: traveling movements and balances	The Circus Performers	K-1	Partnership
Visual arts: repetition in patterns Physical education: tossing, catching, and bouncing to self	Patterns in Action	3-6	Shared
Music: tempo and rhythm Physical education: shapes—straight, twisted, and round	Tempo Dance	2-4	Connected
Music: choosing or creating music to express a mood or feeling Theater arts: creating a character that will travel on a pathway Visual arts: drawing different types of lines to express an idea Physical education: creating a dance emphasizing pathways	Lines of Expression	4-6	Shared

The Circus Performers

Suggested Grade Level

Primary (K and 1)

Interdisciplinary Teaching Model

Partnership

The students, while studying the circus, create their own circus as part of the unit of study. You and the theater arts teacher research and collect information on the circus and plan a series of learning experiences. Both of you will teach in the classroom and the gymnasium.

Theater Arts

Acting as circus animals and performers

Physical Education

Traveling movements and balances

Objectives

As a result of participating in this lesson, the students will

- travel using different directions (forward, backward, sideways);
- practice using forward, backward, and sideways rolls;
- practice balances using different body parts;
- be exposed to basic acting skills; and
- present an improvisational scene based on the actions and characteristics of a circus animal or performer.

Equipment

Mats, hoops, tape lines, individual jump ropes, and circus music

Organization

Groups of three, four, or five students

Description

> This learning experience represents one class in a series of sessions in which you and the classroom teacher have integrated your curricula around the theme of the circus. In preparation for this class, previous classroom activities have focused on the characters, history, events, and activities that relate to a circus. The physical education gymnastics curriculum has prepared the students for this event, and the gymnastics skills will be used to facilitate the movements of the circus performers and animals. You and the theater arts teacher will use creative dramatics as a means for the children to express their knowledge and understanding of a circus and its components.

"During the next few classes, we will create our own circus. Some of you will be the circus performers, some will be the tightrope walkers, others the trapeze artists, and still others the juggling clowns. You will also have the chance to perform as a lion or a horse doing tricks in the circus. Let's begin to warm up our bodies so that we can

move in many different ways." Lead the children in a warm-up that prepares them for balancing, rolling, and traveling movements.

"Now that we are warmed up, let's start creating movements for the lions and horses." Either you or the theater arts teacher leads the children in a discussion about the characteristics of the lions and horses and records the responses on the chalkboard (figure 7.2).

Figure 7.2 **Brainstorming about lions and horses.**

"Your ideas about lions and horses were great. Let's practice some of the movements you described. First, let's show how the lions travel on their hands and feet. Can someone show us how a lion would walk? How will the lion hold its head? Show me how you take big, strong steps. How can you change your hands into the shape of a lion's paws? How will your arms and legs move when you roar like a lion? When I raise my hand, everyone practice your loud roar and lion movements, and when I lower my hand, you should stop."

- Ask several children to demonstrate their roar and movements using their voice and body. The class observes and discusses how the students use their voice and body to make the roar and movements of a lion.

"This time when you perform your lion roar and movements, decide what kind of lion you will be. Are you a small, shy lion? A big, ferocious lion? A scared lion? Or maybe you are a silly lion. Show me how your lion will move."

- Have the children practice their lion roar and movements; then ask each one to demonstrate.

"Now it's time to practice jumping through the hoop and rolling on the mat. I will hold the hoop as you jump through using your hands and feet. Then you may choose to roll

forward, backward, or sideways on the mat. Now let's put all our lion actions together into a short scene. First, all the different kinds of lions walk out of their cages and sit in a big circle. I will play the lion tamer, and when I raise my hand, you will stretch up and use your hands as paws when you roar. Then when I point to you, you will jump through the hoop, roll over, and return to your cage."

- Several children can play the part of the lion tamer—each assuming this role with his or her own small group of lions.

"Now let's create the movements for the horses using the words on the board. We are going to gallop to demonstrate the prancing rhythm of the horses. You will hold your hands up to act as the front legs of the horse. How can you position your hands to show the shape of the hooves? Amy, would you please show us your creation? Wonderful, now let's practice galloping in a big circle, thinking about how the horses love to perform and show off for an audience."

- Children practice galloping in a big circle.

"The horses stop and slowly turn in place to show their favorite trick of balancing on their rear hooves and turning around. They end the trick by pawing the ground with their rear hooves and bowing to the audience. They are very proud of this trick. Now try standing on your toes and the balls of your feet with your front arms and hands reaching to the ceiling, and slowly turn in place. How can you move your feet to show the horses pawing the ground? Juan, can we see your idea? Excellent, now let me hear from all of you. What type of sound will you make as you do a bow? You are doing a good job of balancing as you make a small turn. Now continue to gallop around in the circle."

- Describe the sequence of movements for the horses: galloping out into the circle, stopping to turn and balance, pawing the ground, taking a bow, and galloping off to the stables. Children practice the traveling and balancing movements as you relate the sequence.

"Next, we are going to create movements for the juggling clowns, the trapeze artists, and the tightrope walkers. First, let's create the clowns."

- The children have previously written descriptions and drawn pictures of the type of clown they would like to be. They take a moment to read their description and view their drawing. Now they will use this information to bring their clown to life. Lead the students through an imaginary scene in which they put on their clown costume and makeup. The children practice smiling and laughing in different ways that represent the type of clown they have become.

"Wow! The clowns look great, very funny. I am sure the audience will have a wonderful time watching these clowns juggle. Now let's invent many different ways to pretend we are juggling. First think about what you will be juggling—balls, scarves, rings. What else can you juggle? How many objects will you have? What size and color are they? Do you juggle high, low, in front of your body, in back of your body, standing on one foot, using one hand? Do you drop any of the objects? When I turn on the circus music, you can create your own way to juggle. Ready, go."

- Students practice different juggling movements; some pretend to drop an object, some juggle with other clowns, others fall down while juggling, and still others create different ways to juggle.

"For this part of the circus performance, the clowns will skip out into the circus ring and begin their juggling acts; then they will take a bow together, fall down, and roll over sideways. Then they get up, brush themselves off, take a second bow, and fall and

roll over again. Finally, they stand up, bow together, and do not fall down. They skip out of the space waving to the audience. Let's practice this scene."

- The children practice the scene together and then participate in a discussion about the different ways they juggled.

"The next two circus acts will take us high above the circus ring. First, we will move as a tightrope walker, and then we'll pretend to be the high-flying trapeze artist swinging across the space. Let's look at these pictures of people walking on the tightrope."

- Present three pictures: one from a picture book about a circus, a second from a printed program distributed at a circus, and a painting of a tightrope walker that one of the students brought to school. The children discuss what the performers are wearing, how they feel when performing, where they live, how they became interested in tightrope walking, and what happened to them if they have ever fallen. They create a background for the character.

"You are going to become tightrope walkers and pretend you are many, many feet up in the air walking on a rope. Now, each of you should find a tape line to stand on, with space in front of you to walk forward. Slowly begin to walk forward, stepping only on your line. Try walking backward, walking sideways, turning, balancing on one foot or in a squat or a straddle position. Now create a tightrope routine that uses walking, turning, and two balances. Practice your routine, staying on the line the entire time."

- You and the other teacher visit each of the children, observe their practice, and make suggestions to help them improve their performance.

"The last performer is the amazing, high-flying trapeze artist. We can't really fly across the space; however, we can create the feeling of flying across the space using rocking, running, and leaping. Now, let's look at a video of a trapeze circus act."

- Show a video of a trapeze act and lead a discussion with the children about the cooperation and trust needed between the performers to ensure their success. The discussion continues about how cooperation and trust help people attain success in everyday life.

"Now you will practice rocking, running, and leaping, first by yourselves and then with a partner. Find a space so you have some room in front of you to complete a short run and a leap. To begin rocking, place one foot in front of the other and shift your weight forward and backward. Reach up with your hands as if you are holding on to the trapeze bar. Let's practice rocking forward and backward for eight counts. Ready, one, two, three, four, five, six, seven, eight. At the end of the eighth count, you will take six running steps and leap up into the air. Then take a couple of steps to recover from the leap, stop, turn around, and repeat the rock, run, and leap going back across the space. Let's try it together. Ready, rock, two, three, four, five, six, seven, eight; run, run, run, run, run, run, and leap; recover; and stop. Turn around, and let's try it again. Now I will give each of you a jump rope. Fold the rope in half and hold each end like a trapeze bar. Now try the trapeze movement again holding the rope."

- Students practice the trapeze movement sequence individually, moving smoothly from one movement to another.

"The next part of the trapeze movement will be done with a partner. After I give you a partner, stand side by side with him or her. Practice performing the trapeze movements so that you both are moving at exactly the same time. You and your partner should rock forward and backward at the same time, run at the same time, leap into the air at the same time, and recover and stop together." (See figure 7.3.)

Figure 7.3 Partners performing trapeze movements simultaneously.

- Students practice together to match their movements as closely as possible. You and the other teacher visit each pair and comment on the positive cooperation exhibited by the two students that has enabled them to successfully move together.

"Now that you have tried each of the different circus acts, we are going to put together the entire circus. You will be asked to select a role as either a lion or a horse, and then you will choose to perform either as one of the clowns, as one of the tightrope walkers, or as one of the trapeze artists."

- Organize the students into small groups that represent the selected circus performers. Several students are selected to be the lion tamers, horse trainers, and ringmasters. Over the next several days, in their classroom space, the students finalize the development of the sequence of circus scenes, create a script for the ringmasters, add simple costumes, and create scenery. On returning to the gymnasium, the students are ready to bring their circus to life.

"Today we will practice each part of the circus so that the movements are performed well and everyone is clear about the order of the performance. First, the ringmasters will make their announcements; then each circus act will be performed."

- The students acting the part of the ringmasters read their scripted introduction. They welcome everyone to the circus and introduce the first act, the tightrope walkers. Students who have elected to perform in this act do their walk, turn, and balance sequences and take a bow. The ringmasters continue to introduce each

of the acts: the lions, the clowns, the horses, and finally the trapeze artists. Each student makes the necessary costume and scenery adjustments for each act. The audience is composed of the classmates in the other acts.

Assessment Suggestion

Have a checklist of the movement sequences for each act. Keep a record indicating whether the students can perform the complete sequence or only parts of the sequence. In addition, the students can represent, through some form of visual arts, one of the acts they elected to perform, or they can write about their experience and choices in an entry in a journal.

Look For

- Whether students are able to perform combinations of movements smoothly.
- Correct use of the body in rolling and traveling movements.
- Students using control moving in and out of balances. Students should not fall out of a balance.
- The different ways students use their body and its parts to express the animals and human performers in the circus.
- The ability to cooperate and move with other children in pairs and small groups.

How Can I Change This?

- Use other circus performers, such as elephants, tumblers, bears, or equestrians.
- Take the ringmaster role yourself, so that all the students can perform in all the acts.
- Each group of students creates a mini-circus.
- Ask the visual arts teacher to help with scenery, costumes, drawings, paintings, or three-dimensional representations of the circus.
- Ask the music teacher to recommend different types of music or percussion instruments that can accompany each circus act.

Teachable Moment

Students can create their own gymnastics sequences to represent the movements in each of the circus acts. This is good way to teach them to make smooth transitions between movements and create a sequence of movements.

Patterns in Action

Suggested Grade Level

Intermediate (3 through 6)

Interdisciplinary Teaching Model

Shared

You and the visual arts teacher teach about patterns in your own programs at more or less the same time. Meet to discuss how you will teach patterns in the respective disciplines. When teaching, both of you will be able to refer to the other discipline to help students make the connection.

Visual Arts

Repetition in patterns

Physical Education

Tossing, catching, and bouncing to self

Objectives

As a result of participating in this lesson, the students will

- practice tossing a ball to different heights;
- practice catching a ball from different heights;
- practice bouncing a ball while stationary and while traveling;
- practice coordinating the transition from bouncing to tossing a ball and from catching to bouncing;
- create patterns that can be accurately repeated using tossing, catching, and bouncing to self; and
- understand how the concept of patterns is used in physical education and the visual arts.

Equipment

One 8½-inch (21.6-centimeter) playground ball (about the size of a soccer ball) for each student

Organization

Students work individually.

Description

"Good morning! Today we are going to create a pattern as you toss, catch, and bounce a ball to yourself. Your art teacher and I have agreed to teach patterns over the next several weeks. This will give you the chance to experience the different ways patterns exist in the world, and it will also give you the opportunity to create your own patterns in art and in physical education. First, let's look around the room and at our clothing for patterns. Tell me about one of the patterns you see."

- Several students describe patterns in their clothing, the patterns of the cement blocks forming the walls, and the patterns of the lights in the ceiling.

"You are going to warm up by repeating the pattern of running for 30 seconds and walking for 15 seconds. I will give you a signal when it's time to change the pattern. Begin with the run. Ready, go."

- Students repeat the run-and-walk pattern for several minutes.

"Now I would like you to warm up your arms by creating a pattern composed of three different arm movements. Each arm movement is performed three times. Keep repeating your pattern until I signal you to stop."

- Students create an arm pattern and practice the sequence.

"Now I would like for each of you to get a ball and practice tossing the ball to yourself and catching it without dropping it. Change the height of the toss each time so that it is sometimes only a foot above your head and sometimes as high as you can toss it without hitting the ceiling. Practice catching the ball falling from the different heights.

What are some of the different ways to toss the ball into the air? How are your hands placed on the ball, and where is the ball when you begin the toss?"

- Several students demonstrate tossing the ball in different ways and describe how they change the force to attain different heights. The other students observe and try the different strategies suggested by the demonstrators.

"You are now going to practice bouncing a ball while stationary and then while traveling. I will call out a series of bouncing tasks for you to practice. Ready, find a space. Begin bouncing with your dominant hand with the ball at waist level. Try the same with your other hand, now with alternating hands. How fast can you bounce the ball while alternating hands? Bounce the ball around your body, keeping your feet still. Now lift your right leg and bounce the ball under it, now under the left leg. Can you alternate bouncing under your right leg and then under your left? Can you bounce the ball while changing the height of the ball, sometimes very low to the floor and sometimes at waist height? Travel forward and then backward while bouncing the ball. Now try sliding to the right and then to the left while bouncing. Can you move forward, backward, right, and then left while doing five bounces in each direction? Create your own bouncing idea that alternates using bouncing in a stationary space with bouncing while traveling."

- As students practice their bouncing idea, circulate among them to observe their progress and offer feedback.

"The next task is to create a pattern that uses tossing, catching, and bouncing to yourself. You can choose your own arrangement; however, you must have control of the ball at all times. Having control means that you do not drop the ball when tossing and catching. You are using control when you are bouncing if the ball does not roll away from you as you bounce it."

- Demonstrate what losing control looks like.

"Combine ways to toss, catch, and bounce the ball that you can do well, and practice a smooth transition between the toss, the catch, and the bounce."

- You can demonstrate a pattern you have created or have the students begin working on their own patterns. Circulate among the students and comment on positive ball control, assist students where necessary to achieve success, and offer additional challenges to students.

"Now I will assign you to a group of three or four, and each person will take a turn to demonstrate his or her pattern to the group. After you perform your pattern, you will complete the self-assessment form."

Assessment Suggestion

Have a checklist for assessing the students' ability to accurately perform the pattern without losing control of the ball. For example, a plus sign indicates accurately repeating the pattern twice without losing control of the ball. A check indicates losing control of the ball once in two repetitions of the pattern, and a minus sign indicates repeating the pattern twice but losing control of the ball two or more times. Students can practice their pattern and repeat the assessment to demonstrate improvement.

Look For

- Control during tossing, catching, and bouncing to self.
- A controlled transition between the toss, catch, and bounce.

- Students who need help to organize their ideas into a repeatable pattern. Some children may have many wonderful ideas but need help to select only two or three for the pattern.

How Can I Change This?

- Have students teach each other their patterns.
- Use a different type of ball.
- Have students add traveling movements to the pattern, such as walking, skipping, galloping, hopping, or jumping.
- Have students work with a partner to create a pattern and perform the same pattern in unison.
- Add music to the performances.

Teachable Moment

Students can draw symbols that represent the different parts of their pattern, such as a circle to represent the toss and catch and a triangle to represent the bounce. They create a visual pattern on paper that represents the sequence of their pattern (figure 7.4).

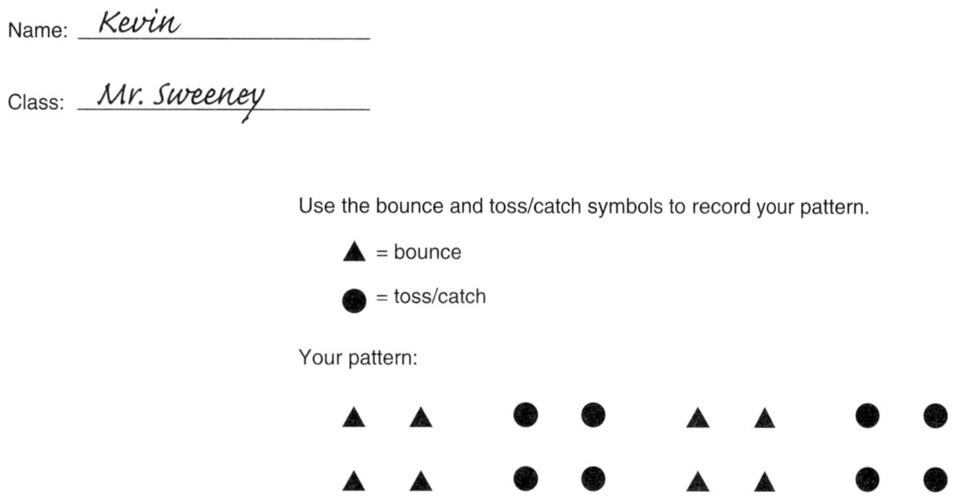

Name: *Kevin*

Class: *Mr. Sweeney*

Use the bounce and toss/catch symbols to record your pattern.

▲ = bounce

● = toss/catch

Your pattern:

▲ ▲ ● ● ▲ ▲ ● ●

▲ ▲ ● ● ▲ ▲ ● ●

Figure 7.4 **Using symbols to record a pattern.**

Tempo Dance

Suggested Grade Level

Primary/Intermediate (2 through 4)

Interdisciplinary Teaching Model

Connected

Music is used to accompany dance movements.

Music

Tempo and rhythm

Physical Education

Creating shapes—straight, twisted, and round

Objectives

As a result of participating in this lesson, the students will

- create straight, twisted, and round shapes with their bodies;
- practice traveling movements in a forward, backward, or sideways direction;
- design a short dance that has a beginning, a middle, and an end;
- coordinate the tempo and rhythm of the dance movements with the tempo and rhythm of the music; and
- change dance movements to reflect different types of music.

Equipment

Tape or CD player; two pieces of music—one with a fast tempo and a strong rhythm and the second with a slow tempo and a light quality; handheld drum and mallet

Organization

Students work individually.

Description

"In this lesson you will compose a short dance that uses straight, twisted, and round shapes with traveling movements, and then you will perform the dance using two very different pieces of music. You will explore how the same movements can be performed to fast music and then to slow music. Let's begin with a warm-up using slow and fast music."

- Prepare a warm-up movement sequence using different body parts. First, the sequence is performed slowly; then the same warm-up is repeated at a fast tempo.

"Now that you are ready to move, I want you to create a straight shape with your whole body. Practice making different straight shapes. Find a way to move very slowly from one straight shape to the next. I am going to play a slow, steady beat on the drum as you move from one straight shape to the next. Let's try it. . . . Great job! Now, you'll try making a different straight shape as quickly as you can. I will beat the drum once and you will quickly make a straight shape. Ready, go. Now make another straight shape and another different straight shape each time I beat the drum. . . . Fantastic! Now we'll alternate slowly making a straight shape and quickly making a different straight shape. I will play four slow, soft beats on the drum for the slow shape and one strong, loud beat for the quick, straight shape. . . . Nice straight shapes!"

- Play the alternating sequence several times.

"Now let's try the same idea of making shapes quickly and slowly using round shapes, and then we'll make twisted shapes."

- Repeat the same sequence of tasks for making the round and then the twisted shapes.

"Next let's explore different ways to travel in the space using a fast and slow tempo. First, the fast tempo. I will play a tape of fast music. I want you to listen to the music and think about three ways you can travel to the music."

- Play the music for 30 seconds and then ask the students to share their suggestions for traveling fast. Students can demonstrate and verbally explain their answer.

"Now each of you will try your first answer. When I play the music, you travel, and when the music stops, I want you to stop and slowly make a straight shape. Ready, travel."

- Play the music; the students travel quickly around the space and slowly make a straight shape when the music stops. You can ask several students to demonstrate how they changed from the fast traveling movement to making a straight shape slowly. Then the students repeat the sequence twice, using their second and third ideas for traveling fast. Instruct them to add a round shape after the second way to travel and a twisted shape after the third way to travel.

"The next way to travel in the space is using the slow music. First, listen to the slow music I have selected, and picture in your mind how you can travel slowly."

- Play the slow music and leave it on as you present the next task.

"Now as the music continues, I want you to slowly begin to move your arms and then your whole body. Use one of your traveling ideas to move slowly in the space. Think about what steps you will use. Add a slow turn as you travel. Now change direction, moving forward sometimes, then backward, and maybe sideways."

- Students explore different ways to travel slowly forward, backward, and sideways. Circulate among the students and comment on the different types of steps they are using.

"In the next part of this lesson, you will create a dance using the sequence I have written on the chalkboard." (See figure 7.5.)

"Begin your dance in a straight shape, slowly move out of the shape, and then travel to another place in the space. Stop and quickly make a twisted shape, holding the shape as you count to four, then travel to another place in the space, and end your dance by slowly

Figure 7.5 Using straight, twisted, and round shapes in a sequence while traveling.

making a round shape. Now you have 5 minutes to create the shapes and the traveling movements and to choose where you will move and make the shapes in the space."

- The students begin to create their dances using the sequence outlined. No music is played while they are working on the dance.

"Now that you have completed your dance, I will play two different types of music, and I want you to make changes in your movements to coordinate with the tempo and rhythm of the music. Listen to the first piece of music, and picture in your mind how you will perform your dance to the music. The first selection is a slow piece of music."

- The students listen to the music.

"I will play the music again, and this time try your dance to the music. Everyone take your places and begin in your straight shape. Ready, begin."

- Students practice their dances using the slow-tempo music. Encourage them to practice their dances several times.

"The next music selection is fast music with a strong rhythm. Listen and think about how your dance movements will be performed to this type of music."

- The students listen to the music and then try their dances several times to the music.

"Would anyone like to share how you changed your dance movements to fit the different tempo and rhythm of the music? Tonya, what a wonderful change, great job! Is there anyone else who would like to share his or her changes?"

- Several students orally share their perceptions, and several volunteer to demonstrate their dance using the two types of music. The class comments on the similarities and differences they have observed in the dances.

"The last part of the lesson requires each of you to make a personal choice about which type of music you would prefer to use for your dance. Think about your choice as I play each piece of music once more."

- Play each selection once more. Then ask the students to perform their dance to the music they have selected. Play the slow music first; the students who selected this music perform their dance. Then the second group performs to the fast music.

Assessment Suggestions

- Students can describe in writing the type of music they selected for their final dance and include a statement on why they chose the slow or fast music.
- Students can make a drawing of their body in a straight, twisted, or round shape to accompany the writing.

Look For

- Clarity in making the straight, round, and twisted shapes. Is the whole body involved? How is the student using his or her torso, arms, legs, and head to express the shape?
- A variety of traveling movements—more than walking to the slow music and running to the fast music.
- The ability of the student to accurately repeat the dance using the shapes and traveling movements he or she has selected.
- Active participation in the discussions by many different students.

How Can I Change This?

- Use levels to define the shapes, such as a high-level, straight shape; a medium-level, twisted shape; or a low-level, round shape.
- Use music from different cultures that emphasizes changes in tempo and rhythm.
- Have students create their own dance sequence. First they can write the sequence and then they can practice the dance.
- Students can collaborate in pairs or small groups to create the dance.
- Students can select their own music that reflects two different types of tempo and rhythm.

Teachable Moment

You can show videotapes of professional dancers performing to different types of music. A discussion can follow about how the movements of the dancers coordinate with the music's tempo and rhythm. You can use dances from different cultures or different forms of dance, such as tap dance, ballet, hip-hop, or dancing on ice skates.

Lines of Expression

Suggested Grade Level

Intermediate (4 through 6)

Interdisciplinary Teaching Model

Shared

You and the visual arts, music, and theater arts teachers have agreed to focus on the concept of how lines represent a feeling or a mood. The students complete their study of lines in the visual arts class, compose music in the music class, and write descriptions of characters and scenes during a lesson in the theater arts. These lessons precede the dance lesson on lines that is taught in the physical education class.

Music

Choosing or creating music to express a mood or feeling

Theater Arts

Creating a character that will travel on a pathway

Visual Arts

Drawing different types of lines to express an idea

Physical Education

Creating a dance emphasizing pathways

Objectives

As a result of participating in this lesson, the students will

- learn to draw different types of lines using pencil, chalk, and pastels;
- interpret a feeling or a mood based on a line drawing;
- create a character and scene based on a line drawing;
- choose or create music that represents a feeling or a mood;

- use the line drawing to create a floor and an air pathway; and
- create a sequence of movements that is performed using a floor or an air pathway.

Equipment

Line drawing from the visual arts class, music selected or created in the music class, character and scene descriptions developed during a theater arts lesson, chalkboard or chart paper, chalk or markers, 8½ × 11 paper and crayons, four or five tape recorders

Organization

Individuals, partners, or small groups

Description

"Over the next few lessons you will create a dance using the line drawing from your visual arts class, the music you selected or created in your music class, and the descriptions of characters and scenes you wrote during your theater arts session. Before you get started on creating your dances, you will need to warm up your body. You are going to organize into groups of five or six and stand in a circle. Then one person will perform a warm-up exercise, and the rest of the group will follow. After each person has had a turn as the leader, you may add any other exercises you feel will help your own body warm up."

- ▶ Students in small groups perform the warm-up exercises.

"Now I will explain how you will create your dance, and then you can choose to work by yourself, with a partner, or in a group of three or four. The line drawing you worked on in the visual arts class will become a floor and air pathway for your movement. Let's try an example together. Look at this line drawing." (See figure 7.6.)

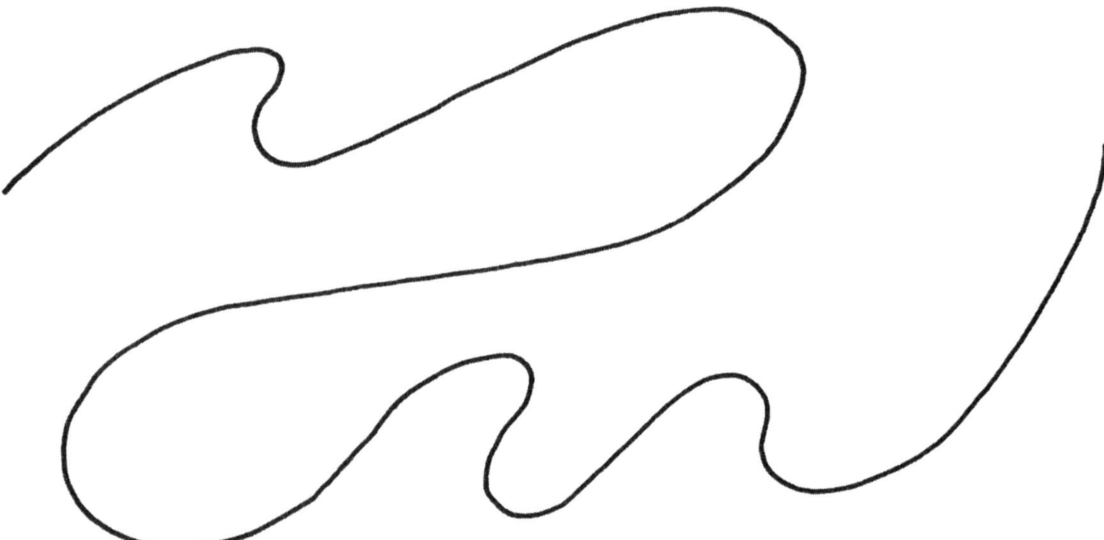

Figure 7.6 **Example of a student's drawing using curvy lines.**

"What types of lines do you see?" Carmen responds, "Lots of curvy lines all over the page." "Can someone show the class how you can move your arm in a pathway in the air that would look like one of the curvy lines in the drawing?"

- ▶ Carmen volunteers to demonstrate. Then have all the students move their arms in a curving pathway. Discuss possible musical selections with the class.

"Has anyone brought music today that could accompany moving on a curvy pathway?" Ryan responds, "We could use slow, smooth violin music." "Great! Let's use your tape. Now try moving your whole body on a curvy floor pathway and at the same time use your arms to draw the air pathway. Move all around the room, just as the drawing filled the whole page. Describe the small and big curves in the drawing with your feet. Move your feet in different ways: Run, skip, or walk and use different directions—forward, backward, or sideways—as you move on the curvy pathway."

▶ Students practice and make changes as suggested.

"Now let's add a character and a scene that would be represented by the movement on a curvy pathway. Did anyone write a character description, or can someone suggest one now?" Rashad suggests, "Someone is digging in a field, and a strong wind blows by, and the person is blown all over the field." "Thank you, Rashad. Now try your curvy line movements again, and this time begin moving as if you were digging in a field. As the music comes on, begin to move as if you are being blown around by the wind. Travel on a curvy floor pathway changing directions. Your arms are moving in a curvy pathway and have the feeling of being blown around by a strong wind."

▶ The students begin the dance with a digging movement and travel on the curved pathway when the music begins. They return to the digging movements when the music stops. Next, the students can try a second example using a similar series of directions and a drawing of zigzag lines.

"Now I will help you organize to create a dance. You can choose to work as an individual dancer, in partners, or as a group of three or four."

▶ Some students are in pairs; several students want to work individually; and the rest of the class is organized into small groups.

"Now that you are organized, let's create your dance. First, select a drawing from your collection that you put together in the visual arts class. Then think about the different characters and scenes you wrote in the theater arts session. Remember, they reflected the different types of drawings. You can use the writing ideas or think about a feeling or a mood that the drawing represents. Then create movements that follow the lines in the drawing. Some of the lines can be a floor pathway and others can be an air pathway. Use different traveling movements and directions. Consider the tempo of your movements."

▶ Students spend a few minutes looking at the drawing, talking with each other about what character or feeling they will use, and begin to try out different movements. Visit each student, pair, or group to offer suggestions or ask questions about how they are using different lines in the drawing.

"Now I want you to add a still beginning and ending shape to your dance. Use a line or part of a line from the drawing in your shape. Perhaps you can use your arms or back to demonstrate the shape of the line. Think about using a different level for the beginning shape and the ending shape. Maybe the beginning shape is standing, and the ending shape is low or on the floor. Your character or feeling may help you determine a good shape for the beginning and ending of your dance."

▶ Students continue to work on their dances. Ask them questions to see what movements they have completed.

"The final addition to your dance is the music. Choose one of the selections from your music class and try performing the dance to the music. You may want to make some changes to fit the dance to the music."

- Students share tape recorders, taking turns using the music as they practice their dance.

"After each person, pair, or group has finished creating their dance and has practiced the movements so that they can remember the dance, we will perform for each other. I will group the class so some people are the audience and others are performing. You will share your dance with a couple of people, not the whole class. Before you perform, show the audience the drawing you have selected, and talk about the characters, scene, or feeling represented in the dance."

- Divide the class into four groups. Each group includes individuals, pairs, and one or more small groups. The students take turns performing for each other.

Assessment Suggestions

- Students as audience members or as performers can answer the following questions in writing: What part of the dance was the most interesting? Why? What changes would you make in the dance?
- You can also assess the dance to see whether all the components of the dance were present (figure 7.7).

Date: ____________________ **Class:** ______________________________

Student: ____

Dance component?	Air pathways follow some of the lines?
Yes No	Yes No
Still beginning shape?	Uses change of direction?
Yes No	Yes No
Still ending shape at a different level?	Uses two or more traveling movements?
Yes No	Yes No
Floor pathway follows some of the lines?	Can remember the sequence of the dance?
Yes No	Yes No

Figure 7.7 **Teacher checklist for assessing dances using line drawings.**

Look For

- Students who need help with suggestions to vary their movements.
- Controlled movement in and out of the beginning and ending shapes.
- The different ways students use their body and its parts to represent the lines in the drawing. Do they need help engaging more body parts in the dance?
- Accuracy with which students represent the line with their bodies.

How Can I Change This?

- Use the same drawing for all students as you did in the examples.
- Students can use percussion instruments instead of recorded music.
- Students can use the drawing of another student instead of their own.
- The students can add props or costumes.

Teachable Moments

- Students working individually can perform their separate dances at the same time in the same space and find ways in which their individual dances match or coordinate.
- Students in pairs can start the same dance at different times, as if one person is the echo of the other.
- Students in groups can work on unison movement and practice moving together at the same time.

Breaking It Down

Suggested Grade Level

Intermediate (3 through 6)

Interdisciplinary Teaching Model

Shared

The theme of friendship brings you and the art and music teachers together to create a shared interdisciplinary experience. While the music teacher presents a unit on creating rap songs to the theme of friendship, you present a unit on hip-hop dance and the art teacher focuses on creating friendship graffiti-style posters. When the posters and rap songs are completed, the students create dances using the hip-hop movements they learned to reflect the friendship message in the rap and graffiti.

Music

Creating compositions using rhythms

Visual Arts

Exploring different letter styles and paint techniques

Physical Education

Learning and creating dance movements

Objectives

As a result of participating in this lesson, the students will

- increase their understanding of how the message of friendship can be expressed in multiple ways,
- collaborate with others to create a dance,
- learn and create new dance movements, and
- express their interpretation of the friendship theme through creating dances to rap songs.

Equipment

CD, player, rap songs and graffiti posters created by students, chalkboard, whiteboard, or poster paper and markers

Organization

Groups of three or four students

Description

- This physical education learning experience can be presented over three lessons. The first lesson teaches a menu of hip-hop moves; the second includes using the learned moves to create dances to the rap songs composed in the music class; and in the third lesson students perform their rap song, dance their dance, and show their graffiti posters to the other students.

Lesson One

"Today you are going to learn five new hip-hop movements and then use the movements to create your own sequence. First, we will warm up using body-part isolations. Everyone find a self-space and face me."

- Play appropriate rap or hip-hop music and lead the warm-up.

"Move your head side to side. Look right, then left. Do it for 16 counts.

"Right shoulder up and down for eight counts, then the left shoulder up and down for eight counts, now both shoulders up and down for eight counts.

"Reach up and down with the right arm for eight counts, then the left arm for eight counts, and then both arms for eight counts.

"Cross arms in front of your chest, then open. Cross and open for 16 counts.

"March in place for 16 counts.

"Kick the right leg forward, out to the side, and then backward and back to place for four counts; then repeat with the left leg. Switch right and left leg kicks four times.

"Bend and straighten knees for 16 counts."

- Add other movements that you feel are appropriate.

"We are going to create a hip-hop movement menu. Does anyone know any hip-hop moves he or she can share with the class? Tell us the name of the movement and demonstrate how it is performed. Then I will write the name of the movement, and we will all learn it and include it as an item in our hip-hop menu."

- Students in the class offer movements from their experiences dancing or viewing hip-hop in movies or on TV. Be sure to assess whether moves are safe and appropriate for the students.

"Any other moves you could suggest? Now let's review the names and how to perform each of the moves you have presented."

- Review the names with the students, then practice the moves listed on the hip-hop menu.

"I will arrange you into groups of three or four. In your group you will cooperate to choose three or four of the movements from the menu and organize them into a sequence. You determine the order and the number of times the move is repeated."

- Students select, organize, and practice the hip-hop sequence. Observe and offer assistance when needed.

"Practice your sequence with your group one more time so you can remember it for the next lesson. Next time you will add to the dance one or more of the rap songs you have created. Bring the rap songs you created in your music class to the next physical education lesson."

Lesson Two

"Today you will return to the groups you worked with in the previous lesson and practice your dance sequence. You can change moves or add new moves."

- Students get together with their group and practice the dance sequence they created in the previous lesson. Students can discuss changes or add movements.

"Share with your group members the rap songs you created in music class. You can choose one of the songs or combine songs. The rap song will be the accompaniment to your dance. Then coordinate your dance sequence to go with the rap song."

- Students select a song and coordinate their dance sequence movements to go with the rhythm of the song. Observe and offer assistance where needed.

"Use the remaining time in class today to make changes in the song and dance and to practice for a performance in the next lesson. Also, for the next lesson, bring the graffiti poster you created in your art class. You will combine the rap song, the hip-hop dance sequence, and the graffiti poster into your performance."

Lesson Three

"Today's lesson has two parts. First you will practice your dance and your song and plan how to use the graffiti posters in the performance. Then you will perform your dance and song for another group. We will switch groups several times so you can perform to different groups instead of to the whole class at once.

"Consider how your posters will be incorporated into the performance. Will you use them as a backdrop, will you move around the posters, or will you move them during the performance? There are endless possibilities."

- Students try out several ideas for including the graffiti posters in their performance. They can move with the posters; move around, over, and between the posters; or use the posters as a backdrop.

"Now that you are finished practicing your performance, I will place two groups together to perform for each other. Then I will switch groups so you can perform for another group. In this way, you will perform your dance and song and use the posters several times and also be able to see other groups' performances."

- While the students are performing, observe each group and change the groups after each performance. Students should perform and observe a minimum of three times.

Assessment Suggestions

- Use a checklist (figure 7.8) to note whether the following criteria are present in the performance.
- Students can write a song and dance script. Under the words of the rap, the students write the corresponding dance moves.

Look For

- Students who need help with coordinating the movements. Suggest ways to change the movements to ensure that all group members are successful.

Date: ____________________ Class: ______________________________________

Student: ____

All group members were included in the performance. Yes No

The rap song, hip-hop dance, and poster were included in the performance. Yes No

Comments:

Figure 7.8 **Breaking It Down checklist.**

- Different ways in which the students use the graffiti posters. Suggest ideas for placement or movements.
- How students simultaneously perform the singing and dancing. Can they do both at the same time?

How Can I Change This?

- Use other themes as the integrating topic, such as rejection and acceptance, health, positive behaviors, ecology, or sports.
- Add percussion instruments to the rap songs.
- Ask the students to create graffiti T-shirt designs instead of posters and to wear the T-shirts as costumes during their dance.
- During the group dance, each dancer can take a solo turn to do eight counts of his or her own movements.

Teachable Moments

- Introduce the concept of moving in unison. This means that all the dancers do the same movement in the same way at the same time.
- Suggest different formations for the dancers. They can all perform in a line, side by side, or in a triangle, square, or circle for the entire dance or can change formations during the dance.

Music in the Movies

Music

Study of how music sets a mood, establishes a character, and enhances the drama of a film

Physical Education

Manipulative skills: bouncing a ball

Grade Level

4 through 6

The students use different movie themes to create ball-bouncing routines that involve stationary and traveling movements. The routine can reflect the tempo, rhythm, or mood of the music or changes in the music. Students can imagine they are a character from the movie and use the bouncing skills to express the character's actions. Music from silent movies can also inspire students to create their own characters and actions.

Theme and Variation

Music

Theme and variation

Physical Education

Locomotor and nonlocomotor movements

Grade Level

4 through 6

This activity works best after the concept of theme and variation has been introduced in the music program. The students select three locomotor and two nonlocomotor movements and organize the movements into a repeatable sequence. This sequence becomes their theme. They create variations by changing the order of the movements, changing the tempo, making the movements bigger or smaller, or altering the amount of force.

Warm-Up Music

Music

Listening to music from various cultures, from different time periods, and of disparate styles

Physical Education

Rhythm and tempo for warm-up exercises

Grade Level

K through 6

Select music for warm-up or cool-down exercises. Choices such as African drumming music provide a strong rhythm to initiate movement; popular music that students enjoy is great for motivation; a jazz piece, a classical selection, a movie theme, or a children's song can also be used. Listen to the music before using it in class so that you are familiar with the rhythm, tempo, melody, and lyrics.

Music Interpretation Through Dance

Music

Interpretation of music through narration

Physical Education

Creating a dance based on images evoked by a musical selection

Grade Level

3 through 6

In their music program, the students are focusing on listening to different styles of music. The music teacher asks students to interpret the music through creation of a poem, painting, or dance. During the physical education class, have the students create short dances based on their interpretation of the music. Have them complete a list of words that create images or convey feelings reflected by the music and then illustrate them through movements using space, time, and force. For example, using the words *scared* and *afraid,* guide the students by asking what shape the body would have if someone were afraid. You can follow up with questions about how fast or slow the person would move, what type of steps he or she would take, which direction he or she would go in, or where he or she would be looking.

Echo Rhythms

Music

Reproduction of different rhythms

Physical Education

Reproducing rhythms using body movements

Grade Level

K through 3

Play a tape of different rhythms, or play the rhythms on a percussion instrument. Students respond to the rhythms using different body movements such as clapping, jumping, twisting, making shapes, running, or shaking. Students can also create their own movements and rhythms.

Grade Level

2 through 6
The students develop a list of objects, animals, and emotions and create a vocal sound to accompany each word. Then they create movements that express the sound. Students can make the sounds as they perform the movements, or some students can be the voices while others are the movers. Consider creating a fire engine sound accompanied by running and leaping; a jackhammer accompanied by jumping and shaking; a purring cat accompanied by slow, stretching movement; or an angry yell expressed through a sequence of jumps.

Imaginary Ball Pass

Theater Arts

Developing acting skills using an imaginary prop

Physical Education

Performing manipulative skills with an imaginary ball

Grade Level

2 through 6
The students stand in a circle with one student holding an imaginary ball. This student shows the size and weight of the ball through the movement of his or her hands and body. He or she throws, rolls, kicks, volleys, or bounces the ball to another person, who pretends to catch the ball. That person then changes the size and weight of the ball. Each time the ball is passed, it changes size and weight, and the person doing the passing changes his or her body to reflect the new size and weight. The ball can be very big and light, like a giant balloon, and held by two hands, or it can be very tiny and pushed across the floor with one finger.

VISUAL ARTS

Pathways in the Air and on the Floor

Visual Arts

Line drawings

Physical Education

Pathways

Grade Level

K through 3
Students draw horizontal, vertical, diagonal, zigzag, or curved lines with colored pencils on a piece of paper to form a design using only one type of line or a combination of types. The

drawings can be used as floor or air pathways for movements. Students can also pretend to draw designs in the air. They can perform different movements such as walking, skipping, running, galloping, bouncing a ball, or foot-dribbling a ball along the pathway.

Partner Balances

Visual Arts

Symmetrical and asymmetrical balance

Physical Education

Balance

Grade Level

4 through 6

In this activity students create several symmetrical and asymmetrical partner balances. Then they develop a gymnastics sequence emphasizing a smooth transition between the partner balances.

The Sculpture Garden

Visual Arts

Free-standing sculpture and modeling for a sculpture

Physical Education

Balance and shape

Grade Level

4 through 6

Students working in pairs designate one partner to be the clay and one partner to be the artist. The clay person can begin by lying on the ground, sitting, or standing. The artist creates a sculpture by moving the clay person's head, arms, legs, fingers, back, and feet into different positions. Students can switch roles several times to form different types of sculptures. Themes for the sculptures can be sport actions, emotions, monsters, or dancers.

Cloud Shapes

Visual Arts

Design in nature

Physical Education

Creating shapes

Texture Toss

Visual Arts

Texture in different art media

Physical Education

Throwing and catching

Grade Level

K through 3

You and the art teacher agree to teach about texture at the same time. In the physical education class, the students practice throwing and catching individually, in pairs, or in small groups. They use a variety of objects that have different smooth and rough textures, such as foam balls, rubber balls, Frisbees, newspaper balls, marbles, yarn balls, tennis balls, beanbags, basketballs, soccer balls, field hockey balls, or balloons. Students discuss how the different textures feel and how the throw or catch is changed by the texture of the ball.

THEATER ARTS AND VISUAL ARTS

Masks

Theater Arts

Creating a character using a mask and an environment for that character

Visual Arts

Creating a papier-mâché mask relief that represents a mood or feeling

Physical Education

Creating dance movements for the character wearing the mask

Grade Level

4 through 6

You and the theater arts and visual arts teachers collaborate on an interdisciplinary unit of study based on the use of masks in African rituals. In the art class students create masks that reflect a specific mood or feeling and that they can wear while moving. A theater artist is working with the students to create a scene that depicts a character wearing the mask in an imaginary environment. In physical education class, the children create the movements and sequences needed to bring the scene to life. The three-discipline collaboration requires planning time for coordination of activities and can result in a grand performance for an audience.

Ongoing Strategies for the Physical Education Classroom

- Use music during warm-ups and practice sessions. The tempo and rhythm of the music support the tempo and rhythm of the movement and make participation fun.
- Ask students to act out classroom rules to show appropriate behavior.
- Encourage drawing to illustrate answers on written assessments. Using drawing can help students represent their understandings through multiple forms of expression.
- Ask students to design and put up bulletin boards that support a specific instructional unit. Students can create a bulletin board about a tennis unit by using pictures, tennis terms, and drawings of a net and racket and can include colorful backdrops and lettering.
- Charge students with creating a team cheer that coordinates body movements with a vocal rhythm.
- Use pictures and book illustrations as stimuli for creative dance lessons. Students will have a visual representation of the idea or topic for the dance.
- Organize students for activities by colors they are wearing or designs on their clothing.

Summary

Music, theater arts, and visual arts, like physical education, can be taught as discrete disciplines with their own body of knowledge, concepts, and skills. Each art form is unique and essential in the curriculum because of the particular avenues of perception that it develops. The arts teach children how to use verbal and nonverbal symbols to communicate and express their thoughts and feelings more effectively and to analyze and understand messages communicated to them. Connections can be made between any art form and other disciplines through the transfer of learning that occurs when students learn to apply the process, skills, and concepts used in a particular arts discipline to other areas. The interdisciplinary possibilities are infinite. The content standards for each of the arts disciplines include a specific standard that addresses developing relationships between art disciplines and with disciplines outside the arts.

The descriptions of learning experiences in this chapter suggest how a student assumes the character of a circus performer and explores the movements characteristic of that performer; how the use of patterns in art parallels many activities involving throwing, catching, or bouncing; how tempo and rhythm come alive as twisted, straight, or round shapes; and how traveling along a pathway is all the more enjoyable with music, character, and illustration. The suggested ideas at the end of the chapter can serve as the genesis for wonderful learning experiences in music, theater arts, visual arts, and physical education.

in September 2000, the sport of geocaching has mushroomed. Now more than 600,000 caches are located around the world, in all 50 states and in more than 220 countries. Today geocaching sites are listed by zip code, state, city (those with populations of over 20,000), and country.

Types of Caches

There are now many variations of geocaching and different types of caches, including traditional caches, multistage caches, virtual caches, Webcam caches, event caches, benchmark caches, locationless caches, and Earthcaches.

TRADITIONAL CACHE

Traditional caches vary from small (micro) to medium and large containers and are found at the exact location of the coordinates. Containers vary from magnetic key boxes and film containers to plastic ware, ammo boxes, and buckets. Generally, a special effort is made to keep them waterproof. Each cache has a log book for registering a find. Many contain small treasures (trinkets). The general rule is that if you take something from a cache, you are to leave something of equal or greater value.

MULTISTAGE CACHE

A multistage cache involves two or more locations. While there are many variations of multicaches, in most cases the seeker uses a hint to find a set of clues that will lead to the next set of coordinates; the process continues until it eventually leads to the final destination.

VIRTUAL CACHE

A virtual cache is a cache that exists in the form of a location, most often a historical site or another place of significance. When visiting a virtual cache one most often has to post an answer to a question and contact the owners of the cache to receive credit for the find. Virtual caches are now referred to as waymarks on Waymarking.com.

WEBCAM CACHES

Webcam caches use existing Web cameras, placed by individuals or agencies, that monitor areas like entrances to buildings and public places or that survey road conditions. The idea is to get yourself in front of the camera to log your visit. The trick is that you need to call a friend and ask him or her to look up the Web site that displays the camera shot. The friend then needs to save the picture to log the cache.

EVENT CACHES

Currently, local geocachers and organizations that they form have regular meetings in their area to discuss topics of interest. Time and location of meetings are posted. After the event, the caches are archived. An outgrowth of event caches is the Cache In, Trash Out (CITO). While out on a local cache hunt, a group agrees to collect litter and properly dispose of it, thus benefiting the community at large.

BENCHMARK CACHES

Benchmarks are locations set up by the United States Geological Survey. They are geodetic control points permanently affixed to locations all across the United States to enable land surveying, civil engineering, and mapping. These objects are usually metal discs but can be any other object that serves as a control point. The control points are used to help establish vertical (elevation) and horizontal (triangulation station).

LOCATIONLESS CACHES

A locationless cache is in a sense the reverse of a traditional cache. Instead of finding a hidden container (treasure), you are given the task of finding one or more specific objects or locations, such as a British phone booth, types of fire trucks, names of cities beginning with the letter "X", or college or high school mascots, and log their coordinates. For a list of types of locationless caches go to Waymarking.com.

EARTHCACHES

An Earthcache is a special place that people can visit in order to learn about a unique geoscience feature or aspect of our earth. Visitors to Earthcaches can see how the planet has been shaped by geological processes, how the earth's resources are managed, and how evidence is

gathered by scientists in order to learn about the earth. To find out more about Earthcaches, go to earthcache.org or access the Earthcache section on Waymarking.com.

Getting Started With Geocaching

To get started with geocaching in a school, you will need a GPS, a computer, and access to the Internet. GPS units range from $100 to $1,000. There are various models; the best way to determine what type of unit will best suit your needs is to go to www.geocaching.com/faq, Guide to Buying a GPS Unit (for Geocaching).

While cost may be prohibitive, there are several possible solutions. One is to survey parents in your school or discover a local geocaching club in your city. Because of their enthusiasm for the sport, club members may be willing to offer support by coming to your class and teaching you how to use the GPS units or may lend you their unit for a short time. Another possibility is to write the purchase of GPS units into your annual physical education budget. You might consider writing a small grant to purchase a few units or getting the PTO to contribute money for the purchase of a few units. Students could then work in small groups depending on the number of units available.

Once you have access to GPS units, all you need is a computer and access to the Internet (no problem)! Log onto geocaching.com. Then click on Getting Started, Frequently Asked Questions (FAQ), Guide to Finding a Geocache, Guide to Hiding a Geocache, Groundspeak Support, geocaching.com Glossary (all about terminology), and so on. You will be amazed at the information at your fingertips. You will find that geocaching has the potential to enhance all areas of your interdisciplinary teaching efforts.

Uses in Education

Because of the interdisciplinary nature of geocaching and the use of handheld technology in the classroom, there are many opportunities to use geocaching across the curriculum. Example suggestions in the areas of physical education, language arts, mathematics, science, and social studies follow. Suggestions for family and recreational uses are also provided as examples of out-of-school opportunities to enhance learning, physical activity, and a sense of adventure.

PHYSICAL EDUCATION

Create several cache sites on your school grounds. Students can walk or jog to each site and thereby increase their physical activity level.

Locate caches within your zip code or another local area. Encourage children to go caching with their parents as a family activity, thereby increasing physical activity time outside of school.

LANGUAGE ARTS

Although children in the early grades (K-2) may not be capable of reading about caching, children from third grade on can read about geocaching and the various subcategories mentioned earlier.

- Children can create their own cache as a class assignment. Find an interesting place. Get permission to plant the cache. Give it a name. Provide information of significance about the site. Maintain the site. Discover who visits the site.
- Children can provide clues to their cache or encrypt and decrypt messages using the reverse alphabet method on all geocache sites. In this system, a letter equals the one below it and vice versa.

A	B	C	D	E	F	G	H	I	J	K	L	M
N	O	P	Q	R	S	T	U	V	W	X	Y	Z

Each of the 13 letters must correspond for decryption: A = N, B = O, etc.

Examples:

GUR CYNDHR VF BA GUR JNYY = The plaque is on the wall.

LBH PBHYQ OR FVGGVAT BA VG = You could be sitting on it.

- Children can participate in the various forums and discussion groups about geocaching on the Internet.

Selected Readings

Allen, V. (1996). A critical look at integration. *Teaching Elementary Physical Education, 7,* 12-14.

Alperstein, C., and Weyl, R. (1992). *Arts for everykid: A handbook for change.* Trenton, NJ: New Jersey State Council on the Arts/Department of State and Alliance for Arts Education.

Altman, S., and Lehr, C. (2003). Integrating sport, physical activity, and the arts in education. *Strategies, 16*(4), 15-18.

Ashlock, R.O., and Humphrey, J.O. (1976). *Teaching elementary school mathematics through motor learning.* Springfield, IL: Charles C Thomas.

Association for Supervision and Curriculum Development. (1994). Teaching across disciplines. *Education Update, 36*(10), 1-4.

Atlanta Committee for the Olympic Games. (1994-1995). *Olympic day in the schools* (Vols. 1-3). Atlanta: Author.

Baker, K., and Wagner, J. (1977). *A place for ideas—our theater.* New Orleans: Anchorage Press.

Ballinger, D., and Deeney, T. (2006). Physical educators as teachers of literacy. *Journal of Physical Education, Recreation and Dance, 77*(5), 18-23.

Banks, J. (1985). *Teaching strategies for the social studies.* New York: Longman.

Barnfield, G. (1968). *Creative drama in schools.* New York: Hart.

Behrman, E. (2004). Writing in the physical education class. *Journal of Physical Education, Recreation and Dance, 75*(8), 22-32.

Beijing 2008 Olympic Games: http://en.beijing2008.cn/.

Belka, D. (1994). *Teaching children games.* Champaign, IL: Human Kinetics.

Bennett, J., and Hanneken, L. (2003). Physical education and academic performance. *Teaching Elementary Physical Education, 14*(6), 27-30.

Benzwie, T. (1987). *A moving experience: Dance for lovers of children and the child within.* Tucson, AZ: Zephyr Press.

Boorman, J. (1973). *Dance and language experiences with children.* Don Mills, ON: Longman Press.

Boorman, J. (1987). *Pompous potatoes* [cassette recording and instruction manual]. Edmonton, AB: University of Alberta.

Brazelton, A. (1975). *Clap, snap, tap* [sound recording]. Freeport, NY: Educational Activities.

Brazelton, A. (1977). *Only just begun* [sound recording]. Freeport, NY: Educational Activities.

Bredekamp, S., and Copple, C. (Eds.). (1997). *Developmentally appropriate practice in early childhood programs* (rev. ed.). Washington, DC: National Association for the Education of Young Children.

Britannica. (1993). *Science system.* Berkeley, CA: Lawrence Hall of Science, University of California.

Brophy, J., and Alleman, J. (1991). A caveat: Curriculum integration isn't always a good idea. *Educational Leadership, 49*(2), 66.

Bucek, L.E. (1992). Constructing a child-centered dance curriculum. *Journal of Physical Education, Recreation and Dance,* 63(9), 39-42.

Buchoff, R., and Mitchell, D. (1996). Poetry workouts. *Strategies, 10,* 18-23.

Buschner, C. (1994). *Teaching children movement concepts and skills.* Champaign, IL: Human Kinetics.

California Department of Education. (1989). *Visual and performing arts framework.* Sacramento, CA: Author.

Carpenter, A., and Stevens-Smith, D. (2003). Locomotor skills skip to a new level. *Teaching Elementary Physical Education, 14*(1), 37-39.

Cecil, N., and Lauritzen, P. (1994). *Literacy and the arts for the integrated classroom.* White Plains, NY: Longman.

Chard, S., and Flockhart, M. (2002). Learning in the park. *Educational Leadership, 60*(3), 53-56.

Chen, W., Cone, T., and Cone, S. (2005). A collaborative approach to developing an interdisciplinary unit. *Research Quarterly for Exercise and Sport, 76,* A-61.

Clements, R., and Osteen, M. (1995). Creating and implementing preschool movement narratives. *Journal of Physical Education, Recreation and Dance, 66*(3), 24-29.

College Board. (1983). *Academic preparation for college—what students need to know and be able to do.* New York: Author.

College Board. (1985). *Academic preparation in the arts—teaching for transition from high school to college.* New York: Author.

College Board. (1996). The role of the arts in unifying the high school curriculum. *National Center for Cross-Disciplinary Teaching and Learning Newsletter, 2*(2), 2.

Collom, J., and Noethe, S. (1994). *Poetry everywhere.* New York: Teachers and Writers Collaborative.

Colvin, A., and Walker, P. (1996). Map out excitement. *Strategies, 9,* 26-29.

Cone, S., and Cone, T. (1998). *Moving across the curriculum: An interdisciplinary approach to physical education and dance.* Abstracts: EDA 1998 Convention. N. Kingstown, RI: Eastern District Association of the American Alliance for Health, Physical Education, Recreation and Dance.

Cone, S., and Cone, T. (1999). The interdisciplinary puzzle: Putting the pieces together. *Teaching Elementary Physical Education, 10*(1), 8-11.

Cone, S., and Cone, T. (2001). Language arts and physical education: A natural connection. *Teaching Elementary Physical Education, 12*(4), 14-17.

Cone, T., and Cone, S. (2005). *Teaching children dance* (2nd ed.). Champaign, IL: Human Kinetics.

Cone, T., and Cone, S. (2007). Dance education: Dual or dueling identities. *Journal of Physical Education, Recreation and Dance, 77*(9), 6-8, 13.

Connor-Kuntz, F., and Dummer, G. (1996). Teaching across the curriculum: Language-enriched physical education for preschool children. *Adapted Physical Activity Quarterly, 13,* 302-315.

Consortium of National Arts Education Associations. (1994). *National standards for arts education.* Reston, VA: Music Educators National Conference.

Cottrell, J. (1977). *Teaching with creative dramatics.* Skokie, IL: National Textbook.

Cratty, B. (1971). *Active learning: Games to enhance academic abilities.* Englewood Cliffs, NJ: Prentice Hall.

Cratty, B. (1973). *Intelligence in action.* Englewood Cliffs, NJ: Prentice Hall.

Cratty, B. (1985). *Active learning: Games to enhance academic abilities.* Englewood Cliffs, NJ: Prentice Hall.

DeFrancesco, C., and Casas, B. (2004). Elementary physical education and math skill development. *Strategies, 18*(2), 21-23.

DePaola, P. (1975). *The cloud book.* New York: Holiday House.

DePice, D. (1996). Stirring imaginations: Connections among the disciplines. *NJEA Review, 69,* 36-39.

Dewey, J. (1934). *Art as experience.* New York: Perigu Books.

Drake, S., and Burns, R. (2004). *Meeting standards through integrated curriculum.* Alexandria, VA: Association for Supervision and Curriculum Development.

Eisner, E. (1980). Why public schools should teach the arts. *New York Education Quarterly, 11,* 2-7.

Eisner, E. (1988). *The role of discipline-based art education in America's schools.* Los Angeles: Getty Center for Education in the Arts.

Eisner, E. (1998). *The kind of schools we need: Personal essays.* Portsmouth, NH: Heinemann.

Elliott, S. (2003). Creating interdisciplinary lessons in elementary physical education. *Strategies, 16*(6), 19-21.

Evans, J., and Brueckner, M. (1990). *Elementary social studies: Teaching for today and tomorrow.* Boston: Allyn & Bacon.

Feelings, M. (1971). *Moja means one.* New York: Puffin Pied Piper.

Feelings, M. (1971). *Jambo means hello.* New York: Puffin Pied Piper.

Fleming, D. (1987). Social studies goals: U.S. Department of Education style! *Social Education, 77,* 141-144.

Fogarty, R. (1991a). *The mindful school: How to integrate the curricula.* Palatine, IL: IRI/Skylight.

Fogarty, R. (1991b). Ten ways to integrate curriculum. *Educational Leadership, 49*(2), 61-65.

Fowler, C. (1988). *Can we rescue the arts for America's children?* New York: ACA Books.

Fowler, C. (1994). *Music: Its role and importance in our lives.* New York: Glencoe.

Fraser, D. (1991). *Playdancing.* Pennington, NJ: Princeton Book.

Freeman, S. (1984). *Books kids will sit still for.* Hagerstown, MD: Alleyside Press.

Gabbei, R., and Clemmens, H. (2005). Creative movement from children's storybooks: Going beyond pantomime. *Journal of Physical Education, Recreation and Dance, 76*(9), 32-37.

Gallahue, D., and Cleland, F. (2003). *Developmental physical education for today's children* (4th ed.). Champaign, IL: Human Kinetics.

Gardner, H. (1983). *Frames of mind: The theory of multiple intelligences.* New York: Basic Books.

Gega, P. (1994a). *Concepts and experiences in elementary school science.* Columbus, OH: Merrill.

Gega, P. (1994b). *How to teach elementary school science.* New York: Macmillan.

Gilbert, A. (1977). *Teaching the three Rs through movement experiences.* New York: Macmillan.

Gilbert, A. (1992). A conceptual approach to studio dance, PreK-12. *Journal of Physical Education, Recreation and Dance, 63*(9), 43-48.

Gilbert, A. (2004). *Brain compatible dance education.* Reston, VA: National Dance Association/American Alliance for Health, Physical Education, Recreation and Dance.

Gillespie, J., and Nadea, C. (1996). *Best books for children.* New Providence, NJ: Bowker.

Graham, G. (1992). *Teaching children physical education.* Champaign, IL: Human Kinetics.

Graham, G., Holt/Hale, S., and Parker, M. (2007). *Children moving: A reflective approach to teaching physical education* (7th ed.). Mountain View, CA: Mayfield.

Greene, M. (1978). *Landscapes of learning.* New York: Teacher's College Press.

Griffin, J., and Morgan, L.K. (1998). PE—write on!: Language integration in physical education. *Strategies, 11*(4), 34-37.

Grube, D., and Beaudet, B. (2005). Physical education and the ABC's: An interdisciplinary approach. *Strategies, 18*(6), 11-14.

Hatch, G., and Smith, D. (2004). Integrating physical education, math, and physics. *Strategies, 11*(4), 34-37.

Heard, G. (1989). *For the good of the earth and sun.* Portsmouth, NH: Heineman.

Hoban, T. (1972). *Count and see.* New York: Macmillan.

Holabird, K. (1987). *Angelina and Alice.* New York: Crown.

Holt music: Scope and sequence. (1988). Austin, TX: Holt, Reinhart & Winston.

http://hogmanay.net.

Horrigan, O. (1929). *Creative activities in physical education.* New York: Barnes.

Horwood, B. (1994). Integration and experiences in the secondary curriculum. *McGill Journal of Education, 29*(1), 89-102.

Huck, C. (1976). *Children's literature in the elementary school* (3rd ed.). New York: Holt, Reinhart & Winston.

Humphrey, J. (1965). *Child learning.* Dubuque, IA: Brown.

Humphrey, J. (1974). *Child learning through elementary school physical education.* Dubuque, IA: Brown.

Humphrey, J. (1987). *Child development and learning through dance.* New York: AMS Press.

Hunt, S. (1964). *Games and sports the world around.* New York: Ronald Press.

International Council for Health, Physical Education and Recreation. (1967). *ICHPER book of worldwide games and dances.* Washington, DC: Author.

International Reading Association. (1970). *Poetry and children.* Newark, DE: Author.

Jacobs, H.H. (1989). *Interdisciplinary curriculum: Design and implementation.* Alexandria, VA: Association for Supervision and Curriculum Development.

Jensen, T. (1971). Creative ropes. *Journal of Health, Physical Education and Recreation, 32*(5), 56-57.

Johnson, E., Sickels, E., Sayers, F., and Horovitz, C. (1977). *Anthology of children's literature.* Boston: Houghton Mifflin.

Johnson, L. (1976). *Simplified lummi stick activities PK-2* [sound recording]. Freeport, NY: Educational Activities.

Joyce, M. (1994). *First steps in teaching creative dance to children.* Mountain View, CA: Mayfield.

Kalyn, B. (2005). Integration. *Teaching Elementary Physical Education, 16*(5), 31-36.

Kirchner, G. (1991). *Children's games from around the world.* Dubuque, IA: Brown.

Kunitz, S. (1985). *Next to last things.* Boston: Atlantic Monthly Press.

Kupka, C. (1982). Windsails. *Modern Dance Technique Environments* [sound recording]. Waldwick, NJ: Hoctor Records.

Lamme, L. (1984). *Growing up writing.* Washington, DC: Acropolis Books.

Lee, M. (1993). Learning through the arts. *Journal of Physical Education, Recreation and Dance, 64*(5), 42-46.

Lickona, T. (2004). *Character matters: How to help our children develop good judgment, integrity, and other essential virtues.* New York: Simon & Schuster.

Lima, C., and Lima, J. (1996). *A to zoo: Subject access to children's picture books.* New Providence, NJ: Bowker.

Locker, T. (2000). *Cloud dance.* New York: Harcourt.

Locker, T. (2002). *Water dance.* Florida: Harcourt.

Mahan, C., and Sanders, C. (1996). The two minute mental workout. *Teaching Elementary Physical Education, 7*(6), 26-27.

Martinello, M., and Cook, G. (1994). *Interdisciplinary inquiry in teaching and learning.* New York: Macmillan.

Mathematics. (1995). Morristown, NJ: Silver Burdett Ginn.

Mathematics in action. (1994). New York: Macmillan/McGraw-Hill.

The mathematics experience. (1995). Atlanta: Houghton Mifflin.

Maurer, R.E. (1994). *Designing interdisciplinary curriculum in middle, junior high, and high schools.* Boston: Allyn & Bacon.

McCaslin, N. (1990). *Creative drama in the classroom* (5th ed.). New York: Longman.

McElmeel, S. (1988). *An author a month for pennies.* Englewood, CO: Libraries Unlimited.

McLaughlin, J. (2005). High on the Hogmanay. *Sky Magazine, 12,* 90-93.

Memmel, R. (1953). Arithmetic through play. *Journal of Health, Physical Education and Recreation, 24,* 31.

http://memory.loc.gov/learn/lessons.

Michael Herman's Orchestra. (1980). *First folk dances* [sound recording]. LPM 1625. New York: RCA Victor.

Miller, A., and Whitcomb, V. (1969). *Physical education in the elementary school curriculum.* Englewood Cliffs, NJ: Prentice Hall.

Minton, S. (2003). Using movement to teach academics: An outline for success. *Journal of Physical Education, Recreation, and Dance, 74*(2), 36-40.

Mittler, G., and Ragans, R. (1992a). *Exploring art.* Lake Forest, IL: Glencoe.

Mittler, G., and Ragans, R. (1992b). *Understanding art.* Lake Forest, IL: Glencoe.

Moulton, J. (2006). Penguin Olympics. *Teaching Elementary Physical Education, 17*(2), 35-37.

Music (1974) [text and sound recording]. Morristown, NJ: Silver Burdett.

National Art Education Association. (1991). *Your child and visual arts.* Reston, VA: Author

National Assessment Governing Board. (1994). *Arts education assessment and exercise specifications.* Washington, DC: Author.

National Association for Sport and Physical Education. (1992). *The physically educated person.* Reston, VA: Author.

National Association for Sport and Physical Education. (2000a). *Appropriate practices for elementary physical education.* Reston, VA: Author.

National Association for Sport and Physical Education. (2000b). *Appropriate practices in movement programs for young children ages 3-5.* Reston, VA: Author.

National Association for Sport and Physical Education. (2003). *National standards for beginning physical education teachers* (2nd ed.). Reston, VA: Author.

National Association for Sport and Physical Education. (2004). *Moving into the future: National standards for physical education* (2nd ed.). Boston: McGraw-Hill.

National Council for Social Studies. (1994). *Curriculum standards for social studies.* Silver Springs, MD: Author.

National Council of Teachers of English and International Reading Association. (1996). *National standards for the English language arts.* Newark, DE: Author.

National Council of Teachers of Mathematics. (2000). *Principles and standards for school mathematics.* Reston, VA: Author.

National Dance Association. (1994). *National standards for dance education: What every young American should know and be able to do in dance.* Reston, VA: Author.

National Research Council. (1996). *National science education standards.* Washington, DC: National Academies Press.

Nebraska Department of Education. (1993). *K-12 visual and performing arts curriculum framework.* Lincoln, NE: Author.

New Jersey Department of Education. (2004). *New Jersey core curriculum standards.* Trenton, NJ: Author.

Nielsen, M.E. (1989). Integrative learning for young children: A thematic approach. *Educational Horizons, 68*(1), 18-24.

Nilges, L. (2003). Interdisciplinary learning: Feature introduction. *Teaching Elementary Physical Education, 14*(4), 6-8.

Orlando, L. (1993). *The multicultural game book.* New York: Scholastic Professional Books.

Overby, L., Post, B., and Newman, D. (2005). *Interdisciplinary learning through dance: 101 MOVEntures.* Champaign, IL: Human Kinetics.

Padgett, R. (Ed.). (1987). *The teachers and writers handbook for poetic form.* New York: Teachers and Writers Collaborative.

Palmer, H. (1969). *Modern rhythm band tunes* [sound recording]. Freeport, NY: Educational Activities.

Palmer, H. (1973). Enter sunlight. *Movin* [sound recording]. Freeport, NY: Educational Activities.

Piaget, J. (1969). *Psychology of intelligence.* Totowa, NJ: Littlefield, Adams.

Pica, R. (1995). *Kids on the move.* Kennebunk, ME: Moving and Learning, Spring.

Pontious, M. (1986). *A guide to curriculum planning in music.* Madison, WI: Department of Public Instruction.

Purcell, T., and Werner, P. (1996). *Teaching children through interdisciplinary programming.* Atlanta: AAHPERD National Convention.

Raftis, A. (1991). *Dance in poetry.* Princeton, NJ: Princeton Book.

Ragans, R., and Rhoades, J. (1992a). *Exploring art: Teacher's manual.* Lake Forest, IL: Glencoe.

Ragans, R., and Rhoades, J. (1992b). *Understanding art: Teacher's manual.* Lake Forest, IL: Glencoe.

Rahn, M.L., Alt, M., Emanuel, D., Ramer, C., Hoachlander, E., Holmes, P., Jackson, M., Klein, S., and Rossi, K. (1995). *Getting to work module two: Integrated curriculum.* Berkeley, CA: National Center for Research in Vocational Education, University of California.

Ratliffe, T., and Ratliffe, L. (1994). *Teaching children fitness.* Champaign, IL: Human Kinetics.

Rayala, M. (1995). *A guide to curriculum planning in art education.* Madison, WI: Department of Public Instruction.

Rovegno, I. (2003). Children's literature and dance. *Teaching Elementary Physical Education, 14*(4), 24-29.

Science anyone. (1995). Orlando, FL: Harcourt Brace.

Science anytime. (1995). Orlando, FL: Harcourt Brace.

Science insights. (1996). Menlo Park, CA: Addison Wesley.

Sendak, M. (1963, 1988). *Where the wild things are.* Boston: Harper Collins.

Shaw, C.G. (1947). *It looked like spilled milk.* New York: Harper & Row.

Silvey, A. (Ed.). (1995). *Children's books and their creators.* Boston: Houghton Mifflin.

Social studies. (2005). New York: Harcourt Brace Jovanovich.

Social studies. (2005). Boston: Houghton Mifflin.

Social studies. (2005). Glenview, IL: Scott Foresman.

South Brunswick Township Public Schools. (1995). *Language arts curriculum K-6.* Monmouth Junction, NJ: Author.

South Carolina Department of Education. (1995). *South Carolina science framework.* Columbia, SC: Author.

State of Delaware Department of Public Instruction. (1997). *Visual and performing arts curriculum framework.* Dover, DE: Author.

Stevens, D. (1994). Integrated learning: Collaboration among teachers. *Teaching Elementary Physical Education, 5*(6), 7-8.

Stinson, S. (1988). *Dance for young children: Finding the magic in movement.* Reston, VA: American Alliance for Health, Physical Education, Recreation and Dance.

Temple, C., and Collins, P. (Eds.). (1992). *Stories and readers: New perspectives on literature in the elementary classroom.* Norwood, MA: Christopher-Gordon.

Umminger, W. (1963). *Supermen, heroes, and gods: The story of sport through the ages.* New York: McGraw-Hill.

United States Army Infantry School. (1971). *The orienteering handbook.* Fort Benning, GA: Author.

United State Olympic Committee. www.usoc.org.

United States Olympic Committee. (1984). *The Olympics: An educational opportunity K-6.* Colorado Springs, CO: Author.

Waber, B. (2002). *Courage.* Boston: Houghton Mifflin.

Wall, J., and Murray, N. (1990). *Children and movement: Physical education in the elementary school.* Dubuque, IA: Brown.

Warren, L. (1975). *The theater of Africa: An introduction.* Englewood Cliffs, NJ: Prentice Hall.

Wasley, P. (1994). *Stirring the chalk dust: Tales of teachers changing classroom practice.* New York: Teachers College Press.

Weikart, P. (1989). *Rhythmically moving* [sound recording]. Ypsilanti, MI: High Scope.

Werner, P. (1971). Effects of integration of physical education with selected science concepts upon science knowledge and selected physical performance skills of boys and girls at fourth, fifth and sixth grade levels. Unpublished doctoral dissertation. Indiana University, Bloomington, IN.

Werner, P. (1994). Whole physical education. *Journal of Physical Education, Recreation and Dance, 65*(6), 40-44.

Werner, P. (1996). Interdisciplinary programming in physical education: What goes around comes around. *Teaching Elementary Physical Education, 7*(4), 28-30.

Werner, P. (2004). *Teaching children gymnastics* (2nd ed.). Champaign, IL: Human Kinetics.

Werner, P., Bowling, T., and Simmons, M. (1989). Combining the arts and academics. *Journal of Physical Education, Recreation and Dance, 60*(7), 55-57.

Werner, P., and Burton, E. (1979). *Learning through movement.* St. Louis: Mosby.

Whitin, D., Mills, H., and O'Keefe, T. (1991). *Living and learning mathematics: Five stories and strategies for supporting mathematical literacy.* Portsmouth, NH: Heineman.

Whitin, D., and Wilde, S. (1992). *Read any good math lately?* Portsmouth, NH: Heineman.

Why do we say it? (1985). Edison, NJ: Castle Books.

Wigginson, W. (1985). *The haiku handbook.* Tokyo: Kodansha International.

Wilcox, E. (1994). An interview with Susan M. Tarnowski. *Teaching Music, 2(2*), 44-45.

The world around us. (1991). New York: Macmillan/McGraw-Hill.

About the Authors

Theresa Purcell Cone, PhD, is an assistant professor in the department of health and exercise science at Rowan University in Glassboro, New Jersey. A coauthor of the first edition of this book, she is a past president of the National Dance Association and has held numerous leadership roles in physical education, including being president of New Jersey AHPERD and Eastern District AAHPERD. She has taught physical education and dance for 35 years in public schools and college and university settings.

Dr. Cone is also a frequent presenter at national conferences on interdisciplinary teaching, dance, and physical education. She has published extensively on these topics, and with her husband she is coauthor of Teaching Children Dance, Second Edition. In her leisure time, she enjoys time with her family, travel, and the arts.

Peter Werner, PED, is a distinguished professor emeritus at the University of South Carolina. His doctorate includes a specialization in physical education for children with a minor in elementary education. He is the coauthor of the first edition of this book and author of Teaching Children Gymnastics, Second Edition, among other titles, and has also written more than 100 journal articles on physical education for children. In addition, he has presented on interdisciplinary physical education for the past 35 years at the state, regional, and national levels.

Dr. Werner, a lifetime member of AAHPERD, edited the film series for the American Master teacher program. He has also served as senior editor of Teaching Elementary Physical Education from 2000 to 2003 and as the chair of the Editorial Review Board for Strategies from 2007 to 2008. In his spare time, his pursuits include whitewater canoeing, broom making, and fly fishing.

Stephen L. Cone, PhD, is a professor in the department of health and exercise science at Rowan University. He coauthored the first edition of this book with his wife and has served as AAHPERD president. He has published and presented extensively in physical education, dance, and interdisciplinary teaching and has taught physical education and dance for 35 years in public schools and college and university settings. He also has served as president of Eastern District AAHPERD and New Hampshire AHPERD. Along with his wife, he enjoys time with his family, travel, and the arts in his leisure time.